THE
COMPLETE
MOBILE HOME
BOOK

Also by Nicholas M. Raskhodoff:
  Set Ceramic Tile Yourself
  Electronic Drafting Handbook
  Electronic Drafting and Design (four editions)

THE
COMPLETE
MOBILE HOME
BOOK

The Guide to Manufactured Homes

Nicholas M. Raskhodoff

𝕊𝔹

A SCARBOROUGH BOOK

To Julie, my wife

Figs. 1–15, 9-4, and 10-10 courtesy Selma H. Wade

First published in 1982
Copyright © 1982 by Nicholas M. Raskhodoff
All rights reserved

Designed by Louis A. Ditizio
Printed in the United States of America
STEIN AND DAY/*Publishers*
Scarborough House
Briarcliff Manor, N.Y. 10510

Library of Congress Cataloging in Publication Data

Raskhodoff, Nicholas M.
    The complete mobile home book.

    Bibliography: p.
    Includes index.
    1. Mobile homes—Handbooks, manuals, etc.   I. Title.
TH4819.M6R37   643'.2   80-5798
ISBN 0-8128-2781-3   AACR2
ISBN 0-8128-6137-X (pbk.)

CONTENTS

ACKNOWLEDGMENTS

I wish to express my gratitude to the mobile home industry, its various companies and corporation officials, who provided many of the photographs, drawings, and data for use in this book, and to the various industry associations which supplied relevant information. Several of the most helpful are listed below.

Carrier Corporation (United Technologies Corporation)
Champion Home Builders Company
Coast Mobile Home Sales, Torrance, California
Duo-Therm Division (Goodyear Tire and Rubber Corporation)
Epco Mobilehome Products, Inc.
Fleetwood Enterprises, Inc.
Fuqua Industries, Inc.
General Electric Company
Golden West Homes
Highland Springs Village
Immobile Home Company®, Inc.
Jenkins Mobilehome Printers
K-S-H, Inc.
Kaiser Steel Corporation
Mrs. Edna Meyer
Mastic Corporation
Minute Man Anchors, Inc.
Morgan Drive Away, Inc.
Silvercrest Industries, Inc.
Tropicana Mobile Homes, Inc.
Woodall Publishing Company

Gratitude is also due to the nationwide municipal, county, and state officials who, with the exception of New Jersey, provided information, copies of their laws, assessment values, and other valuable information to assist in the preparation of this book.

The following governmental agencies supplied requested information and copies of standards and regulations involving the mobile home industry:

Department of Consumer Affairs, Sacramento, California
Department of Housing and Urban Development (HUD)
Federal Housing Administration (FHA)
Federal Trade Commission (FTC)
Veterans Administration (VA)

My special thanks are extended to Norma J. Turrill, who contributed advice and assistance in the preparation of this book.

®Registered trademark of Immobile Home Company, Inc.

Nicholas M. Raskhodoff
Largo, Florida

INTRODUCTION

This guide to mobile homes can be of great value to prospective buyers and to those who already own these manufactured homes. It is a reference as well as a practical manual.

The sales of mobile homes have risen tremendously over the past fifteen years. Their great advantage, compared to conventional housing, is price. Many persons who are not yet familiar with mobile homes will shortly seriously consider such a purchase; this text presents all the facets of this investment in much detail.

The book is organized under several headings—mobile home construction, checkpoints for purchasing, mobile home parks, accessories, mobile home problems, improvements and maintenance, and other topics of importance to buyers and owners.

Considerable space has been devoted to the manufacture of mobile homes. This is a subject likely to be unfamiliar to most prospective buyers, whose only notions may have been gained from the models on a dealer's lot. While they may be impressed with the interiors, decorated with luxury furniture, they should consider the rest of the structure as well.

A "stripped down" mobile home is probably not what you want, so at purchase you'll want to include such accessories as an air-conditioning/heating unit, a shed, skirting, a carport, and other items. With their installation you'll have a complete home.

Parks may present various problems—management, escalating rents, location, or even regimentation.

On the positive side are the park facilities and entertainment. These contribute to enjoyable living among people with similar interests, and in many instances, similar ages.

The detailed comparison list of mobile home vs. conventional home features (Table 1–1) provides insight into the variations to be expected in living accommodations. The other guidelines for mobile home selection should be helpful in making a final decision. Two or three copies of this list will allow you to make notations as you inspect the various models. To their regret, too many people have purchased a mobile home without a thorough examination of the product.

Details of the construction standards have been presented at some length to better acquaint the purchaser with existing government standards.

I have also dealt with fire safety. Although present standards still allow the use of thin, imitation paneling, some manufacturers are switching over to the thicker, genuine paneling, used in conventional homes. The extra cost is only about one percent of the mobile home's price, a small price to pay for a safer home.

CHAPTER 1

MOBILE HOMES

The major attraction of buying a mobile home is its price—compared to the price of what the mobile home industry often calls "stick-built" or conventional single-family housing.

The mobile home industry has spent, and continues to spend, great sums on publicity and promotion illustrating the advantages of mobile home living. They are even starting to call their product "manufactured housing." However, too many of these comparisons of features are as apt as comparing oranges with apples. For example, mobile home prices are often compared directly to those for conventional homes but the promoters frequently fail to offer a comparison of square feet of living area. When homes of equal living area are compared the overall price advantage of mobile homes is reduced considerably.

Also, in comparing mobile homes against conventional housing, the mobile home industry usually fails to include the price of the lot—an oversight which can cost the unwary several thousand dollars. The lot is included in the price of a conventional home.

Instead, the industry seems to prefer to have the purchaser depend upon a rental park site which, in monthly rent payments over 10 or 15 years, will cost the owner much more than if he had purchased a lot outright when he bought his mobile home.

The prospective buyer is faced with a selection of mobile homes available in many different floor plans, widths, and lengths, and he is often encouraged to situate on someone else's land. He'll also find that a multitude of extra cost accessories must be contracted for before his mobile home is really complete.

However, his choice is often limited to only one or two builders' products. That's because many mobile home parks restrict the sorts of models they'll admit; despite the potential homeowners' preferences, and the availability of other good or better builders.

There are significant differences in mobile home appearance, quality, equivalent equipment and parts, sturdiness of construction, stability, maintenance effort and cost, and many other factors.

Appearance

For most people who've lived in a conventional home for much of their lives, the mobile home presents a radical change. Its box-like shape has been one of the objections faced by mobile home manufacturers and park owners. Very little change has occurred until recently. Manufacturers are finally trying innovative design to overcome buyers' resistance to their product. Their latest, more expensive offerings are shown in figures 1-1 and 2 and interiors in figures 1-3, 4, and 5.

Mobile home appearance has also influenced many zoning authorities who will keep a mobile home park from being placed anywhere near conventional homes. Residents of conventional homes frequently voice their feelings to local zoning boards and until the problem of appearance is fully resolved, zoning for new parks will continue to meet obstacles.

Another appearance drawback is the typical use of space blocks or plastic or metal skirting to cover the area below the mobile home. These devices give the mobile home a makeshift look compared with the solid brick or concrete block foundation of a conventional home.

Quality of Construction

The early mobile homes, starting with the movable trailer, had metal skin sidewalls and a metal roof. This type of construction is still being followed today even though the sheet metal roof usually requires painting every two or three years and often rumbles in heavy winds. Compare this to a conventional home with asphalt shingles that need to be replaced only once in 20 years. The mobile home, without a permanent brick or block foundation and without a concrete floor or pad, also requires periodic settlement checks. Unless it has been set up properly on the site, its underside may develop openings that will attract rodents and insects.

Figs. 1-1, 2. The latest in double-wides.

Fig. 1-3.
A modern kitchen.

Fig. 1-4.
A bedroom with mirrored closet doors.

Fig. 1-5.
Living room/ dining room

Stability

Some mobile homes, supported on piers that extend to their steel framework, were originally expected to stay in place after they had been set up. It was presumed that their weight would prevent shifting. High winds have repeatedly invalidated that premise, however (figures 1-6, 7). To prevent these hazards, the Department of Housing and Urban Development (HUD) now requires that mobile homes be built with over-the-home anchoring straps that can be secured to the ground. However, many older mobile homes still are not tied down. To protect the neighboring homes, the insurance industry may begin to charge higher rates for these.

Tying down a mobile home with straps is not the whole answer. For instance, anchors imbedded in rocky or clay soil provide better anchoring than those in sandy soil. Another variable is the length of the anchors themselves. If they can be implanted in the soil with very little effort they will pull out just as easily. In addition, HUD has designated no specific authority to inspect tie-downs. One is simply left to follow manufacturer's instructions.

Quality

Since mobile home designs have developed to double- and triple-wide, the burden of quality control on the completed product has partially shifted from the manufacturer to the installer at the mobile home park. His ability to produce a satisfactory final assembly depends upon such factors as these: his experience; cost limitation imposed by the park owner or the dealer; effects of transporting the mobile home sections from the plant to the site; provisions made by the manufacturer, such as brackets or other means to tie the sections together, in addition to conventional spiking; and complete sealing of all openings on the bottom side of the mobile home. This last concern may be complicated by the installation of air conditioning and additional plumbing, which may introduce new bottom openings.

The conventional home does not have these problems. It is an integrated structure, built complete by one set of workmen, and may have been inspected by the purchaser a number of times during its construction. The mobile home buyer generally does not see his purchase until it is completed and thus he's unlikely to discover any deficiencies until later.

Figs. 1-6, 7. (Above) A tornado upset this mobile home. (Right, below) A close-up.

Mobile Home Equipment

There are appliances and there are appliances. The difference depends upon quality built-in by the manufacturer, the availability of replacement parts and service facilities, the length of time required for repairs, and the strength of the warranty. Unfortunately, too many mobile homes have appliances made by relatively unknown firms with limited repair parts and service facilities. The purchaser should demand first-class merchandise, preferably of the same brand throughout, to simplify servicing and maintenance contracts.

Increased Maintenance

In spite of the industry's advertising that very little maintenance is required for mobile homes, the presence of many service trucks in parks belies that claim. When you consider that most roofs have to be repainted every two or three years; that homes need to be releveled periodically (especially in soft-soil areas); that new roofs sometimes need to be installed over the original roofs; that the homes require washing; and that they often need plumbing repairs, pest control, and external repairs to the metal skin, it is understandable that most lenders are not anxious to extend long-term loans for mobile homes. The usually thin internal paneling and floors also contribute to higher mobile home fire insurance rates.

Advantages of Mobile Home Living

Mobile homes may include many appliances as standard—often a refrigerator, wall oven, and an electric or gas range. Others may be optional, such as a garbage disposal, dishwasher, central air conditioning (except in Southern states where it is almost always standard), and washer and dryer. Before signing the contract, the buyer may have the option of changing some of the items—for instance, a larger refrigerator of the frost-free type with ice maker, a name brand for all appliances, built-ins in the dining room or bedrooms, and other items at additional cost. All such changes should be reflected in the purchase contract.

Many people find an advantage in the type of living enjoyed in mobile home parks. Recreation facilities such as a modern clubhouse, swimming pool, and shuffleboard courts, combined with a recreational program, give the residents a feeling that they live in a small town where they are free to organize affairs of their own. The similarity in age

groups and occupational backgrounds encourages residents to organize trips, as well as intra-park activities such as kaffee-klatsches, pancake breakfasts, potlucks, fiftieth wedding anniversary parties, and the like. This certainly compares well with apartment, town house, or conventional home neighborhood living. More will be said on this subject in Chapter 5.

Disadvantages of Mobile Home Living

A mobile home cannot be readily altered. The few possible alterations include an enclosed porch, a patio, or an additional room, and these are rather expensive. The owner must presume that professional help will be required for the change. These usually constitute greater problems and greater *relative* expense than with a conventional house where such additions are commonplace, many made by the owner himself.

Mobile homes built only a few years ago had only a little insulation. That's because energy costs were low. New government standards now require more insulation to decrease energy waste. However, since all double- and triple-wide mobile homes are site assembled, there is always the possibility of poor workmanship, undetected even if inspected, resulting in less than expected savings. Manufacturers, too, have been known to skimp. For example, as figure 1-8 shows, the specified roof insulation of 4-inch thickness was actually only one-half inch.

Fig. 1-8. Roof insulation only ½″ thick.

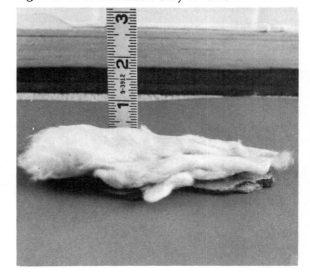

The Differences

A prospective mobile home buyer should find the following comparisons useful. Since many purchasers do not realize the differences in housing until they have bought a mobile home, table 1–1 provides enough detail to help prevent disappointment. Most of these differences between mobile and conventional homes are out of sight, so they are usually not apparent right away. Even though the list entries are not organized in a rigorous fashion you should find them of great help.

With so many variations in mobile homes, the list represents some of the highlights found in earlier and present models. Without doubt, improvements will continue to be made as the mobile home industry attempts to secure a greater share of the housing market. Continuing government regulation will also force changes to increase safety.

TABLE 1–1

Conventional Housing and Mobile Homes: A Comparison

Item	Conventional Home	Mobile Home
1. Floor joists	2 by 8s, if with a basement.	2 by 6s (except 2 by 8s in high-priced homes).
2. Floor	¾″ by 4″ finished hardwood flooring and a subfloor ¾″ by 4″.	⅝″ or ¾″ particle board, one layer. Better models have one-layer plywood.
3. Basement floor, walls	4″ concrete floor. 4″ cinder block plus brick facing.	None.
4. Floor joist bridging	1 by 4s. Prevents tilting of floor joists.	None.
5. Walls	¼″ by 4′ by 8′ paneling or ½″ by 4′ by 8′ gypsum wallboard, nailed on.	5/32″ luan paneling, stitched in place. Some may have ¼″ paneling.
6. Framing, interior walls	2 by 4.	2 by 2s, some 2 by 3s of non-bearing walls.
7. Roof	20-year asphalt shingles or tile.	Galvanized metal on lower priced models; requires painting every 2–3 years.
8. Angular roof rise	3″ in 12″ to 6″ in 12″.	¾″ in 12″ to 1¼″ in 12″.
9. Window sills	Wood, some marble.	None.
10. Windows and doors	Prefinished, anodized if aluminum.	No finish—subject to corrosion.
11. Interior doors	Have sills.	None.
12. Air ducts	Plastic in some homes. Heavy sheet metal in most.	Many use aluminum, noisy and has poor cooling/heating efficiency.
13. Air duct location	Ceiling, usually.	Floor.
14. Built as a complete unit	Yes.	Multi-wides are not.
15. Garage	Often.	No, only carport, roof and supports added later, extra cost.

Item	Conventional Home	Mobile Home
16. Fire hazard	Not if well maintained.	More so, especially with 5/32″ luan paneling.
17. Cabinet shelf surfaces	Finished smooth.	Unifnished in many models.
18. Roof overhangs	Yes.	No, added later at extra cost.
19. Gutters and downspouts, built-in	Yes.	Added later at extra cost.
20. Floor leveling	No.	Releveling needed after six months at extra cost.
21. Storage shed	Not usually needed.	Needed for storage. A requirement at parks, at extra cost.
22. Plumbing	Copper tubing, galvanized piping.	Copper tubing, plastic piping.
23. Air conditioning/heating unit	Built-in.	Added at installation at extra cost.
24. Insurance rates	Lower by comparison.	Higher than conventional homes.
25. Hurricane straps and anchors	No.	Necessary at installation at extra cost.
26. Blocks or skirting	No.	At installation at extra cost.
27. Heat tapes	No.	Required in colder climates to protect outside pipes, extra cost.
28. Formaldehyde fumes	No.	Requires chemical treatment or lengthy airing.
29. Fasteners, outside walls and gutters	No.	Zinc- or cadmium-plated steel screws that rust easily.
30. Electrical wiring	Code requires wiring is to be secured close to outlet and switch boxes.	Wiring is subject to movement when mounted on thin paneling, increasing the fire hazard.
31. Insect and rodent entrance	Foundation usually prevents entrance.	Extent of closure of bottom hardboard and skirting determines ease of entrance.
32. Fire safety	½″ thick gypsum walls and ceiling.	Thicker paneling or gypsum walls available at extra cost.
33. Door hinges (figure 1–9)	Large and heavy, 3 per door, recessed in door, 3 screws per side.	Small, stamped from one piece of metal, surface mounted, with 2 screws per side.
34. Door sills	Provided at most doors, thus helping to isolate each room in case of fire.	None, except entrance doors. Two-inch opening below each door required for return air.
35. Entrance	One or two steps above ground level in most modern homes.	Two or three steps to reach floor level, at extra cost.
36. Height, inside	8′.	7′6″; sometimes 7′.

Item	Conventional Home	Mobile Home
37. Walls	Fire resistant.	No.
38. Moisture resistant floors	Yes.	No.
39. Ample space under roof for insulating effect and storage	Yes.	No.
40. Escape windows needed	No.	Yes.
41. Extra fire escape door needed	No.	Yes.
42. Outer walls supported throughout	Yes.	No.
43. Carport roof	No.	Attached separately, develops leaks at junction.
44. Average home size (1978)	1,650 square feet.	1,150 square feet.
45. Average lot size	60′ by 100′ and larger.	40′ by 100′.
46. Average home set back from curb	25′–50′.	5′–15′.
47. Relative position of home on lot	Lengthwise, facing street.	Endwise.
48. Permanent foundation	Yes.	No*.
49. Lot price included	Yes.	Not in rental parks.
50. A complete package	Yes.	To mobile home price must be added many extras increasing the basic price by 20–35%.
51. Labor used	Mostly skilled, union.	Mostly non-skilled, non-union in building and installation.
52. Awning window control (figure 1–10)	Large gears and gear box.	Pot metal gears do not last and often require early replacement.

* Except in California

Note: If a phrase such as "2 by 4s" carries neither the single prime (′) nor the double prime (″), the unexpressed unit of measure is the inch (double prime).

Fig. 1-9. Hinges (left) for conventional home and (right) for mobile home.

Fig. 1-10. The awning window controls on mobile homes (left) are not as durable as those on conventional homes.

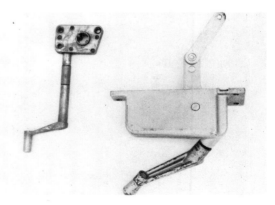

Relative amounts of necessary maintenance, as well as safety, and customer satisfaction are all reflected in the differences in table 1–1. For example, narrower floor joists (item 1) results in a weaker floor. The floor is, of course, already weaker, (item 20) since it is only of one-layer construction. The reduced joist height contributes to another problem. If a drain line is run from the kitchen sink, the 2 by 6s do not allow the pipe to run at the normally required angle. Consequently, if a garbage disposal is used, in a few years the drain will often become clogged. The only satisfactory method is to run another drain pipe outside the mobile home floor with sufficient pitch to prevent such stoppage, and this requires a plumber.

Cross bridging (item 4) stiffens the floor joist assembly. One-quarter inch paneling or gypsum walls (item 5) is needed to stiffen the whole mobile home assembly, a characteristic it lacks with only 5/32-inch paneling.

A metal roof (item 7) containing many soldered seams may leak after a few years. This is particularly likely if it has been walked on while being painted. Roof rumbles in high winds can occur if the roof is insufficiently fastened to the roof rafters, a deficiency that cannot be seen from the top.

Prefinishing of windows and doors (item 10) would stop corrosion on mobile homes located near coastal areas.

Smoothly finished cabinet shelves (item 17) allow the housewife to cover them with contact-type shelf paper which will not stick to the rough surfaces found in many mobile home cabinets.

The extra items (18, 20, 21, 23, 25, 26, 27, 32, and 35) add to a mobile home's cost, but some of them will determine whether you will be satisfied with mobile home living.

Due to possible fire hazard, an electric wall oven and/or electric range is preferable to the gas type where the choice is offered.

Table 1–1 indicates some of the differences between *average* conventional and mobile homes. You must understand that typical mobile home construction keeps some of the items from view—the thickness of roof or floor insulation, the diameter of air conditioning ducts connected to the air conditioner, whether or not the electrical wiring is in compliance with the National Electric Code, and so forth.

Sizes

While the Department of Housing and Urban Development (HUD) does not allow any radical changes in floor plans that have been submitted and approved, small variations are possible to meet the purchaser's desires.

Mobile homes are available with one, two, three, or more bedrooms, and with one, two, or more bathrooms, family rooms, dinettes, dining rooms, Florida rooms, living rooms, etcetera. They are available in lengths of up to 80 feet in single-, double-, and triple-wides of 12-, 14-, and 16-foot widths. The industry has been attempting to bring the amount of living area they provide up to the standard of conventional housing, with corresponding increases in cost, of course.

The major limitation is the size of the mobile home lots. Many of the older parks do not have space for double-wides or longer models. Fire regulations and lot size will determine the location of your mobile home.

Transportation Problems

Should you wish to move your mobile home, you may find yourself facing other serious obstacles. Many states, due to variations in building codes, will not allow you to have it moved through their jurisdiction. Nor will some states allow a mobile home built in another state to be located in their territory.

Another disadvantage is that when one purchases a mobile home, it is usually part of a package deal, involving a dealer or park operator, and many subcontractors, good or bad, on whom the purchaser must depend to secure an enjoyable residence. The quality of their work may determine whether or not you will be satisfied with mobile home living.

A "Motor Vehicle"?

Many states, including Florida, still treat a mobile home as a motor vehicle when it is located in a rental park. In the past, the then prevalent single-wide mobile homes, 8 feet wide and 30 feet long, could be moved readily over the highways. Such is not the case with most mobile homes today; double- and triple-wides require extensive preparation before and during the actual move.

The motor vehicle tax, however, has been a good source of state revenue for years, with a registration tag required for each mobile home section. To add insult to injury, the hitch length is added to mobile home length when the tax is determined, even though the hitch is removed after the mobile home is on its site.

Some progressive states do not penalize the mobile

home owner. They issue labels or stickers for as low as $3, to be paid only once when the mobile home is located on its site. Compare this to the annual tax in Florida of approximately $100 for a 62-foot double-wide, with an actual length of 59 feet.

The same "motor vehicles" are treated differently when located on an owned lot. They no longer require a yearly motor tag or sticker for each section but are taxed annually as a conventional home. Taxes are reduced further by one or more homestead exemptions, an advantage denied to residents in mobile home rental parks.

Financing

Buying a conventional home is usually a simple transaction between the purchaser and his bank or savings and loan association. Loans can sometimes be obtained for a period of 30 years or longer.

On the other hand, banks are usually not anxious to finance mobile homes except through the dealer and then for a shorter term. So far, banks have considered mobile homes as a greater than normal risk, with the loan rate determined by the type and size of the mobile home. The Veterans Administration has one set of regulations for mobile home loans, while the Federal Housing Administration has another.

It is usually advisable to finance the home's furniture on a separate loan, if necessary, and for a shorter term. It is probably safe to assume that it will not last as long as the mobile home itself.

Further details on financing are given in Chapter 6.

Maintenance

Despite the industry's claims, mobile homes require more maintenance than conventional homes. For example, the metal roofs normally need painting white every three years to avoid leaks and keep the roof temperature down. This is an expensive process for many persons unable to handle that task themselves. Most mobile home faucets are of the competitive type, i.e., they require washer replacement occasionally—a plumber's job for many people. In conventional homes single-lever faucets are to be found with ceramic or other seats not requiring a replacement.

Mobile homes settle in certain types of soil, sometimes due to poor preparation of the original site. In any case expensive releveling is necessary. You will find further discussion of maintenance in Chapter 11.

Fire Hazard

This has been a problem for many years due primarily to the use of flammable construction materials by most companies. Not only are such materials usually cheaper, but their use is encouraged by the relatively light weight of 5/32" luan paneling, a favorite on wall assembly lines because it is easier to staple rather than nail the paneling to the studs.

Because of this hazard, builders are required to install readily demountable "safety windows" in each bedroom. These allow a person to escape by releasing the catches on the window frame. However, the lower edge of these windows is often as much as 4 feet above floor level, necessitating a small ladder, chair, or stool in order to climb up to the window. Many handicapped persons are unable to do so. Outside window awnings sometimes also hinder escape. Adding the height of the floor above the ground, the distance from the window to the ground is often 5 or 6 feet, with an attendant possibility of an injury.

Although manufacturers have been compelled to install smoke detectors to give a fire warning, they could better enhance the safety of their products by eliminating the use of hazardous materials and by more thoughtful design.

High Winds

In spite of claims of their safety in high winds, hurricanes, or tornadoes, mobile homes, even when properly anchored, should be evacuated in a severe storm in favor of a safer building such as the park clubhouse. The destruction may be total (figure 1–11), since even the best mobile home anchors do

Fig. 1-11. The same home as shown in Figs. 1-6, 7. Only the floor frame was left. Note conventional house in background—still standing.

not secure as well as a conventional foundation. A conventional house may lose its roof but not be demolished.

Mobile home occupants are also subject to the danger of falling debris from neighboring mobile homes. Window awnings can be a great help in these circumstances as they can be lowered to protect the windows.

Floor Plans

Choosing a suitable floor plan is a matter of great importance. Your selection should not be based on a visit to a model home display at a dealer's lot. This is a favorite method of selling mobile homes. The salesman hopes that your first impression will overcome your natural caution about such a large expenditure.

The furnishings and color scheme in one model may influence your decision, but you should remember that many options are available, and that you should call your own good judgment into play. It is amazing how many people fail to inspect the entire mobile home, and simply confine their inspection to the living room or kitchen.

Single-Wides

Basically, only 12- or 14-feet wide (16 feet in Nebraska), they have an aisle along one side, similar to a European railway car. Two entrance doors are now required, both located on either side of the home.

The relative location of rooms is limited in a single-wide to allow space for the aisle. The only choice is their order of placement: whether the kitchen is at one end and the bedrooms at the other; living room and kitchen at one end and the bedrooms at the other; the two bedrooms at opposite ends; and living room and dining area at one end and the kitchen in between (figure 1–12).

These are but a few of the floor plans available, and the choice depends upon the number of persons who will occupy the mobile home. Many people find it desirable to have the youngsters' bedroom away from the master bedroom to reduce noise.

One important consideration in selecting the floor plan is whether the design will resell readily. A one-bedroom plan has limited resale value since most people want a spare room for guests.

Some floor plans show a complete bath adjoining the master bedroom and another bathroom with only a shower and toilet facilities, the so-called ¾ bath.

The maximum inside width is 11 feet, 4 inches for the 12-foot single-wide; and 13 feet, 4 inches for the 14-foot single-wide. The dining area, not a dining room, may share space with the kitchen and has limited space for furniture. Some models have one door opposite the bath entrance, not usually considered a desirable feature. The minimum distance between the two doors is specified by the HUD standard; some homes have entrance doors on the carport side so as to gain the protection of the carport roof.

The length of the rooms is governed by the overall mobile home length. A double-wide mobile home is often preferable in order to preclude uncomfortably narrow rooms.

Remember that the choice of a floor plan should be governed by your living requirements. Some persons prefer a kitchen up front while to others a living room with a good outside view is desirable. No one plan is the complete answer.

Enlarging Single-Wides

In the past, before the advent of the double-wides, more space in the single-wides was obtained by adding "expando" units alongside the mobile home. For example, they could provide extra space for a living room. Their use has decreased as sales of double-wides have increased.

An enclosed porch could also be added on the side of the single-wide. Again, the lot determines whether such additions are practical.

Double-Wides

The double-wide mobile home has become increasingly popular and some parks allow only double-wide models. Their larger space allows flexibility in floor plans, (figure 1–13), and they look more like a conventional home. The interior open spaces allow good traffic flow, and the narrow aisle, present in single-wides, is either very short or completely eliminated. Full-height living room windows, bay windows, round kitchens, and other modifications have become standard. More refrigerator-freezer space is available as well as plenty of kitchen cabinets. The owner is no longer confined to threading the long, narrow path from one end to the other.

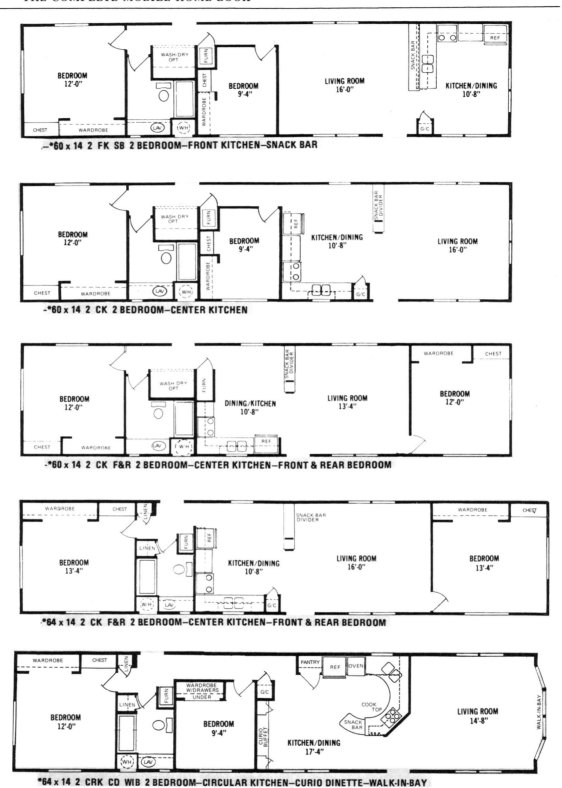

Fig. 1-12. Floor plans of single-wides.

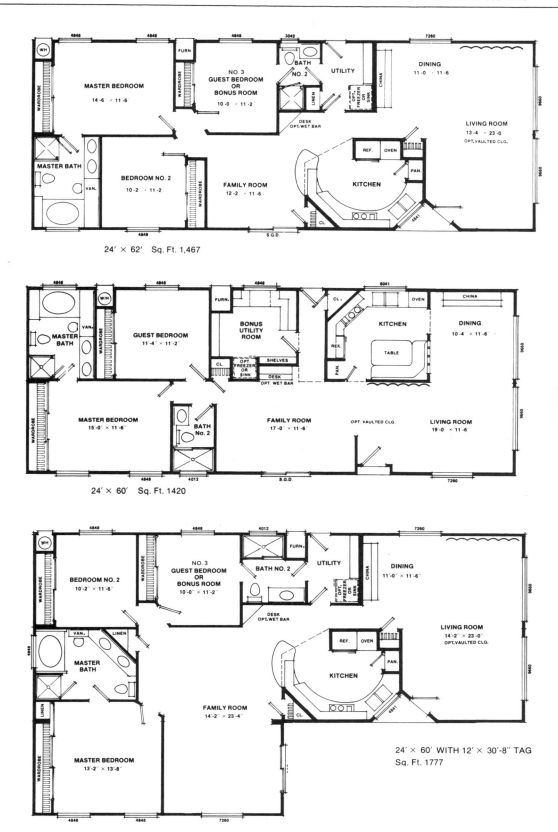

24' × 62'   Sq. Ft. 1,467

24' × 60'   Sq. Ft. 1420

24' × 60' WITH 12' × 30'-8" TAG
Sq. Ft. 1777

Fig. 1-13. The larger space of a double-wide allows more flexibility in floor plans.

Options

To please the prospective customer, manufacturers will alter the basic floor plans (within HUD limitations) often, however, at an increased price. If possible, examine the options you believe you want; see them in an actual model before placing an order for them. Obtain the exact increase in price from the salesman in writing. Remember, too, that extra time must be allowed for delivery. The dealer or park owner selling the mobile home can check with the factory to obtain the delivery date. Get that in writing, too.

Some possible options are:

1. A different brand of appliances, preferably from the same manufacturer
2. Garbage disposal
3. Dishwasher
4. Separate wall oven
5. Single-lever washerless faucets
6. Larger hot water heater
7. Shut-off valves on all plumbing facilities
8. A frost-free refrigerator-freezer. Top freezer type is preferred in smaller mobile homes
9. Better grade carpeting—different color or type
10. Quarter-inch paneling or ½-inch gypsum board
11. Better grade or different color draperies
12. Built-ins
13. Different outside-door types—wood, separate screen doors.
14. Different windows—up-and-down sash instead of awning type
15. Better kitchen floor covering
16. Overhead room registers for air conditioning
17. Provision for installation of heat-pump type air conditioning and heating
18. Plywood flooring instead of the customary particle board

Some manufacturers offer a greater choice of options than do others but remember that some parks limit the buyer's choice to one or two manufacturers as a proviso for rental space. Inquire about this before you make your home selection at a dealer since you may not be able to buy the mobile home of your choice.

To relieve the monotony of a mobile home paneled throughout, consider the possibility of ordering wall-papered bathrooms. Tiled areas around the kitchen sink are becoming popular, and molded plastic counter tops, which eliminate the possibility of dirt catching in the corners, are also available.

Mobile Home Inspection

One of the problems with mobile homes derives from the quality of construction inspection.

With hundreds of mobile home plants in some states, and with only a few inspectors assigned by the state to monitor manufacture, there are bound to be instances where substandard construction, not up to code standards, gets by.

For example, my own personal inspection of models of several manufacturers at the 1979 and 1981 Tampa, Florida, mobile home shows, disclosed that electrical wall receptacles were not supported as required by the HUD construction standard, Part 280.808(n). This standard specifies that outlets must be mounted so that no movement occurs when an electrical plug is inserted into them. Otherwise, the wires connected to their terminals may loosen after a period of time. This may result in a fire hazard from arcing at the terminals. The practice of installing electrical receptacles *after* the walls have been erected in place may explain this common problem.

By contrast, conventional homes receive several inspections of electrical, plumbing, foundation, and other work after a building permit has been secured. Other typical problems include insufficient floor frame protection to prevent corrosion of frame members and to prevent weld failure.

Many more problems derive from lack of reliable inspection after the mobile home has been set up on its site. Adequate anchoring, suitable for the type of soil; correct external plumbing connections; complete sealing of the hardboard on the bottom of the mobile home *after all* plumbing, electrical, air conditioning, and telephone connections have been made; and safe electrical interconnections between mobile home sections are some of the problems that the mobile home buyer faces as he accepts his purchase. His own personal inspection is unlikely to disclose all of these potential problems, and others may occur later.

More stringent inspection of mobile homes and their site erection would preclude some of the many complaints and dissatisfaction of purchasers.

State inspection of mobile home construction plants has improved since the inception of the nation-wide system of inspection checks by the newly created National Conference of States on Building Codes and Standards (see Chapter 2). Unannounced visits by inspectors of this agency will help to reduce the shoddy workmanship which otherwise might be practiced. There is intense competition among the hundreds of manufacturers. Too many sustain their competitive price position by undercutting quality.

Mobile Home Furniture

Built-in furniture is found in many mobile homes and is one of the attractions of mobile home living because it leaves more space for storage and reduces the need to buy additional furniture (figures 1–14 and 15). It also enhances appearance, a not inconsequential incentive for the buyer.

Fig. 1-14. This built-in shows an attractive display of china.

Dining room and bedroom built-ins are most favored. The additional space which they leave for storing dishes, clothes, and other items helps to reduce the problem of mobile home space limitations.

Yet it's hard to say much else that's good about the furniture usually sold as part of the mobile home package. Frequently, buyers have found that its quality, dictated by price, is low and that it is likely to need replacement in a short time. Youngsters, particularly, require sturdy furniture, not something made of plastic which is, incidentally, an additional fire hazard.

Fig. 1-15. Built-in desk and storage space can be very handy.

On the other hand, you should exercise caution when inspecting mobile home models with expensive and elaborate furniture. The homes themselves may be of low quality but the furnishings may lend an aura of luxury and thus sway the buyer's judgment.

Mobile Home Purchasers

There are two distinct groups of mobile home buyers—the younger 20–35-year-old group and the older 55-and-up—many of them retirees.

Both of these groups include single and married persons who find mobile home living an easy lifestyle. The largest percentage of mobile homes are occupied by two persons, according to the U.S. Census.

Due to their lower price, especially of the single-wides, they offer many people real advantages over apartment rental and provide recreational facilities as well. While some parks cater to families, most parks limit occupants to adults or retirees, setting a minimum age for occupants.

Many retirees, having sold their former conventional home, are able to purchase a mobile home with cash, due to the lower cost of the latter. However, caution must be exercised if you expect to pay for the mobile home in cash. Complete payment should only be made after you have thoroughly inspected your mobile home as delivered.

Mobile Home Prices

With the never-ending inflation and continued improvements as well as size increases of mobile homes, their prices have been rising steadily. Back in 1970, $6,100 would buy a single-wide, 60-feet long. By 1976 it took more than $12,000 to buy a 14-foot single-wide, 69 feet long. These figures include appliances, draperies, and built-in furniture, but do not include such items as set-up charges, cost of land, skirting, carport, anchoring, air conditioner, and other charges. These add a minimum of 20 percent to mobile home cost.

Today's prices of double-wides are even higher. Mobile homes have been built in price ranges of $30,000 to $75,000 and even more for luxury double-wides and triple-wides in lengths up to 80 feet. The price does not include the above-mentioned items needed to complete the installation. The mobile home you purchase should be in the same price range as others in the park, so that if some day you have to sell, your mobile home will be sufficiently attractive to the potential buyers to allow a quick sale.

Fig. 2-1. Mobile home construction details.

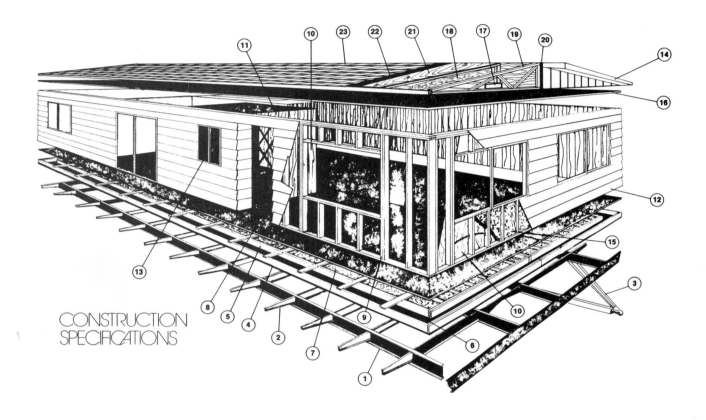

CONSTRUCTION
SPECIFICATIONS

1. Heavy duty "I" beam frames
2. Outriggers and cross members spaced 48" on center (typ.)
3. Detachable hitches
4. ⅜" asphalt impregnated industrial board for close up
5. 2x6 floor joists spaced 16" on center (typ.)
6. Perimeter air return system
7. 3½" R-11 fiberglass insulation
8. ⅝" sub floor
9. Studs spaced 16" on center (typ.) on exterior walls

10. Stress rated plywood throughout
11. Studs spaced 16" on center (typ.) in interior partitions
12. House type horizontal siding with ⅜" backing
13. House type sliding windows with removable screens
14. Front overhang eave (additional rear overhang eave on 34 wide models)
15. 3½" R-11 fiberglass insulation
16. ½" tongue and grooved accoustical type ceiling

17. Overhead heating and cooling system with ⅝" fiberglass ducts
18. 7" R22 fiberglass insulation
19. Truss type roof rafters spaced 16" on center (typ.)
20. 2 layer ⅝" laminated plywood ridge beam
21. ⅜" plywood sub roof
22. Two layers 15 lb. felt
23. Asphalt shingle roof

CHAPTER 2

MOBILE HOME CONSTRUCTION

A mobile home is a factory-built structure. If double- or triple-wide, it is transported to its site in sections, and assembled with various accessories to provide a habitable home.

It is the product of some skilled, but mostly semi-skilled workmen and is built on a small-scale production line reminiscent of an automobile assembly line. To qualify as a mobile home it must be larger than 8 feet wide and 32 feet long, and it must have a steel chassis to support it on its home site.

Mobile homes are built in various widths and lengths. The older models of 8- or 10-foot width have been superseded by 12-, 14-, and 16-foot units for a single section. The more popular double-wides come in 24- and 28-foot widths. Some triple-wides have even been built in 36-foot widths. Lengths vary from 36 to 80 feet.

Transporting a mobile home from the factory to the setup site is the factor that restrains size. Many states do not allow movement of unit sections wider than 14 feet. Nebraska, so far, is the only state that allows movement of 16-foot-wide singles within its boundaries.

Mobile Home Construction

Mobile homes, both single-wide and multi-wide, are built by firms whose capacity ranges from one per day to a single corporation which operates 30 plants and produces 100 units or more daily.

In order to keep costs down, build a quality product, and meet HUD construction and inspection standards, such plants must be operated like automobile plants. Subassemblies such as floor, walls, and roof must be built separately and then assembled to form the end product—a single-wide home or a section of a multi-wide (figure 2–1).

The starting point is the welded frame assembly (figures 2–2 and 2–3). It consists of two ten-inch channels, to which are welded the cross members or outriggers. Notice the hitch assembly in front in figure 2–3. Figure 2–4 shows the wheel-and-axle assem-

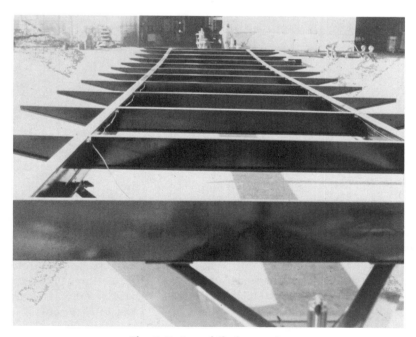

Fig. 2-2. A mobile home frame.

Fig. 2-3. A frame hitch.

Fig. 2-4. Axles and wheels support the frame.

bly. It supports the frame during assembly to the floor unit and allows the eventual transportation of the mobile home to its destination.

Some construction details are shown in the next seven illustrations. Figure 2-5 shows a partial end view of the plant producing Tropicaire mobile homes. Figure 2-6 illustrates the floor assembly after insulation has been installed, while figure 2-7 shows wiring added to the assembly. A partial wall assembly is shown in figure 2-8, with outer wall in the foreground. Figure 2-9 is another view with the exterior wall in place. Figure 2-10 shows roof trusses and figure 2-11 pictures the completed section of a double-wide, ready for shipment.

Fig. 2-5. A mobile home manufacturing plant.

Fig. 2-6. A floor assembly in process.

Fig. 2-7. Wiring is added to the floor assembly.

Fig. 2-8. A partial wall assembly.

Fig. 2-9. An exterior wall.

Fig. 2-10. View of roof trusses.

Fig. 2-11. A completed section ready for delivery.

The Codes

The standards under which mobile homes are built and transported differ from those of the conventional home. They include specifications for construction, plumbing, electrical systems, and air conditioning/heating details. To date, the industry lacks an adequate bracing standard for transportation of mobile homes over long distances.

The original code or standard was written by the industry itself and became known as the "A119.1 standard." It included so many generalities that it was possible to circumvent the standard's requirements. This standard existed for many years and was finally adopted by the American National Standards Institute as the "ANSI A119.1 Standard."

The National Fire Protection Association (NFPA) also established mobile home standard NFPA 501B, which covers construction, plumbing, heating, cooling, fuel burning systems, and installation of the electrical system. In addition, various states had their own standards of mobile home construction. Such standards varied from state to state, and as a result mobile homes manufactured in one state frequently could not be sold in another because of conflicting regulations.

In 1976 the Department of Housing and Urban Development (HUD), which monitors the construction and safety requirements of mobile homes in every state, issued the "Mobile Home Construction and Safety Standards." This standard replaces the ANSI A119.1 standard.

The HUD standard is very specific on many points in mobile home construction. Some of the more important are listed here:

1. *Data Plates.* Each mobile home shall bear a data plate affixed permanently near the main electrical distribution panel. This data plate shall bear the manufacturer's name and address, serial number, model number, and date of manufacture, manufacturer's name for factory-installed equipment, and model designations of factory-installed appliances.

It should have a reference to the structural and wind zones for which the home is designed, and also include copies of wind zone and cooling/heating maps (figures 2–12A and 2–12B).

A mobile home serial number is to be stamped on the front cross-member of the mobile home's frame.

2. *Light and Air.* Each habitable space shall have windows or doors not less in size than 8 percent of gross floor area. The kitchen may have artificial light and mechanical ventilation capable of producing change of air every half hour.

3. *Toilet facilities.* Bathrooms and toilet compartments must have artificial light and have either windows of a minimum of 1½ square feet or mechanical ventilation that is capable of producing change of air every twelve minutes.

4. *Ceilings.* Ceilings must be at least 7 feet high over a minimum of half the space of the room's area and a minimum of 5 feet over the remainder.

5. *Doors.* Two exit doors are to be provided. In single-wides the doors shall not be less than 12 feet apart, center to center. They shall provide an opening a minimum of 28 inches wide and 74 inches high, with locks that do not require the use of a key from the inside.

6. *Room requirements.* A living area must have a minimum of 150 square feet of floor area.

7. *Bedrooms.* Bedrooms must have a minimum of 50 square feet of floor area or 70 square feet for bedrooms for two or more people. Clothes closet, minimum depth of 22 inches, shall have a shelf and rod.

8. *Hallways.* They shall be at least 28 inches wide.

9. *Safety glass.* It shall be used on all entrance or exit doors, shower and tub enclosures, storm doors, and in door panels within 12 inches of exit and entrance doors.

10. *Fire safety.* Interior finish of all walls, partitions, and ceilings shall not have a flame spread of over 200, ASTM E84 standard. This includes kitchen cabinet doors, exposed bottoms, and countertops, surfaces of plastic bathtubs and shower units.

11. *Fire detection equipment.* At least one smoke detector is to be installed in the hallway nearest the bedroom area, unless bedrooms are widely separated; in which case a separate smoke detector shall protect each bedroom area.

12. *Construction details.* Lumber used shall not exceed 19 percent moisture content.

13. *HUD approval.* Each mobile home shall be designed and constructed as an integrated structure subject to approval by HUD. Roof framing shall be securely fastened to wall framing, walls to floor structure, and floor structure to chassis.

14. *Floors.* Wood, particle-board, or plywood floors in kitchens, bathrooms, laundry rooms, and water heater compartments shall be moisture resistant by sealing or overlay of nonabsorbent material, such as plastic floor covering.

15. *Anchoring systems.* Means shall be provided in the form of straps or cables.

16. *Miscellaneous.* All exterior surfaces shall be sealed to prevent entrance of rodents.

17. *Window Size.* Fire escape windows shall have a minimum opening of 5 square feet. *Note.* There is

MANUFACTURING PLANT

COMPLIANCE CERTIFICATE

Date of Manufacture
_____

Manufacturer's Serial Number and Model Unit Designation
_____

Design approval by (D.A.P.I.A.)

If questions regarding the operation, maintenance, warranty or performance of this mobile home should arise please contact the dealer from whom it was purchased, the manufacturing plant listed below or:

Answers to most questions regarding operation, installation, maintenance and design capabilities are found in the appropriate sections of the owner's maintenance and information manual and installation instructions furnished with each mobile home.

This mobile home is designed to comply with the federal mobile home safety standard in force at the time of manufacture.

The factory installed equipment includes:

Equipment	Manufacturer	Model No.	Equipment	Manufacturer	Model No.
For heating	_____	_____	Washer	_____	_____
For air cooling	_____	_____	Clothes Dryer	_____	_____
For cooking	_____	_____	Dishwasher	_____	_____
Refrigerator	_____	_____	Garbage Disposal	_____	_____
Water heater	_____	_____	Other	_____	_____

STRUCTURAL DESIGN BASIS CERTIFICATE

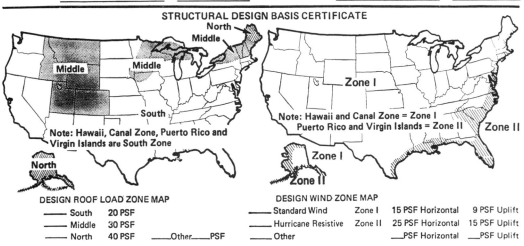

DESIGN ROOF LOAD ZONE MAP
_____ South   20 PSF
_____ Middle 30 PSF
_____ North   40 PSF   _____Other_____PSF

DESIGN WIND ZONE MAP
_____ Standard Wind   Zone I   15 PSF Horizontal   9 PSF Uplift
_____ Hurricane Resistive Zone II 25 PSF Horizontal   15 PSF Uplift
_____ Other   _____PSF Horizontal _____PSF Uplift

Fig. 2-12. Heating and Cooling Design Basis Compliance Certificates showing (a) roof load and wind zone maps and (b) winter climate zone.

HEATING AND COOLING DESIGN BASIS CERTIFICATE

DESIGN WINTER CLIMATE ZONE
This mobile home has been thermally insulated to conform with the requirements of the Federal Mobile Home Construction and Safety Standards for all locations within climatic Zone I _____

Zone II _____   Zone III _____

INFORMATION PROVIDED BY THE MANUFACTURER NECESSARY TO CALCULATE SENSIBLE HEAT GAIN.

Walls (without windows and doors). . . . ."U" = _____

Ceilings and roofs of light color . . . ."U" = _____

Ceilings and roofs of dark color . . . ."U" = _____

Floors . . . ."U" = _____

Air ducts in floor . . . ."U" = _____

Air ducts in ceiling . . . ."U" = _____

Air ducts installed outside the home . . . ."U" = _____
Heat transfer area to outside of home from air ducts located:

Inside home . . . . "Sq. Ft." = _____

Outside home . . . . "Sq. Ft." = _____

The above heating equipment has the capacity to maintain an average 70° F temperature in this home at outdoor temperatures of ____°F.

To maximize furnace operating economy, and to conserve energy, it is recommended that this home be installed where the outdoor winter design temperature (97½%) is not higher than ____°F.

The above information has been calculated assuming a maximum wind velocity of 15 MPH at standard atmospheric pressure.

The air distribution system of this home is suitable for the installation of central air conditioning.

The supply air distribution system installed in this home is sized for Mobile Home Central Air Conditioning Systems of up to _____B.T.U./Hr. rated capacity which are certified in accordance with the appropriate Air Conditioning and Refrigeration Institute Standards. When the air circulators of such air conditioners are rated at 0.3 inch water column static pressure or greater for the cooling air delivered to the mobile home supply air duct system.

Information necessary to calculate cooling loads at various locations and orientations is provided in the special comfort cooling information provided with this mobile home.

To determine the required capacity of equipment to cool a home efficiently and economically, a cooling load (heat gain) calculation is required. The cooling load is dependent on the orientation, location and the structure of the home. Central air conditioners operate most efficiently and provide the greatest comfort when their capacity closely approximates the calculated cooling load. Each home's air conditioner should be sized in accordance with Chapter 22 of the American Society of Heating, Refrigeration and Air Conditioning Engineers (ASHRAE) Handbooks of Fundamentals, once the location and orientation are known.

no protective finish for aluminum window members or aluminum doors specified in this standard.

18. *Heating/cooling.* A certificate that covers heating system shall be affixed in a mobile home, listing the name of the manufacturer, plant location, and mobile home model, and including the winter-climate-zone map. The manufacturer certifies that the heating system will maintain 70° F. temperature inside the mobile home when the outside temperature is down to the temperature specified on the heating certificate. The heating plant may be located within the mobile home or outside as part of the electrical heating/cooling unit.

19. *Certificates of compliance.* A "Comfort Cooling Certificate," which may be combined with the "Heating Certificate," shall be affixed inside the mobile home, containing the name of the manufacturer, air conditioning model, and certified capacity in BTUs.

20. *Water supply systems.* Supply connection to a mobile home shall be equipped with a ¾-inch threaded inlet connection, tagged FRESH WATER CONNECTION (figure 2–13). A relief valve is to be provided for temperature and pressure relief on the water heaters, and a pipe large enough to discharge the overflow.

Fig. 2-13. Tag indicating location of the house water connection.

21. *Water pipes.* Water pipes shall be of brass, copper tubing, galvanized steel, and approved plastic suitable for hot water use.

22. *Freezing.* All pipes and fixtures that are subject to freezing temperatures shall be insulated or otherwise protected to prevent freezing. Only heat tape, designed for mobile home use, is to be connected to an electrical receptacle outlet provided for that purpose.

23. *Rodent resistance.* All exterior openings around piping and equipment shall be sealed to prevent entrance of rodents.

24. *Drainage systems.* There shall be only one drain outlet, terminating in the rear half section of the mobile home (figure 2–14). It shall not be less than 3 inches inside diameter and located with a minimum clearance of 3 inches from any part of the structure. The pipe must be large enough to accomplish its function.

Fig. 2-14. Tag showing the sewer outlet connection.

25. *Venting.* Each plumbing fixture trap must be protected against siphonage and back pressure. Each vent pipe shall terminate vertically through the roof, not less than 2 inches above the roof. Vent caps shall be of the removable type.

26. *Inspection.* All water piping and drainage and vent systems must pass water or air tests at specified pressures.

27. *Oil and gas heating and cooling systems.* For the heating system, liquefied propane (LP) gas containers shall deliver gas at pressure of not more than ½ pound per square inch. They shall be permanently marked to show correct mounting position and the location of service connection.

LP gas valves and regulating equipment shall be installed in a vapor-tight compartment accessible only from the outside. Two vents are to be provided—open and unrestricted to outside atmosphere.

Oil tanks for mobile homes, using oil as fuel, shall be mounted outside and sufficiently high to provide gravity flow to appliances.

28. *Gas piping systems.* They shall be designed for gas pressures of ¼ inch-pounds per square inch

and subjected to a test pressure of 3 inch-pounds per square inch. A shut-off valve shall be installed at each appliance.

The gas supply connection for LP gas shall be located in the rear half of the mobile home, within 2 feet from the left side wall.

Each mobile home shall have affixed on the skin near each gas supply connection a tag, 3 inches by 1¾ inches minimum size (figure 2–15).

LP Gas System

This gas piping system is designed for use of liquefied petroleum gas only

DO NOT CONNECT NATURAL GAS TO THIS SYSTEM.

CONTAINER SHUT OFF VALVES SHALL BE CLOSED DURING TRANSIT.

When connecting to a lot outlet, use a listed supply connector for mobile homes rated at
☐ 100,000 BTU
☐ 25,000 BTU or more

Before turning on gas, make certain all gas connections have been made tight, all appliance valves are turned off, and any unconnected outlets are capped.

After turning on gas, test gas piping and connections to appliances for leakage with soapy water or bubble solution, and light all pilots.

Fig. 2-15. Tag for LP gas system.

Fuel-burning appliances shall be vented to the outside and meet performance-efficiency standards.

29. *Clothes dryers.* They shall have a moisture-lint exhaust duct to the outside wall which shall not terminate beneath the mobile home. A roughed-in dryer system, installed at the factory for a later dryer installation, must contain the moisture-lint exhaust system.

30. *Appliance installation.* Appliances shall be installed in accordance with manufacturers' instructions, which must be left attached to the appliance. There must be a minimum space of 24 inches above the cooking surface. Operating instructions shall be provided for each appliance. Every appliance shall be accessible for inspection service, repair, and replacement without removing permanent construction.

31. **Duct systems.** Built-in ducts must be of gal-vanized steel or aluminum, of adequate size to provide heating or cooling in accordance with the standard tests applied to the home's duct system.

32. *Electrical systems.* The distribution panel board, consisting of a number of circuit breakers or fuses, and equipped with a main supply cutoff circuit breaker, or switch and fuses, shall be located at least 24 inches from the floor, measured to the bottom of the panel board (figure 2–16).

Fig. 2-16. A circuit breaker panel.

33. *Built-ins.* Outlet boxes, fittings, and cabinets shall be securely fastened in place, and supported from a structural member, directly or with a substantial brace.

HOME FIRE HAZARDS

One of the major potential problems of mobile home living derives from the construction materials chosen by the manufacturers.

It has been claimed that the transportation of mobile homes to their sites precludes the use of conventional materials for mobile home walls. Luan paneling, consisting of ⅛-inch base with a glued-on paper face, on which wood patterns are printed, was and still is being used almost exclusively for interior walls.

This type of paneling is attached by stitching to the wall framework. These lightweight walls are easy to handle on the production line.

Conventional ¼-inch paneling requires nails as fasteners, but it is much safer than luan from the fire-hazard standpoint. It also makes much stronger walls and thus stiffens the whole mobile home considerably. With only a 1/32-inch outer aluminum skin, any additional strength one can add to a mobile home is desirable.

Some manufacturers now offer the ¼-inch paneling as an option.

Figs. 2-17, 18, 19, 20. Burning test of gypsum vs. luan paneling. Time—3 minutes between lefthand and righthand photos: (top) gypsum board; (bottom) luan paneling.

The material used in conventional housing is ⅜-inch- or ½-inch-thick gypsum board. The mobile home industry has claimed that such board is impractical because it tends to crack during transportation. However, Champion Building Products, a major producer, has demonstrated that adequate bracing of mobile homes will prevent such cracking.

They have also demonstrated the vulnerability of luan paneling as compared to gypsum board (figures 2–17, 18, 19, 20).

Considering that it only costs a manufacturer some $200 more to install conventional ¼-inch paneling rather than luan it may be only a matter of time before the latter is outlawed by HUD.

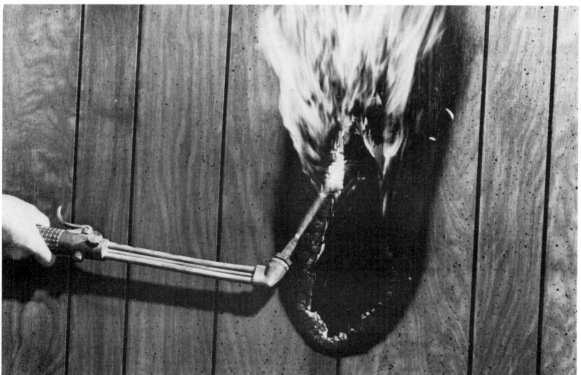

The fire hazard in mobile homes has been underscored by the requirement that fire escape windows be installed in all bedrooms to allow the occupants to escape readily. Your security is not foolproof, because such windows are often installed 3 to 4 feet above the floor and are sometimes difficult to manipulate in the middle of the night, especially without lights. In such a circumstance escape might prove troublesome, if not impossible, for handicapped persons.

Many mobile home owners have had fire escape doors installed later when they learned of problems with their fire escape windows.

Another fire hazard is interior doors that clear the floor by 2 inches. They are built in this manner to allow circulation of air to the return point of the air-conditioning system. However, this shortened door also allows spread of fire.

Because of these fire hazards, smoke-detector alarms are required in new mobile homes built since mid-1970s.

As a final word, in warmer climates it is often advisable to select a mobile home which uses electricity for heating and cooking rather than the open flame of gas or oil. Conveniently located fire extinguishers should also be placed in every mobile home. Fires due to careless smoking have taken a heavy toll in these homes.

MOBILE HOME INSPECTION

A problem encountered in many states has been the lack of adequate trained personnel to inspect mobile homes during the construction phase. In Florida only a few inspectors were available to oversee a hundred mobile home plants. Thus, the chances of buying a fully inspected home there were rather slim. The buyer had to depend upon the manufacturer's will and ability to control the quality of his product.

To correct the situation, the Department of Housing and Urban Development has established a special inspection agency. Hopefully it will result in better quality products.

The National Conference of States on Building Codes and Standards, Inc. (NCSBCS), was designated as the agency to oversee the details of the federal regulation and to inspect mobile homes. Two agencies were also created by HUD: the primary inspection agency (PIA) and the state administrative agency (SAA), the latter to investigate consumer complaints.

PIAs are of two types: design-approval primary inspection agencies (DAPIA), and in-plant primary-inspection agencies (IPIA). Mobile home manufacturers are required to use the services of each of them. HUD contracted with NCSBCS to direct and monitor this interstate monitoring system.

DAPIA's main function is to review and approve mobile home designs.

IPIA's main function is to certify that a given manufacturer is capable of constructing mobile homes in conformance with approved designs and HUD standards, and to check production for conformance with above.

NCSBCS examines reports submitted by various inspection team members for substance and completeness. NCSBCS is also the sole supplier of the HUD label which is affixed to each mobile home section. It charges a $19 inspection fee for each mobile home.

CHAPTER 3

BUYING
A MOBILE
HOME

In some parks buying a mobile home presents many choices, while others, so-called closed mobile home parks, offer models of only two or three manufacturers. Investigate at the outset which type you will be dealing with and make your choice of a park accordingly.

The "open" parks offer you the advantage of buying through a dealer, who maintains a mobile home display lot, presenting models of various manufacturers (figure 3–1). Here a wide choice is available; in

Fig. 3-1. A mobile home dealer's display lot.

addition, the dealer interested in making the sale will try to obtain the home of your choice as well as the options you want.

There is an advantage to the "closed" park, but it will limit you to the models of only one or two manufacturers, since the park owner contracts with these manufacturers to sell only their products in his park. The advantage is the guarantee of a lot if you purchase the home through him.

CHOOSING YOUR DEALER

In large communities you will find several dealers representing the various manufacturers. They can be located through the yellow pages of the telephone directory or the local chamber of commerce.

As do many car dealers, mobile home dealers fly pennants and flags over their lots and purchase television advertising to attract customers. They may also employ salesmen on a commission basis, an arrangement that pressures them to close the sale.

Some favorite sales tactics are those encountered in buying cars: telling the prospect that the price is going up tomorrow; that some one is coming back today to place a down payment; or that the next shipment will not come in for several weeks. If you find a salesman employing such tactics, be cautious.

It is best—even before you start looking at the models on the dealer's lot to be quite certain that you will have a lot for your new mobile home. Get a contract, in writing, that you do have a certain specified lot in a named park, reserved for you by number or other definite description.

Your dealer will not only be your contact with the manufacturer, but he may also take over responsibility for setting up your new home and performing the required inspection. Since HUD has come into the picture, the manufacturer is charged with providing a satisfactory product and making the necessary corrections; the dealer may assume the responsibility of calling shortcomings to the attention of the manufacturer.

In choosing a dealer, consider matters such as these: Is it a small lot and crowded with models, some of which look as though they have been there for quite some time? Do they have such accessories as steps, skirting, and planters, or do you have to climb a couple of cement blocks to get in? Is the model air conditioned in hot weather? Has it been cleared of the formaldehyde fumes?

Is there an office on the grounds? Does the dealer have facilities and a qualified service man for minor repairs if needed? Does he have trucks to set up your mobile home if you buy it from him? Will he take you to the manufacturer's plant if it is nearby, so that you can see the details of construction of your home, or will you have to go alone?

Contact a local bank and inquire about the dealer's reputation and any troubles they may have had with him. A reputable dealer probably will be a member of the Mobile Home Dealers National Association, which closely supervises its members and maintains membership standards. Also, he will probably belong to the local Chamber of Commerce and other business organizations. The length of his membership is a good barometer of his stability in the local business community. Dealers who move frequently may not be around if you need them after purchase.

Is the salesman courteous and willing to spend time with you answering your questions? Does he know his job or merely recite prices? Is he high-pressuring you to buy a home beyond your needs or means? Will he provide the names of previous customers so you can check their experience?

Visit more than one dealer. In talking with another salesman you might discover that the low-priced model offered by the first is really a close-out, and service may be difficult to obtain or that it contains hard-to-correct defects.

Select nationally known manufacturers if possible. They are likely to remain in business long after your purchase. Their product probably is better because of their experience and a desire to maintain a good image. One of the largest manufacturers has added special designs to such items as wall corner posts, which are bound together with steel to reinforce the wall structure against severe weather. This manufacturer has 30 plants which cover areas within a 250-mile radius of each plant. Thus, country-wide coverage is attained, and the advantage that their mobile homes have to travel only a maximum of 250 miles to their park site.

Almost all mobile homes require some type of service, so the service that a dealer will provide is very important, especially in the first year. For example, when buying a home insist that the dealer agree to relevel the entire home after six months. Mobile homes tend to settle on their sites unevenly after the furniture has been put in and the occupants move about. Also, the side containing appliances and bathrooms tends to settle more than the other. Some people object to even such slight—but noticeable—inclination.

A dealer with fully equipped service facilities is to be preferred to one who depends upon a separate contractor, who in turn may have only limited personnel and equipment to perform repairs.

An experience that disturbs many buyers is the presence of formaldehyde fumes from the luan paneling and particle board in many mobile homes. (Pages 154–55 discuss this point in detail.) These fumes can be quite irritating to the eyes; a good dealer will make sure that such an irritant has been aired out before the model is displayed at the sales lot or in your new home.

Preplanning

Before beginning your search, prepare a list of desirable features. Estimate your resources—the maximum price you are able to pay, whether by cash, financing, or both. Unless you take such a planned approach, you might be talked into buying a home beyond your needs or price.

Here are some of the points on which you might decide:

1. Single- or double-wide.
2. Number of bedrooms—one, two, three, or more.
3. Maximum size of mobile home that may be placed on the lot you have selected.
4. Price.
5. Manufacturer.
6. Appearance, inside and out.
7. Does it meet the park's requirements?
8. Construction—type of roof, internal arrangements, and similar questions.
9. Provision for washer and dryer.
10. Warranty provided by dealer or manufacturer.
11. Available options and their extra cost.
12. Length of delivery time from the manufacturer.
13. Length of time required for complete installation on the site, including all of the accessories.
14. Will the dealer provide a complete package, including installation, or must the subcontractor be hired by the buyer?
15. Will the dealer guarantee a lot?

Factory Tour

In conventional housing, the buyer can see the details of construction by visiting the site and watching the progress. If necessary, you can get into the attic of a conventional home and check the insulation, for example; whereas in a mobile home the roof assembly is sealed and the center roof strip has to be removed to determine the amount of insulation used.

However, some dealers will arrange for you to visit the plant to see the mobile home of your choice under construction. This is highly desirable because a home is built in a way that (as in the case of the roof strip) offers little opportunity to inspect its internal construction after completion. Otherwise you must depend largely upon the manufacturer's reputation and other purchasers of his product, since only a certain percentage is inspected because of shortage of personnel or lack of quality control.

When visiting the factory, pay attention to such details as these:

1. Are outriggers welded to frame assembly (vertical channel members) completely? Is the assembly completely painted or coated with a heavier undercoating, with no bare spots showing?

2. The floor assembly is the foundation for the mobile home. It contains the insulation, plumbing, and electrical wiring, as well as duct work. Metal ducts, especially aluminum, develop "cracking" noises on the heat cycle. Two-by-sixes are generally used for floor joists. Only a few manufacturers use the two-by-eights. Floors are mostly of ⅝-inch or ¾-inch particle board (tongue-and-groove type), which is glued and nailed to the floor joists. The floor is only single-layer as compared to the double-layer floor in most conventional houses. Plywood is a better flooring material, since it is more resistant to any moisture collected beneath mobile home. It is also less flexible than particle board, which gives a feeling of "sponginess" when walked on. The particle board is likely to buckle due to expansion from moisture but its lower price makes it attractive as floor material.

3. Wall assemblies. Two-by-four framing members have replaced the two-by-twos in the earlier models. Additional framing members should extend above and below all door and window openings. Interior wall assemblies generally use two-by-two framing members if they are non-bearing walls. Supporting walls use two-by-fours.

In conventional housing many frame members are joined by metal straps, some of them formed to special shapes, whereas in mobile homes they are stapled or glued together. Thus, it is up to the construction crew to accomplish this properly.

The so-called "wall paneling" is luan paneling, 5/32 inch thick. This is ⅛-inch luan base, on which decorative paper simulating wood designs has been glued. You can easily identify this material by inspecting wall interiors since the design repeats itself every few feet. Pressing on the wall between the framing studs will give a feeling of elasticity not present with the conventional ¼-inch paneling or gypsum board. The manufacturers use luan paneling because it is a cheaper material and it can be attached with staples instead of nails.

4. Roof assembly. This consists of roof members or trusses to support the roof covering, which may be galvanized steel, shingles, or other material.

Again, to reduce costs, the manufacturers have departed from the conventional house roof rise of 6-in-12 inches or even steeper, for a 1-in-12-inch rise. This skimping shortens the roof sides and detracts from appearance; it also could create leaks. Where metal roofs are used on cheap commercial buildings, additional material is added over the metal to help make them leak-free.

Whether on conventional or mobile homes, shingled roofs require a higher pitch to prevent the shingles from being torn loose by the wind. They do not require maintenance and will last twenty years on conventional homes.

Ceilings generally consist of prepainted plastic U-shaped panels stapled to the lower side of the roof trusses.

The new HUD requirements specify certain insulation materials of a specified thickness (R rating) to protect the living area from high roof temperature.

To inspect every detail of construction at the factory would indeed be a time-consuming task; but such tours are generally limited to an hour or less.

Inspecting the Model

Much can be discovered by carefully examining the model's exterior and interior. As noted before, many of the construction details are well hidden and, unless a factory tour has been made, they will remain so.

Mobile home exterior. The exterior of a mobile home may consist of painted vertical aluminum panels, fitted together in a special groove on one end of each panel (figure 3–2). This type of construction allows for expansion of the panels in hot weather even while they remain interlocked.

Fig. 3-2. A vertical panel's edge.

Fig. 3-3. Horizontal siding adds to attractiveness.

It may instead be of horizontal siding (figure 3–3) (similar to that used on conventional homes), insulated or not, in white or pastel colors.

The vertical paneling should be sealed from possible leaks by horizontal overlapping panels above and below it. It is attached to the wall framing members by self-tapping screws, driven in by power tools at the factory. Cadmium plated steel screws are used; but because of the electrical potential difference between steel and cadmium, plus the salt water atmosphere present in coastal areas, such screws will rust after a few years. This is one factor in the early depreciation of mobile homes. Substituting stainless steel screws would eliminate this problem; otherwise, the owner is faced with replacing them later.

Driving the screws blind with a power tool is a risky method. In one such instance, a screw had been driven into a power cable directly in back of it—right through a protective metal strip in front of the cable. During removal for replacement, the screw came in contact with the high side of the power line and short-circuited the line. Thus a potential fire hazard had existed all along.

Check the siding and other screws to note if any heads were broken off during their installation. Inadequate quality control would account for such defects; if it does, the entire mobile home may suffer from the same shortcoming (figure 3–4).

Metal roofs are a constant problem. Unless they are stretched at the factory, they will rumble in the wind. The use of thin material is one source of trouble; insecure fastening to the roof trusses is another. Some ways to handle these problems are given in Chapter 12.

Water draining off the roof should drip into the gutter below it, but if the junction between roof and walls is a sharp corner, the water rolls down rather than drip into the gutter. A narrow built-in overhang will eliminate this problem.

Windows and doors should be adequately caulked. The model will indicate if the home is deficient in this respect. Leakage at the windows will eventually rot the woodwork inside.

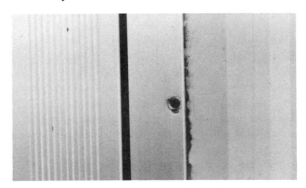

Fig. 3-4. A broken-off screw head.

Mobile home interior. Examine the floor layout and ask the salesman for a complete list of features, if it is not attached to the floor plan (figure 3–5). The list may indicate which optional features—not shown on the model—are available.

Practically every model will be completely furnished as to drapes, curtains, and carpeting. The furniture may vary greatly in quality. For years, furniture especially developed for mobile homes was used, but its quality, based on a large use of plastics, left much to be desired. Today, many models will have furniture of better quality, costing from 10 to 20 percent of the mobile home's price tag. However, if your present furniture is in good condition it will serve just as well in a mobile home. If not, you can purchase new furniture yourself rather than through a mobile home dealer.

Fig. 3-5. A list of standard features.

Paneling. For the many mobile homes finished in luan paneling, the only choice left to you is selection of its color. The darker pecan paneling should be avoided if you expect to add awnings later. Some owners add Solar-X, a darkened film applied to the window panes, or similar materials to reduce sun's glare, but such an addition makes the interior darker. A light color paneling will harmonize with most furniture.

Some manufacturers have ¼-inch regular paneling or gypsum walls as an option. They are to be preferred over the thin luan paneling because they decrease fire hazard and add to the overall strength. Such an option may amount to one percent of the mobile home's cost, but it is well worth the price.

Hot water heater. The tank for these heaters (located within the home) should be of 30- or 40-gallon capacity, instead of the all-too-frequent 20-gallon size. In many low-priced models, water heaters are not glass-lined, and have only a one-year warranty. If a larger heater with glass-lined tank can be obtained as an option by all means get it. A typical heater is shown in figures 3–6 and 3–7. Notice the piping that hinders removal—a factor in high plumber's costs. Note also the absence of shut-off valves.

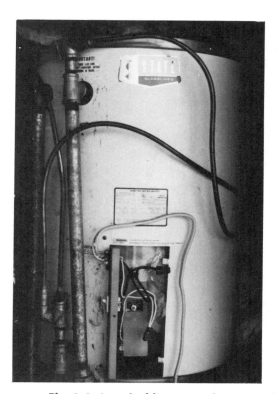
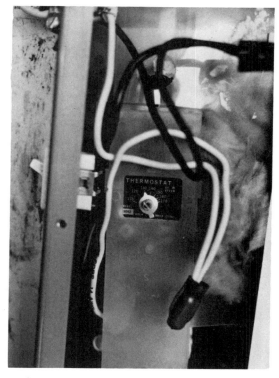

Fig. 3-6. A typical hot water heater and its control (Fig. 3-7).

The water heater is generally located near one of the bathrooms, with an access panel outside the home; it should be isolated from the remainder of the home. The model shown in figure 3-6 was not enclosed on the back side, which would permit insects to get into the mobile home (figure 3-8).

Water heaters, especially of the one-year-warranty type, may present another problem. Since they are on the same level as the floor of the home, if one should develop a leak, water will enter the particle-board flooring in the surrounding areas. Buckling (see p. 33, above) and will probably necessitate costly repairs, especially if the carpeting or rugs near the heater are cemented to the floor.

Much of this problem could be eliminated if manufacturers would adopt a slightly different construction technique. A large metallic saucer, dished out downward, below the heater, could collect any leaking water and drain it under the mobile home. Then water could not get into the particle-board flooring, as it now does regardless of where the water heater is located (figure 3-9).

Appliances

Brand-name merchandise is preferable by far (for reasons explained above) with as many appliances as possible from the same manufacturer. Ask for the model number and other necessary identification of

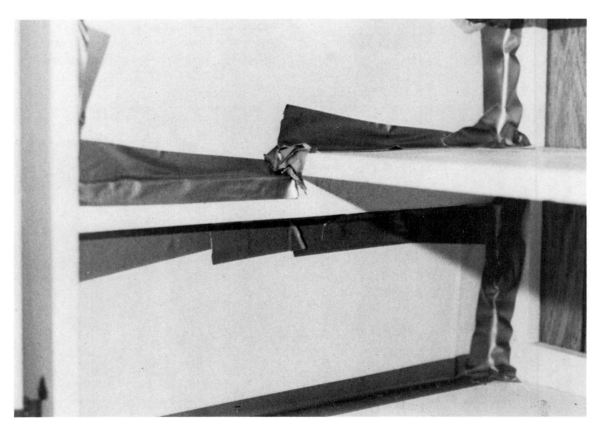

Fig. 3-8. The large opening left in back of this hot water heater would permit insects to get in if not sealed up.

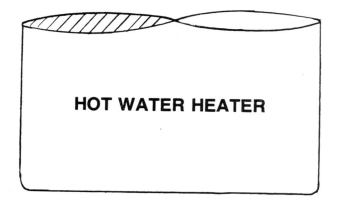

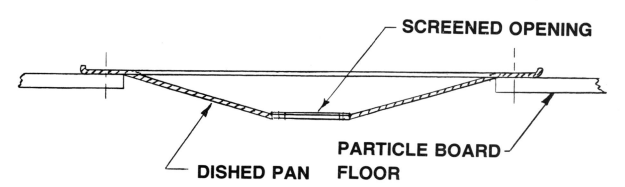

Fig. 3-9. Diagram of a suggested metal drain for a hot water heater.

the appliances if lacking on the display model. If the mobile home manufacturer uses appliance suppliers without warehouse or service facilities, the home owner may be left waiting for days for repair work.

A self-cleaning oven—not a continuous-cleaning type—is preferred. A wall oven should be adequately insulated from the kitchen walls. Electricity rather than gas is preferable as fuel for appliances—including the hot water heater—to limit flame exposure. However, in Northern areas, electric power may be inadequate for this purpose.

A frost-free refrigerator is a desirable appliance if you are willing to pay for its high energy use. If the one shown in the model is not suitable in size to your needs, there may be an option permitting necessary space alterations made at the factory, for the size you need.

If a washer and a dryer are shown in the model, make sure the home you order will have a drain pipe for the washer, cold and hot water connections, as well as a three-wire, 220-volt receptacle connected to the electrical panel for the dryer. Check whether these items are listed as being standard or optional equipment.

Dishwashers and garbage disposals are in favor with many people. Notice if they are a part of the model or must be installed as an option, and the price.

Furniture

Be on guard against elaborate furniture installed in a model as a device to distract your attention from inferior construction. Its cost should not be out of line with that of the model.

Try to visualize your own furniture in the model; if your own is suitable and in good condition, it may do just as well as that on display.

Electrical Wiring

Aluminum wiring was used in mobile homes in the past to reduce cost. However, it proved to be an inferior product. Its outer surface oxidizes very quickly after installation. The oxide tends to intensify any arc forming due to loosened connections at the receptacles and switches. When they are mounted on thin paneling, such as luan, and an appliance plug is pressed into such a receptacle, unsupported except by paneling, the receptacle deflects inward. The wiring connected to the receptacle terminals will eventu-

ally loosen through the repeated receptacle motion, resulting in an arc at the terminals with a possibility of fire. Warm receptacles or a circuit breaker panel indicates aluminum wiring, which is now illegal. So are unsupported receptacles and switches but they will be found just the same.

Check if the model has a 150-ampere-capacity circuit panel, sufficient to take care of a central air-conditioning system or a 15-kilowatt electrical heating unit. Many such panels have only a limited capacity, which precludes installation of heavy-current using appliances such as air-conditioners.

Plumbing

You will find that plastic piping is commonly used in mobile homes for drainage, and copper tubing for cold and hot water supply pipes. Check whether shut-off valves in the model are installed at each point requiring cold or hot water. This will enable you to maintain water supply in other parts of the home while shutting it off at the fixture under repair. This feature is a good indication of a well-constructed model.

In areas subject to cold weather, piping should be insulated against possible freezing. Piping within the walls and floor assembly is subject to such a possibility.

Another indication of quality construction is the faucets in the kitchen and bathroom. They should be of the single-control-lever type, with ceramic or other permanent-type seats. This design does not require washers and so eliminates the need for repair of that sort. Such faucets are well worth any extra cost because they eliminate future maintenance difficulties.

Fixtures in the bathroom and kitchen should be name brands such as American Standard, Moen, Koehler, and Delta, to facilitate servicing if needed. Repair costs of many items will soon absorb any savings realized through cheaper initial cost.

Interiors

A good way to detect inferior manufacture is to inspect the drawers and shelves in the kitchen cabinets and shelving areas. They should have smooth surfaces, not roughly finished surfaces, painted over: Contact paper or similar covering will not stick to a rough surface. Many housewives prefer to cover these shelves, if possible, with such papers.

Doors and windows. Sliding doors should have a substantial locking device, such as a locking bar. Other doors (figure 3–10) should be provided with an overhanging lip to hide the entrance latch bolt, thus making any break-in attempts difficult. Pins in the outside door hinges should, likewise, have a locking device to prevent removal. Check to see if the exterior doors are flush with the frames throughout the entire length; otherwise, poor workmanship is indicated. Nor should there be any broken-off screw heads (figure 3–11), again a sign of poor quality control.

Awning-type windows should be inspected to make sure they close completely and their controls checked for size. Small controls generally have pot metal gears, which will wear out and require replacement in a few years.

Safety windows are essential for all bedrooms. They have small fasteners (figure 3–12) which allow the windows to be removed in case of fire or other emergency. For a handicapped person—if not for all—the windows are often too high and difficult to remove. Fire escape doors are far more practical and are installed in many mobile homes after purchase.

Conventional windows, which slide up-and-down, should be checked for ease of operation and freedom from sticking. Try one or two on the model. A warped window frame will cause binding and indicates poor construction.

Windows and doors should be weatherstripped and caulked. Check whether storm windows and doors are included if you intend to reside in Northern areas. As an option direct from the factory, they may be ordered at a lower cost than when purchased later.

Carpeting. Consider whether the standard grade offered will suit your needs. Since the same type of carpet may extend throughout the mobile home, care should be exercised in selecting the most suitable one.

There are three basic types of pile used in carpets: looped, cut, or combination of both, in quite a few versions.

1. Level-loop pile. It consists of uncut loops of equal height. It wears well and is suitable for heavy-traffic areas.

2. Multilevel loop. It consists of uncut loops of various heights. Conceals dirt and foot prints well but is difficult to vacuum.

3. Plush or cut pile. Loops are cut to an even surface. The velvety look is good for low-traffic areas.

4. Shag. It consists of looped or cut yarns with a minumum height of 1½ inches. It is suitable for medium-heavy traffic, but is difficult to vacuum.

5. Random shear. It is similar to shag, but with only the highest-level loops cut.

6. Level-tip shear. Level looped yarn, some loops cut and others uncut, with a smooth surface, suitable for high-traffic areas.

7. Sculptured or carved. Yarn cut at different levels to create either a pattern or a random appearance. Sculptured pattern hides dirt and footprints of heavier traffic, while carved is more suitable for light traffic.

8. Frieze. Yarns are tightly twisted and set with heat. It is a long wearing carpet.

The carpet's appearance and wear are more directly dependent on the materials of which it is made than on its pile type. Among them are these materials:

Wool. It gives a soft, luxurious appearance, suitable for low-traffic areas. It should be mothproofed at the factory.

Nylon. This is a long-wearing synthetic fiber—extremely resilient, readily cleaned—that does not absorb moisture: a material good for all types of carpeting.

Polyester. Cheaper than nylon, it wears well, and is resistant to fading from direct sunlight.

Acrylic. Probably costing more than nylon, it has all of its better characteristics.

Polypropylene. This is an outdoor-indoor carpeting material, easy to clean, colorfast, and quick drying.

The most important feature in a carpet is its density, with close tufting resisting flattening. The density is lower for high-pile carpets.

Light-color carpets should be selected to give the space a larger appearance and vice versa. Small patterns are less noticeable in a large area, while large patterns make the ceiling appear lower in a small room.

Since the carpet is installed at the factory on each mobile home section of a double- or triple-wide, inspect the seam which occurs at the junction. Poor horizontal alignment of the sections or poor carpet work will result in a bulge. This is especially true with sculptured carpeting and will result in rapid wear at the seam.

Kitchens. Some of the newer models are of the round type (figure 3–13). Observe whether the space lost from such an arrangement has been utilized to install bookshelves or other woodwork.

Cabinets should have a smooth-finished floor and drawers should slide on nylon rollers and have built-in stops. To reduce noise, cabinet doors should have felt bumper stops, with three hinges on tall cabinet doors. Plastic door knobs are not acceptable because

Fig. 3-10. The entrance lock on top is better protected than the one on the bottom.

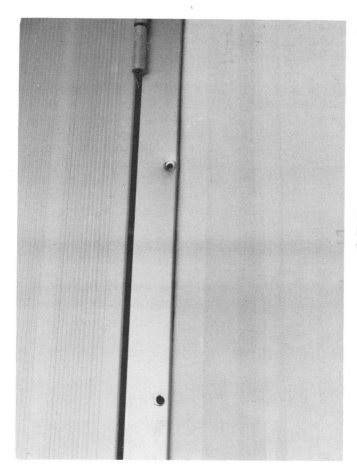

Fig. 3-11. Broken-off screw heads show poor quality control.

Fig. 3-12. A safety fastener for a fire escape window.

they will break after a short period of use.

Most kitchens use long fluorescent lamps in a central lighting area for better visibility. Additional fluorescent lights may be installed over the kitchen sink. The number of electrical outlets should be adequate as required by the code.

Molded countertops are preferable to those with dirt-catching metal corners.

Fig. 3-13. Many newer models have a round kitchen.

Bathrooms. In a conventional home, recessed fixtures and medicine cabinets are the rule, rather than the exception. In mobile homes, recessing the fixtures is impractical because of the thin interior walls. Consequently, such fixtures as toilet paper holders have to be surface-mounted on the thin paneling and may not hold securely.

Bathroom fixtures—bathtubs and shower stalls come in two types. One is a molded plastic shower (figure 3-14), or the molded plastic tub and sidewalls (figure 3-15), eliminating all made-up corners that collect dirt. The other is a composite assembly of laminated plastic walls and metal corners that does collect dirt and surface stains (figure 3-16). The first is definitely to be preferred; time has proved that such molded plastic assemblies will stand up to the rigors of mobile homes and their transportation.

Many mobile homes now use ceramic tile in the bathrooms as well as in the kitchen. The imitation tile board that is still in use is a poor substitute.

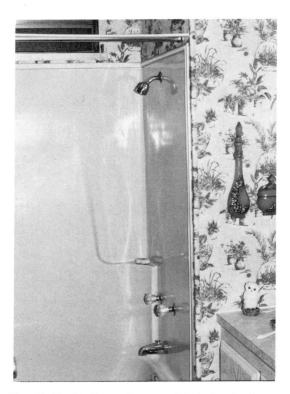
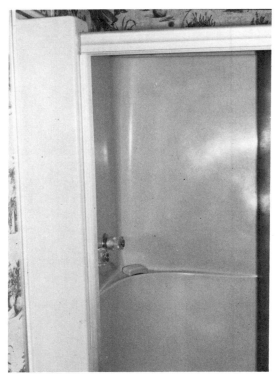

Figs. 3-14, 15. One-piece molded plastic shower and tub.

Fig. 3-16. Rust and accumulation of dirt in a built-up shower.

Air Conditioning

The best system in areas where air-conditioning is a "must" much of the year, consists of plastic ducts with overhead registers, and return registers in the floor. Doors can then extend to the floor, with thresholds to seal off each room. This provides greater privacy and also prevents the rapid spread of fire.

The air-conditioning system itself may consist of large, insulated, flexible plastic ducts installed beneath the mobile home and connected to a large air-conditioning unit. Another type is a heat pump system, requiring only a small duct connected to an evaporator unit in a closet within the home. There will be more said on this subject in Chapter 8. In any case, the system to be used must be selected when placing your mobile home order with the dealer.

Window air-conditioning units are not a practical substitute for central air-conditioning units. They have a limited cooling capacity, place a severe strain on windows not built for such a load, and are being rapidly replaced by the central air-conditioning system.

Insulation

Great improvement has been achieved here over the past few years, mostly through governmental regulation to conserve energy.

The minimum insulation for each area of the country is now specified by HUD. Additional insulation may be requested from the dealer but the additional cost may cancel out potential savings.

The preferred insulation is fiberglass, applied in batt form between wall framing members and in the roof. The use of styrofoam insulation under the roof is not recommended as it slowly evaporates at high temperatures.

The spaced-block approach (figure 7–27) to mobile home skirting increases heat losses beneath the mobile home. An insulated type of metal or plastic skirting cuts down this loss and still provides access and ventilation. Too many parks use only one type of skirting, regardless of its deficiencies.

Smoke Alarms

The ease with which a fire can spread through a mobile home has led to a mandatory requirement that smoke alarms be installed in every home now being sold. Check the model for the presence of this safety device. Smoke alarms may be battery-operated or connected to the 110-volt circuit line. A periodic check should be made of the smoke detector's batteries to maintain it in working order.

Miscellaneous Items

While examining the model, check whether the floor feels "spongy," or squeaks under a heavy person. Such symptoms may be due to inadequate fastening of the floor to floor joists, or to other design faults. Or the model may not be properly set up, with some supports missing underneath.

The furnace compartment has to meet specific HUD requirements, including stipulations as to details of enclosure, vents, door construction, and so forth. Examine these for compliance.

Check the quality of construction by observing the way the trim fits at floor, ceiling, and cabinet levels. Also, make sure that wall paneling appears to be fastened securely, without bulges or movement when you press on it. Check that filler wax has not been removed from the staple indentations in the paneling. These items are indications of possible poor workmanship throughout the remainder of the mobile home.

Warranties of one year should be attached to each major appliance. Such warranties may be either of limited or unlimited type.

"The List"

Don't depend on your memory to make later comparisons between models.

The list below will enable you to make a direct comparison of each feature in all models. Make one Xerox copy of the list for each model involved, and then compare them among themselves, feature by feature. That should tell you at a glance which model appears to suit you best. Options have also been listed. Desirable features have been indicated by a + sign.

"The List"

MANUFACTURER _____
PRICE _____
YEAR _____
DELIVERY PROMISED _____
BRAND NAME _____
SIZE _____
ACTUAL LENGTH _____
SINGLE, DOUBLE, OR TRIPLE _____
NEW OR USED _____
DEALER'S NAME _____
ADDRESS _____
_____

MEMBER OF DEALERS' ASSOCIATION _____
YEARS IN BUSINESS _____
FORMER CUSTOMERS _____

MODELS ON DISPLAY _____
    NUMBER _____
    NAMES _____
SERVICE DEPARTMENT _____
CUSTOMER COMPLAINTS _____
    BETTER BUSINESS BUREAU _____
    CONSUMER AGENCY _____

CONSTRUCTION

Standard stud spacing _____

Floor joists

    2-by-6's _____

   + 2-by-8's _____

Insulation _____

Floor material

    particle board _____

   + plywood _____

Ceiling _____

Interior walls

    5/32″ paneling _____

    color _____

   + ¼″ paneling _____

   + gypsum board _____

Exterior walls

    painted alum. _____

    color _____

    horizontal

        siding _____

        color _____

Roof

    galvanized steel _____

    asphalt shingle _____

    fiberglass

        shingle _____

        other _____

    overhangs

        1 side _____

     + 2 sides _____

     + all sides _____

HUD requirements

    external faucet _____

    ext. electrical

    receptacle _____

Type of furnace

    oil _____

    gas _____

Air conditioning

   + overhead registers _____

    floor registers _____

    ducts

       + plastic _____

        metal _____

    make _____

    size _____

   + heat pump _____

Doors

    wood _____

    metal _____

   + treated metal _____

Windows

    treated aluminum _____

    vent _____

    slide _____

Water heater

    capacity _____

    electric _____

    gas _____

    oil _____

Floor plan

    how many rooms _____

    bedrooms _____

    ¾ bath _____

    family room _____

    den _____

Living room size _____

    wall paneling _____

    color _____

    option _____

    carpeting _____

        color _____

        options _____

    windows

        number _____

        type _____

        bay _____

        picture _____

        regular _____

    furniture space

        adequate _____

        cut up by

           windows _____

Dining room

    dimensions _____

    walls

        paneling _____

        color _____

        other finish _____

        color _____

    floor

        carpeting _____

        color _____

        other _____

    built-in hutch _____

        adequate size _____

    overhead cabinets _____

    drawers

        nylon rollers _____

    accessible to kitchen _____

    adequate size for

        entertainment _____

    lighting fixture _____

Kitchen

    dimensions _____

    walls

        paneling _____

        wall paper _____

        vinyl paneling _____

        tile _____

floors
   vinyl tile _____
   carpeting _____
   linoleum _____
cabinets
   shelves
      smooth _____
   nylon rollers
      & stops _____
sink
   single _____
   double _____
   stainless _____
   porcelain _____
pantry
   washer dryer
      space _____
   plumbing &
      electricity _____
broom closet _____
appliances
   electric range _____
   dishwasher _____
   garbage dis-
      posal _____
   self-clean-
      ing oven _____
   refrigerator
      frost-free _____
      size _____
      side-by-side _____
      top freezer _____
   make of appliances _____
   extra cost appliances
      _____
      _____
      _____
      _____
   range hood _____
   exhaust fan _____
   illuminated ceiling _____
Bedroom, master
   size _____
   wall covering
      paneling _____
      wall paper _____
   flooring
      carpeting _____
      color _____
      other _____
   draperies _____
   curtains _____
   closet/s _____
   windows _____
   built-ins _____

   lighting _____
Bedroom, 1st
   dimensions _____
   wall covering
      paneling _____
      wall paper _____
   flooring
      carpeting _____
      color _____
      other _____
   draperies _____
   curtains _____
   closet _____
   windows _____
   built-ins _____
   lighting _____
   bunk bed space _____
Bedroom, 2nd
   dimensions _____
   wall covering
      paneling _____
      wall paper _____
   flooring
      carpeting _____
      color _____
      others _____
   draperies _____
   curtains _____
   closet _____
   windows _____
   built-ins _____
   lighting _____
   bunk bed space _____
Bathroom, master
   dimensions _____
   wall covering
      paneling _____
      wall paper _____
   flooring
      ceramic tile _____
      others _____
   tub
      standard _____
      plastic _____
      *garden _____
   linen storage _____
   lighting _____
   exhaust fan _____
   + heat lamp
      built-in _____
   shower only _____
      vanity in bedroom _____
   clothes hamper _____
   mirror _____
   indirect lighting _____

medicine cabinet _____	+ exhaust fan _____ _____
dressing space	+ heat lamp _____ _____
adequate _____	mirror _____ _____
Bathroom - bedrooms	medicine cabinet _____ _____

	1st	2nd
dimensions	_____	_____
shower only	_____	_____
bathtub		
standard	_____	_____
plastic	_____	_____
*garden	_____	_____
walls		
paneling	_____	_____
wall paper	_____	_____
vanity in bathroom	_____	_____
clothes hamper	_____	_____
linen storage	_____	_____
lighting	_____	_____

dressing space
   adequate _____ _____
access outside
   of bedroom _____ _____

Miscellaneous factors:
+ electric heat _____
+ electric appliances _____
+ hot water, electric _____
+ heat pump _____
+ owned lot _____
+ washer-dryer within home _____
+ shingled roof _____
+ roof overhangs _____ _____
+ kitchen drain pipe, external _____

_____

*A specially shaped step-in tub with space for plants or flowers.

Diverse Matters

In selecting a model, consider the following from the standpoint of convenience, safety, and maintenance:

1. Electric heat, electric appliances, and electric hot water heater eliminate the fire danger which attends the use of open flame. Still, electric systems have their own fire dangers.

2. A heat pump is more economical and it eliminates plastic external ducts, which can be a fire hazard.

3. Lot ownership means no rent, and no rent increases. Seemingly unjustified rent increases have been the bane of many mobile home owners who site their homes in rental parks.

4. Washer-dryer placement within the mobile home is the logical location if space permits.

5. Vented all around skirting reduces the danger of rodents, snakes, and other pests.

6. A shingled roof eliminates the need to paint your metal roof every two or three years. Many metal roofs eventually develop leaks.

7. Roof overhangs add to the appearance of the mobile home and keep the walls free of washed-down roof dirt.

This List is quite impressive but remember that you are making an expensive purchase in which you may be living for years. Mobile homes cannot be altered easily except by external additions. Thus, you have to consider your choice seriously and possibly add notations of your own to "The List." Be wary of a salesman trying hard to sell you a particular model. It might be a discontinued product on which service or repairs might be difficult to secure later.

To meet customers' requirements, many manufacturers offer options such as these: different types and colors of carpeting, curtains and drapes in various colors, several types of paneling in colors, register location in ceiling or floor, metal or shingle roofs, and similar variety, where feasible.

Many salesmen now have floor plans of the various models on display, together with a list of their features. Ask the salesman for a copy; it will provide a handy reference later to room arrangements and other details.

Dealer's Service

Arrange to see the dealer's service department, an important consideration if repairs become necessary. Some dealers provide their own service, while others hire outside repairmen or firms. The former is preferable since an outside firm often will send its service truck only when it is doing other work in the neighborhood. Thus there could be a delay of many days.

The dealer's service department should stock an inventory of all necessary parts, updated periodically to keep the supply at a high level. Otherwise, he has to order a part at a time, which is a costly, time-consuming process that leaves the customer waiting. (Thus begins the adverse customer reaction to a manufacturer's product which eventually translates into lower sales.)

The large manufacturers have service representatives who keep dealers throughout the country informed on problems and solutions. They also train the dealers' servicemen for corrections or replacement of defective parts. Thus, a small mobile home manufacturer is not to be recommended from the standpoint of the fierce competition possibly causing him to go out of business.

A mobile home dealership has much in common with a car dealership. Both must have good service departments to expand their sales. By buying from a large dealer the customer benefits from good, prompt service on a reliable well-built product. As mentioned previously, many of the construction details of the mobile home are hidden and the customer sees only the finished product.

Many mobile home manufacturers have so many plants (some as many as thirty) that they achieve, in effect, regional coverage; transportation is then limited to a 250 mile radius. This specialization allows the manufacturer to build mobile homes suitable for such requirements as hurricane zones or heavy-snow-roof loads.

Some state transportation laws limit the width of mobile home sections that can be moved over the highways. The limit may be 12-foot width, 14-foot, or 16-foot for a given state, within its own boundaries.

Choosing a Manufacturer

Determine if the manufacturer is a member of the industry's trade association, Manufactured Housing Institute (MHI), which polices the industry. Also, ask previous customers about their reaction to the manufacturer's product. The dealer will be able to refer you to them if he expects to make a sale.

Manufacturers are required to build their product to either ANSI A119.1 code before 1976, or to HUD standard after July, 1976. Either code requires display of a seal on the mobile home.

Warranties

In the early days of mobile home manufacturing, it was difficult to obtain remedial action from the manufacturer or a dealer selling his product. There was a tendency to "pass the buck" from one to the other when time came to correct the defects. The customer was the loser in the long run.

It was only upon passage of the Magnuson-Moss Warranty Act in 1975 that protection was offered to the consumer. The Federal Trade Commission was designated as the agency to oversee the standard warranties offered by manufacturers.

Consumer products manufactured after July 4, 1975, are covered under this act. It allows the consumer to sue for failure to honor a written warranty, a service contract agreement, or implied warranty under state law.

Remedies available include recovery of purchase price, market price of a replacement, or other costs.

This act applies to written warranties, such as written affirmations or promises that the material or workmanship is defect free, or to a written understanding to refund, repair, replace, or otherwise remedy a defective product. The supplier must make the remedy at no extra charge to the purchaser.

In reference to mobile homes, the act specifically sets up the following framework:

1. Service must be performed on the mobile home's site.

2. Repair of defects that make the home uninhabitable or unsafe must be undertaken within three business days and be completed expeditiously.

3. The manufacturer, through its representative, must inspect each home.

4. If a complaint is made, the manufacturer, through its representative, must reinspect each home to determine if defects or setup problems exist.

5. The manufacturer agrees that, if a dispute arises between itself and a representative (dealer) as to which is to handle a warranty or setup problem, corrective action will be taken in a minimum of time by the manufacturer.

6. If the dealer agrees to perform warranty functions for the manufacturer, he will perform as in item 2.

7. The dealer agrees to perform repairs of non-safety defects within a period of 7 to 30 days.

8. The dealer must maintain adequate service personnel and facilities, inspected by the manufacturer.

9. Manufacturers have to maintain records of service rendered.

10. The warranty period is one year.

Table 3–1 presents a typical mobile home warranty, as issued by Fleetwood Enterprises, Inc.

TABLE 3–1

Full One-Year Warranty

For Homes Manufactured by Subsidiaries of
FLEETWOOD ENTERPRISES, INC.

Coverage Provided

Your new home, including the structure, plumbing, heating and electrical systems, and all appliances and equipment installed by the manufacturer, is warranted under normal use to be free from manufacturing defects in material and workmanship.

This warranty extends to the first retail purchaser and his transferee(s), begins on the date of original retail delivery or the date of first occupancy if a rental or commercial unit (whichever comes first), and extends for a period of one year from that date.

This warranty covers only those defects which become evident within one year from the date of original delivery or the date of first occupancy if a rental or commercial unit and where written notice was given to the selling dealer or the manufacturer not later than one year and ten days after such date of delivery or first occupancy.

Owner's Obligations

The owner is responsible for normal maintenance as described in the Owner's Manual.

If a problem occurs which the owner believes is covered by this warranty, the owner shall contact the SELLING DEALER, giving the dealer sufficient information to enable him to resolve the matter.

Dealer's Obligations

By agreement with the manufacturer, the dealer is obligated at no charge to the owner to repair or replace any parts necessary to correct defects in material or workmanship.

When Dealer Does Not Resolve Problem

If the dealer is unable or unwilling to resolve a problem which the owner is convinced is covered by the warranty, he should contact the MANUFACTURER'S FACTORY and provide the manufacturer with a description in writing of the problem and the attempts made to resolve it.

Manufacturer's Obligations

Upon receipt of notice of a claim, where the dealer was unable or unwilling to resolve the problem, the manufacturer will repair or replace any part necessary to correct defects in material or workmanship, or will take appropriate action as may be required.

When Factory Does Not Resolve Problem

If the factory representatives are unable to resolve the problem and the owner is convinced that it is covered by the warranty, the owner should call, toll-free, (800) 854-4755, (800) 442-4804 for California residents, or (714) 785-3562 for Canada and Alaska residents, to describe the problem and the attempts made to resolve it.

(continued)

What Is Not Covered by Express Warranty

This warranty does not cover:

1. Problems resulting from failure to comply with instructions contained in the Owner's Manual and or Technical Installation Manual.
2. Bedding, Draperies, or furniture
3. Defects caused by or related to:
   a. The setup of the home
   b. Abuse, misuse, negligence, or accident
   c. Alteration or modification of the home, or by its transportation
   d. Normal deterioration due to wear or exposure.
4. Loss of time, inconvenience, commercial loss, loss of the use of the home, incidental charges such as telephone calls, hotel bills, or other incidental or consequential damages. Some states do not allow the exclusion or limitation of incidental or consequential damages, so the above limitation or exclusion may not apply to you.

This warranty gives you specific legal rights, and you may also have other rights which may vary from state to state.

The manufacturer is not responsible for any undertaking, representation or warranty made by any dealer, or other person, beyond those set forth in this warranty.

Actual Mobile Home Sizes

For many years, in Florida and other states, the length of a mobile home has been specified as the length of the hitch plus the home's length. The aim is to provide a basis for the transportation charges for towing the mobile home on a highway. Thus, an additional 3 feet or so was added to the actual length; the longer figure appears on the sales papers of the mobile home. To many persons, this appears to be a fraud on the buyer unless he is told about this additional length.

Of course, the longer home length is a source of greater income to the tax assessors or motor vehicle departments that issue the registration tags or labels on this misleading basis. The tax assessed is not on the true length—a sort of an officially sanctioned tax increase. Other, more progressive states do not charge the buyer such a discriminatory tax.

Mobile Home Accessories

The price of a model home may not include accessories that you find necessary or desirable—carport, shed, awnings, planters, roof overhangs, patio, and other items. Remember that they will add considerably to the home's basic price if you decide to buy them.

Inquire whether the quoted price includes transportation to the site, setup on site, carport and shed installation, carport deck and ramp, air condi-tioning, leveling twice, and the like. In other words, is it a "package" deal? Some dealers handle only the sale of the mobile home and leave it up to the park to complete the installation.

Also note the sections on TAXES in Chapter 4.

Final Selection

After you have gathered the facts on several models examined in detail, you should take your time in making the final choice.
making the final choice.

Make a list of the items you want changed in, or added to, the contract, together with their prices as given by the salesman. They must be listed in writing to avoid any misunderstanding. Some salesmen cannot be trusted unless everything is spelled out in detail. Delivery dates are also very important so the remainder of the work can be scheduled.

When you have decided on your choice, make a second thorough inspection of the selected model. You might discover some things that you overlooked originally. If possible, take a knowledgeable friend with you to help you in the final selection.

Remember: the more items you can check out prior to your purchase, the fewer problems you will face later. If buying in a park, check out the manager and his relations with the residents by inquiring of your future neighbors. Residents well pleased with their park is a plus sign. Too many resales in a park is a warning sign.

Buying a Used Mobile Home

This is similar to buying a used, or as some dealers call it, "preowned" house. It is a case of "Let the buyer beware." You will have to examine several actual mobile homes, not models. They may be on a dealer's lot or in a park. They may be being sold by a real estate agent, the owner, or by the park. Also, they may be on a rental lot, or on a lot owned by the mobile home owner. If on a dealer's lot, it will be necessary to locate a site for it, either by the dealer or yourself. Arrangements for the lot must be made before you buy.

Many parks will not accept a used mobile home purchased from a dealer's lot. There are several possible reasons: The park may have used mobile homes of its own for sale; the park loses its commission by not selling a new home for placement on an available lot; or the used home may not conform in appearance with other homes in the park. More will be found on this subject in Chapter 15.

Thus, unless the dealer can arrange for you to get a lot, buying a mobile home already on a lot is preferable. It also saves you problems: site placement, constructing a carport, planters, erecting a storage shed, and other matters.

Situating a used mobile home by itself in a suburban area can be complicated by zoning restrictions and the availability of sewer, electrical, and water connections.

Establishing Value

Placing a value on a used mobile home can be approximated roughly from advertisements appearing in local and mobile home newspapers. Many factors determine the value of a used home, including the types of homes in the park; location of the home in the park; whether it is offered for sale in the park; park's appearance and facilities, etc.

The "List" given above could be used to establish the relative merits of various homes you inspect in buying a resale home.

There are some additional factors to be considered:

1. Age of the various kitchen appliances
2. Age of air conditioning/heat unit or heat pump
3. Appearance of carpeting and walls
4. Appearance of furniture if it is being sold with the home
5. Outside appearance—walls, grass, planters
6. Carport—cracked concrete, stained, grease
7. Discolored outside trim and any other discoloration
8. Appearance of the park itself—neglected lawns, cars under repair, etc.
9. Existing mortgage and its terms
10. Refinancing problems, if any
11. Down payment requirements
12. Insurance—dates covered and extent of coverage
13. Whether any service contracts exist on appliances and air-conditioning/heat unit, or heat pump, and dates of coverage
14. Monthly rental and additional charges, if any
15. Lease—transferable, and changes in rental fee, if any
16. Copy of park rules and regulations
17. Termite inspection certificate
18. Date of last releveling

CHAPTER 4

MOBILE HOME PARKS

You should reserve a space for your mobile home in a park before you actually purchase the home. If you intend to buy a site not in a park, make sure there are no zoning or other restrictions to prevent using your property for that purpose.

Even before you consider a lot in or outside a park, you should decide if the general location is convenient to your place of work, shopping center, school, and place of worship. This is, of course, after you have selected the general area and state that are right for you.

Mobile homes can be placed on your own lot space outside a park, in a rental park, or in a park where you own the site. Most people, especially retired persons, prefer to locate in a park.

"Closed" Parks

Many rental parks are prone to certain shortcomings. Chief among these is the "closed" park, in which the owner or his salesman limits his stock to one or two makes of mobile homes, thus greatly restricting the available selection. The buyer is allowed to rent a lot only if he buys the brand of mobile home handled by the park, and then only at whatever price the park charges. The explanation given for such restrictions is generally that uniformity of appearance within the park is essential. In fact, however, the park owner may simply be making an additional profit by buying mobile homes from a factory at a wholesale rate.

Such practices can seriously hamper the buyer's ability to find the mobile home best suited for his purpose, or even to purchase his home from a large corporation, with plants and service facilities throughout the country. Also, the brands offered in "closed" parks may not be of the latest design or appearance. Thus, the buyer is likely to be a loser.

Also, many such parks require a "package" deal that saddles you with obligations beyond the mobile home itself. For example, if subcontractors are hired by the park to do carport, anchoring, and other work, you will be liable for the work (whether or not it meets your expectations), yet exercise no control over it.

Again, it may be difficult to get satisfaction for defects under warranty because the park manager decides whether the complaint is legitimate, and may decide against you, refusing to notify the manufacturer. That such situations lead to friction and bad feeling between manager and residents is self-evident.

For the foregoing reasons some states have outlawed the "closed" park concept, and suits have been brought by the Federal Trade Commission to stop such practices.

"Open" Parks

If the park is "open" to several dealers to sell their mobile homes, the park may still exercise some control over the size and quality of homes brought in. However, the customer will likely have a wider choice among models and brands than in the "closed" parks.

Dealers with model homes on display are often anxious to please the prospective buyer and may offer to have options added or changes made to suit the customer.

Mobile home dealers are listed in the yellow pages of the local telephone directory. Contact the Better Business Bureau beforehand for information on complaints against particular dealers.

Dealers may recommend certain parks, but caution should be exercised, since the dealer may have an interest in the park, own it, or even collect a fee for referrals.

Park Classification

Once you have decided to settle in a mobile home park, you should make a list of available parks and drive through them.

Your task will be easier if you have a directory of parks in your area, such as the latest edition of *Florida and Southern States Retirement and Resort Communities,* by Woodall, *Florida's Mobile Home Guide, California Mobile Home Park Guide,* or *Pacific Northwest Mobile Home Guide,* which covers Idaho, Oregon, and Washington. These guides are listed in the Bibliography.

A park classification system, originated by Woodall Publishing Company, and based upon examination of individual parks, was used for many years, but was abandoned in 1976. It was a star rating system, with a range of one to five stars in ascending order. The five-star park represented the most desirable type of park, combining all features important to most mobile home owners.

The system can be described as follows:

One-Star Park

In overall appearance, an average park, with old but well-kept homes and a part-time manager, is what this rating says.

Two-Star Park

To one star requirements, a two-star rating also adds some landscaping, neat storage and laundry facilities, and good maintenance and management.

Three-Star Park

Meets all standards of the two foregoing ratings, and adds good overall appearance, hard-surfaced streets, good lawns on all lots, and off-street parking.

Four-Star Park

Offers the sum of the three foregoing categories and, in addition: trees, shrubs, flowers, and grass on all mobile home spaces; at least 75 percent of all coaches with manufactured skirting; underground utilities; minimum coach width of 10 feet; adequate community hall and swimming pool; full-time management; and overall appearance of high quality.

Five-Star Park

Combines the features of the foregoing four requirements with these additions: paved streets; curbing; street lights; street signs; carports adequate for two-car parking; skirting on every home; awnings and storage sheds on all homes; recreation hall with kitchen and tiled bathrooms; all late-model homes; well planned and well laid out park; varied recreation program; excellent swimming pool of adequate size; full-time management interested in the maintenance of the park and comfort of its residents; attractive entrance and park sign.

Unfortunately, many parks have apparently lost interest in meeting these standards, and after a period of more than 20 years the park-rating system has given way to a detailed description of each park in 1976. Such description gives the following information: *park detail*—size of lots available, which gov-

erns the size of mobile homes that can be accommodated; improvements—such as water, sewer, electricity, street lights, sidewalks; *community services*—fire, police protection, refuse collection, medical services available, shopping centers; *fees*—monthly rental, mobile home price, lot prices, fees for lot maintenance; *business history*—length of park operation; *eligibility*—minimum age, adult or family, with or without pets.

The prospective resident makes the selection by comparing park descriptions, localities, rental prices, and other considerations.

When selecting a park be sure to note if it is a rental park or a lot-owned park. In Woodall's listing such information may vary in position from the beginning of the entry to the end.

A typical description of a park where lots are available for purchase may be given as follows:

> FACILITY DESCRIPTION: mobile home park, development/subdivision, 228 sites, single-family homes, purchased from development, lots 60' by 98' to 60' by 138', 100 percent double-wides, level, wooded. IMPROVEMENTS: water and sewer, electric, paved streets, street lights, SECURITY: internal security patrol, manager lives on site. COMMUNITY SERVICES: fire, police, refuse collection, hospital 10 miles, medical services; park public transportation, golf course 5 miles, churches, neighborhood shopping 2 miles. ON-SITE RECREATION: swimming pool, shuffleboard, recreation hall, square/round ballroom dancing, bingo, potlucks. FEES: developments $25,000 to $35,000 purchase price, $25 additional fees per month. BUSINESS HISTORY: facility has been operating for 3 years, corporation has been in business 2 years.

Tenant-Right Protection

Imagine moving a mobile home, an item weighing perhaps ten tons or more to another distant mobile home park. Many parks demand an "entrance" fee; or the park may be owned by a dealer who is more interested in selling one of his own mobile homes to fill any vacant lots than to provide you with a new lot.

Thus, most mobile home owners in rental parks are "captive" in their parks, and under a constant threat of eviction, either from investment corporations owning the parks or from park managers more eager to please their bosses than to assist in solving tenant problems.

The failure of many tenants to stand up for their rights has weakened the efforts of tenants' associations fighting back against such practices.

As a result, the lobbying efforts of mobile park owners' associations in various states have prevented passage of legislation to protect the rental mobile home owner against skyrocketing rents and eviction procedures. The attitude generally exhibited to counter tenant protests is that if you do not like the rent increase you can move, meaning your mobile home as well as yourself.

Florida rental parks are at the top of the list in this regard. The members of the legislature have succombed to the lobbyists' efforts. (Ironically, the lobby's funds have come primarily from the tenants' rents.) However, the twelve-month eviction – no-cause rule is bringing the tenants' plight into the open; see Chapter 14.

This is another reason to consider living in the "own-your-lot" park. Some of the rental worries will be absent, and you will be living in the same way as in conventional housing, with a lower monthly expense rate.

Mobile Home Park Living

There are problems in mobile home park living, but there is a brighter side to it. Although your neighbors may be from many states, you share the common bond of a different type of living.

As compared to apartment living, your neighbors will watch out for you—much like living in a small town. They will notice any changes in your habits and check if they suspect illness or other problems. "You are never alone" in a mobile home park.

Most parks have recreational committees selected from the park residents to provide entertainment programs and plan group trips for residents. Consider the facilities that you are likely to use when making your park selection.

Family Parks. It is the older parks that are likely to provide the features that cater to families with preschool and teenage children. Such parks are likely to have recreational facilities and activities to occupy the spare time and surplus energy of children while their parents are at work.

Some family parks are a part of an adult park, but separated from the remainder of the park.

It takes a patient park manager to overlook the damage that children may inflict in a clubhouse or to recreation equipment. If damage is a continuing problem, he may have to talk with the parents and remind them of the park rules. In any case, such

patience is not likely to be found elsewhere than in a family park.

Pet sections. Many mobile home buyers do not want to part with pets when moving into a mobile home. Practically all parks restrict pets to cats or dogs. Many parks provide sites, generally on the perimeter, for mobile home owners with pets. Most parks restrict them to one or two per home; some even restrict replacement of pets that die.

Pets are generally required to be on a leash at all times when being taken for a walk, except when they are confined to their share of the yard; that part has to be fenced in. Pets are restricted to the pet section of the park and arrangements have to be made if pets are brought in to other park areas by visitors.

There are rules against leaving pets on their own. Even if the owner is away for only a day or two, they must be kept in kennels. Other possible restrictions are those as to the maximum size or weight of the animals.

Older parks. If your interest is confined to a smaller park, with few facilities, you will also find such parks listed in park directories. These parks have been in existance for many years and are confined to single-wide homes, since their lot size will not hold a double-wide. Consequently, replacement homes must be of the same size. The residents are likely to be of advancing years, having lived in the park 15 or 20 years.

Frequently, the older parks are owned and operated by a man and wife who live in the park and are quite familiar with the residents. Rents are probably lower, and tend to stay low, in comparison with the newer, larger parks.

Park Rules

Some sets of park rules bear down so hard on tenants' rights as to drive prospective lot renters away. Some are so voluminous, consisting of so many *don't's* as to overwhelm the few *do's,* that they are apt to upset persons used to conventional home living.

Some rules are necessary, but many parks have gone overboard on the matter. For example, some will not even allow a washer and dryer in the home—they must be placed in the shed (see Chapter 9). From the standpoint of convenience, in cold or hot weather, such placement is not a desirable arrangement. Similarly, some parks will not allow cars to be washed within their boundaries. Again, some will allow only mobile homes with metal roofs, although the industry's trend is away from this. The owners will have to put up with painting such roofs periodically, every two or three years.

An example of a set of rules is given in table 4–1 at the end of this chapter. Note that, like any other such set, this one may be subject to amendment from time to time. However, this is a device unscrupulous management may use to entice persons to settle in a park, with few restrictions, at first, to hamper them. Later, home owners may find new or added rules, not to their liking.

Some parks restrict the number of adults per mobile home, charging extra for additional occupants. Others restrict the number of children or pets. In adult parks, the rules may restrict the number of guests, their length of stay or both, and add charges for them by the week or month. The charge may be $5 or more per week for each additional person. The reason for the additional charge is the cost of extra water used, which may amount to $1 per week per mobile home, a slight markup.

Some parks permit no motorized equipment except cars and self-propelled carts for the handicapped. Prospective buyers in some parks may not see the rules before the contract has been signed, on the ground that the contract may be cancelled within fifteen days of signing. This arrangement is definitely in conflict with existing laws; presumably, the operators hope that you will not change your mind after reading the rules. Any such arrangement, however, should be viewed with suspicion.

Leases

Various states, in response to the thousands of complaints received from residents in rental parks, have finally passed lease laws. These, in many instances, protect you from a possible monthly rent increase.

It may be of interest to note in the lease shown in table 4–2 that FOR SALE signs are not permitted on the tenant's lot or even in the windows of his mobile home, an enchroachment on his right to sell his own property. In one state such a rule has been nullified by the legislature, the action occasioned by the many protests received.

However, many folks believe that leases are made to be broken. If, for example, the park is sold to an out-of-state investment corporation, the new owner could plead that it must make an adequate return on its investment and raise the monthly rental as much as 25 to 50 percent. The tenants are helpless. It is either move or pay the higher rent. To people on fixed incomes, the increased rental becomes a heavy burden. This is one reason for selecting a smaller park, likely to be bypassed by such corporations, which are generally interested only in larger parks. The other problem with corporate ownership is that it is likely to install its own park manager, whose tenure depends upon his ability to cut expenses, with the tenants again the ultimate losers.

Despite periodic rent increases, some parks reduce expenses by turning off air conditioning or heat in the clubhouse, except at designated hours or when the number of residents using the facility reaches a certain minimum number; or they may cut down on grass mowing, or leave the grass clippings in the grass areas.

The mobile home salesman or park manager may promise extras that never materialize, such as a park bus or a heated pool in the winter. Depend only upon what is specified in writing.

Your Own Lot

The preferred way to purchase a mobile home is usually to buy, rather than rent, the lot which it occupies.

Parks in which lots are for sale have been created by developers who improve the property, subdivide it into lots (which may vary in size), erect the clubhouse, pave the streets, install lighting, and provide sewage facilities, electrical services, a swimming pool, and perhaps even a golf course. Mobile home owners pay a small monthly fee for the privilege of using such facilities.

The lots may vary in price, depending upon their size and location within the park, whether they are on canals or a lake, whether they are corner lots, and other variables.

The developer may also sell mobile homes within a particular price range to help maintain a uniform appearance. You, the lot purchaser, may be required to take care of such accessories as carports, sheds, landscaping, and utility wiring and plumbing connections, or the park developer may provide these services, as in a rental park—arrangements vary here.

One important aspect of such park development is that the developer controls the price range of mobile homes to be erected in the park. He will zone the park into two or three price ranges by segregating single-wides, double-wides, and triple wides, a procedure that helps to establish and maintain resale prices.

After the park has been filled, the developer turns over the facilities to a committee formed by the residents. Such a committee, or board of governors, sets up rules and regulations for the park operation, hires a park manager, and sets the monthly fees (item C, below). They may include money set aside as a capital fund for future repairs and improvements.

Here are some more expenses that the purchaser may or may not find included in the contract:

A. The cost of landscaping—whether grass sod and shrubbery, and landscaping helps are to be provided by the buyer or a contractor.

B. Carport driveway and apron—whether to be done by a contractor, or required by the park.

C. Monthly assessment—inquire about it. The cost of recreational facilities, provided by the developer, is borne by the lot owners, at a monthly amount determined by him. There may be an arrangement that, once the park is filled, the recreational costs and all facilities revert directly to the lot owners. They set up a committee that decides upon all affairs in the park, including the monthly maintenance fee.

D. Title insurance and similar matters involving financial and legal knowhow—as in conventional home buying. It's wise to have an attorney to represent you, the buyer, and oversee the various documents to be signed.

Such a document, for example, is the deed which, with certain restrictions, transfers the lot property to the new owner, another reason for hiring an attorney. These restrictions may have many manifestations and aspects: that the lot may be used only for residential purposes; spell out the qualifications of the mobile home to be placed on the lot as to price, age, and size; utility line easements; pet restrictions; garbage and trash placement; limit the number of occupants; park rules must be obeyed; your purchase extends only to the surface of your lot; limitations on reselling your property; whether street parking is permitted; whether individual TV antennas are allowed; that no outside storage is permitted; relative location of mobile home on the lot; the amount of monthly maintenance assessment, which is likely to be increased later; that future special assessments may be made to improve park facilities or to install new equipment; that any improvements outside the mobile home are subject to management's review prior to actual change; age and number of occupants. A sample set of such rules appears in table 4–3.

Advantages of Lot Ownership

There are many advantages, financial and otherwise, to owning your own lot.

Increasing rents. The biggest problem encountered by mobile home owners all over the country has been skyrocketing rents. Since home owners are "captive" on their rental lots, the management has come to think that rents can be raised practically at will: when a corporation purchases the park for investment; when the park owner can blame inflation for the rent increase; when the park has filled up and there is no longer any incentive to keep the rents low; when adjoining parks are no longer competitive and all raise their rents in unison; when associations formed by mobile home owners cannot have their case heard in courts because the courts refuse them a hearing; when state governments and legislators fail to listen to protests from thousands of mobile home owners about high rents. As a result, bitter feelings have developed between the park owners and residents.

But revolt seems to be in the making. For example, one 1,000-unit park in Florida, the Zellwood Station, has found so few buyers of mobile homes on rental lots that the management had to change its policy and now offers to sell lots to all buyers, past and present. This is only the first indication of the consumer resistance to gouging in rental mobile home parks.

Taxes. As a lot owner you become a real estate owner and thus have to pay taxes directly to the city or county. However, your expenses will be less than rent, since there is no profit involved; you can get "homestead" exemptions in some states, which reduce your tax bill. Some states allow a reduction in taxes if you are age 65 or over.

Mobile home taxes. I recently conducted a survey of mobile home taxes in various states. County and city assessors throughout the country were requested to furnish the same sort of information on this subject.

A glance at tables 4–4 and 4–5 may influence your selection of the state in which to settle upon your retirement. The information in these tables is "for comparison only." Obviously, no one lives in an "average" county, and, as we all know, real estate taxes can vary widely from one jurisdiction to another.

Some states still use vehicle registration tags to license mobile homes while others have shifted to labels. Some, such as Florida, still require high yearly label payments of residents in rental parks, whereas others may issue either a once-a-year label at a nominal price, or issue a one-time only label, as does New Mexico.

Increase in value. As real estate increases in value over the years, so does your lot. Owning the lot also has the advantage that, if you sell later, you—not the park owner—get the profit.

Management change. As the rental parks began increasing their rents beyond prevailing inflation and tax rates and thereby increasing revenues at the expense of the park residents, large corporations started to buy them as an investment. With no controls they could increase the rents, regardless of the existing rates, to a level which they considered sufficient for their stockholders. When the residents own their lots they are protected against such a takeover.

Other costs. In addition to the yearly city or county taxes for your mobile home and lot, there is the monthly maintenance charge levied on all the lot owners. This covers garbage collection, grass cutting, in some parks a capital improvement fund, salary of the park manager, and other expenses prorated among the residents owning lots.

While there will be added costs such as carports, shed, air conditioning, and landscaping, these same costs have to be borne in rental parks, either directly or hidden in the monthly rental. Thus, they do not increase the cost of owning your own lot.

A comparison between two adjoining parks finds that while the residents of a rental park were paying $104 per month, the residents in a lot-owned park were paying a total of $45 for taxes, maintenance, garbage disposal and trash collection, and capital improvement fund. Also the value of their owned lots had quadrupled in value from their original cost.

Having to move. There is always the threat of having to move in a rental park. This may be occasioned by a change in park ownership, or the management simply taking a disliking to you. One Florida county judge decided that any rental park resident can be forced to move for no reason at all if he is given a year's notice. The Florida State Supreme Court has upheld the ruling, even though it is unfair and not based on any state law. This decision has been cited in a number of eviction cases in Florida. Residents affected by this decision would be forced to sell their mobile homes at a possible loss, since the cost of moving them would be high, and depend upon finding another park that would rent them a space.

The decision by this county judge was made despite the fact that the legislature has specified only four acceptable causes for eviction. The "no reason" eviction clause in the proprietor-renter agreement was not included among them.

Lot restrictions. Restrictions, inserted in the deed, are to your benefit because all the lot owning residents then abide by the rules as they do in a rental park but with a considerable difference. In rental parks, the management inserts many *don't's* and few *do's* for the residents so as to be self-protective in any situation. Additional ones may be made by the park manager thus circumventing the lease which the residents have signed.

Your choice. Buying a lot for a mobile home is additional initial expense, but consider that you may pay $10–15,000 over a period of 10 years for a rental lot and have nothing to show for it at the end of that time. When you own your lot it is likely to increase in value and you have something to say about the park's operation through your representatives.

It seems clear that rental parks should be your second choice. The owned-lot parks usually allow you a monetary advantage and more peace of mind.

"Liaison" Committees

Some parks attempt to cut down on the number of complaints that the rental park manager may face from mobile home owners. That helps explain the establishment of so-called "liaison" committees which act as a buffer between the residents and the park manager. The committee acts to dispose of some of the complaints by holding hearings at specified times.

The trouble with this method is that the manager often handpicks the committee members from the park residents, and, naturally, those favorable to him. Thus the committee members often form what may be called the "company union" in union circles and are not likely to look with favor on some complaints even though they may be justified. After all, most complaints would not exist without an underlying cause in the first place. Thus, complaining residents frequently receive short shrift from the "liaison" committee and the manager escapes the wrath of the residents who may be totally justified in their complaints. All too often the only qualification for committee membership appears to be friendship with the management, not any special technical skill or talent.

TABLE 4–1

A Rental Park's Rules and Regulations

I. The management declares rules and regulations to be necessary in order that you have a neat, clean and attractive mobile home community of which both management and residents can be proud.

II. It is the resident's responsibility to do his share in helping to keep the community a pleasant, safe and desirable place to live. Therefore, the following rules and regulations supersede all other rules and regulations previously written:

1. Rents are payable in advance by the 3rd of the month. Make checks payable to _____ . Office hours are: 9:00 a.m. to 3:00 p.m. (Weekdays). Only emergency telephone calls (interpreted as serious illness, accident, or death) can be accepted and delivered to residents without phones.

2. Clubhouse, shuffleboard, pool room and other recreational facilities are provided for your pleasure. You are asked to treat them as you would your own personal property. No children under 18 may use shuffleboard courts unless under resident supervision. No children under 18 permitted in the pool room unless under resident supervision. Residents are responsible for pool table damage. Further, any additional rules governing the use of the shuffleboard courts, pool room, game and card rooms and swimming pool, posted in these facilities shall become a vital part of these rules and regulations.

3. a. _____ is a park for adults only. All visitors (guests) will be registered at the office. A visitor (guest) is anyone (member of the family, relative or non-relative) staying overnight in a mobile home. Visitors (guests), adults and children, exceeding two weeks stay will pay $5.00 per week, per person.

b. The monthly lot rent, as charged, covers those occupants who were residing in the mobile home when it was originally purchased. Any additional adult person residing in a mobile home exceeding the two weeks visitation period will either pay $5.00 per week or $10.00 per month, whichever is applicable. Residents will be held responsible for the conduct of their visitors and any damage caused by them. Visitors are to be advised of the *15 MPH SPEED LIMIT.*

4. All residents are required to sign out and sign in at the office when leaving for two weeks or more.

5. Disorderly conduct, abusive language, noisy disturbances, or disregard of the rules and regulations contained herein shall be grounds for immediate removal of the resident from premises.

6. No peddling, soliciting, or commercial enterprise is permitted in the park without the prior consent of the management.

7. Accidental damage to awnings, skirting, screening, etc. must be repaired within 60 days.

8. Management reserves the right of access onto the lots at all times for the purpose of inspection, utility maintenance and mowing. Maintenance workers are not to be stopped when they are mowing or working.

9. Management shall be notified immediately of any hazardous condition known to be a violation of these rules and regulations.

10. Discretion in the use of water is requested.

11. *Sale and Rental of Mobile Homes:* Management must be informed of all mobile homes for sale or for rent. No signs shall be displayed within the boundaries of the park. In order to expedite resales, management has available the facilities and experience to sell your mobile home. Before a home can be sold, the prospective buyer must be approved by the management. Renting of mobile homes is not encouraged. Only long term rentals are acceptable. Prospective renter-resident must meet with management. Further, renter-residents can be expelled under the same set of rules and regulations as owners.

12. *Pets.* Pets are restricted to pet section. They must be walked in that section on leash. Pets of visitors to residents outside the pet section must be boarded outside the park. Constant barking of dogs will not be tolerated. Grass will not be cut when pets are loose in the enclosed area of the pet section.

13. *Swimming Pool.*

a. All residents must wear white bracelets with tags and visitors must wear black bracelets with tags when in swimming. Only overnight visitors are privileged to go into the pool.

b. All persons must shower before entering pool.

c. All persons with long hair (male or female) must wear bathing caps or hair coverings while in the pool.

d. No rafts or floats are allowed in the pool.

e. No food or drink is allowed in pool area except on the patio.

f. Residents or visitors in swimming attire will remain in the pool area—not in and out of clubhouse or in the office. Further, residents and visitors are requested not to ride bicycles or walk through the park wearing only swimming attire.

g. Anyone using suntan oil must stay out of the pool. A large towel may be used to cover a pool lounge or chair if suntan oil is used and that person is *only* sunbathing.

h. Courtesy is the way of life at _____
—let's keep it that way, particularly in the swimming pool.

i. Children under 18 can use the pool *only* from 10:00 a.m. to 2:00 p.m. and must be accompanied by an adult park resident.

14. No changes, alterations, or additions to exterior of the mobile homes and lots may be made by the residents without prior approval of the management. Skirting, porches, awnings and other additions approved by the management shall be maintained in good repair.

15. Placement of shrubs, fences, trees or any outside structure must be approved by the management. Further, shrubs and trees planted in the future must have a 3- or 4-foot-diameter of rocks placed around the base.

16. It is the responsibility of the resident to maintain his site sewer line and water line from the perimeter connection. Also, the electrical system is the responsibility of the resident from the pedestal to the mobile home including the circuit breaker system or fuse boxes.

17. If a lot or planter is neglected, the management reserves the right to take over its care at a reasonable charge.

18. Storage of boats, travel trailers and other vehicles will not be allowed on individual lots.

19. No major repairing or overhauling of cars is permitted around the mobile home lots or in the roadways. Engine oil or motor oil drained from automobiles will not be poured in the storm sewers.

20. Garbage cans are to be placed in back of storage room. Decorative enclosures approved by management must be provided for each garbage can.

21. There shall be no exterior clothes lines or racks or drying of clothes under carports. Umbrellas are acceptable under controlled conditions.

22. No extra covering is to be placed over doors and windows when residents are away from the home.

23. TV masts are to be placed at the rear of the mobile home and are not to exceed 20 feet in height.

24. Management assumes no responsibility for theft or damage.

25. General notices and notices of odd articles for sale may be posted on the Bulletin Board for two weeks.

26. *SPEED LIMIT.* The speed limit of 15 MPH in the park must be observed at all times by residents and visitors, and all drivers must be alert for pedestrians and cyclists.

27. Automobiles must be parked in spaces provided on your own lot or in the space around clubhouse. Cars will not be permitted to stand on streets. Streets must be kept open for emergency vehicles. Motorbikes, motorcycles, and scooter bikes are not allowed in the park. Bicycles and tricycles must be equipped with a light and reflector if ridden at night. Residents are asked not to park their bicycles or tricycles on sidewalks, near windows and doors around clubhouse.

28. Complaints, recommendations, etc. are to be discussed with management and not neighbors. Avoid passing rumors onto others. Come to the office—we will be glad to give you the facts and do everything possible to correct unfair situations. Complaints by a resident regarding rule violations must be submitted to management in writing over his or her signature.

29. The management reserves the right to evict anyone who refuses to comply with the rules and regulations as herein provided.

These rules and regulations are hereby effective _____.

TABLE 4-2

A Rental Park's Lease Agreement

THIS LEASE AGREEMENT, entered into and between _____ , hereinafter called the "LANDLORD," and _____
hereinafter called the "TENANT,"

WITNESSETH:

WHEREAS, the LANDLORD is the owner of _____ , a mobile home park; and

WHEREAS, the LANDLORD is willing to lease to the TENANT under the following terms and conditions:

NOW, THEREFORE, in the consideration of the premises and the other terms and conditions hereafter contained, the parties agree as follows:

(1) LANDLORD leases to the TENANT Lot No. _____ for a term of one year commencing first day of January, 1979 and terminating on the first day of January, 1980.

(2) In consideration of the foregoing, the TENANT agrees to pay to the LANDLORD the sum of _____ Dollars ($_____) in advance per month. Said sum entitles TENANT to the use of the mobile home park facilities, cutting of TENANT'S grass and lot rental. If LANDLORD renews the term of this Lease, LANDLORD reserves the right to raise the rent by giving thirty (30) days notice, in writing, of a new rental amount and new terms of conditions of Lease, if any.

(3) The LANDLORD shall pay for the TENANT'S water, garbage collection and sewer charges. The LANDLORD'S payment of these utilities as a commitment is made for the term of the existing lease. The TENANT shall be responsible for the payment of any sales taxes, licenses, tag, tangible or intangible personal property taxes and any other taxes hereunder. The LANDLORD shall pay taxes only on the land and park improvements. The TENANT shall provide for his own liability and casualty insurance.

(4) There are no entrance fees or assessments to the TENANT by the LANDLORD except that may be contracted for and agreed to between the parties in writing hereafter.

(5) The Rules and Regulations of _____ _____ dated _____ are by reference made a part of this Lease Agreement. TENANT ACKNOWLEDGES RECEIPT OF A COPY OF SAID RULES AND REGULATIONS PRIOR TO SIGNING OF THIS LEASE.

(6) The TENANT shall be responsible for the compliance of all the laws of the State of Florida, Pinellas County, and other governmental agencies specifying requirements concerning the use, health, safety, sanitation, maintenance of the TENANT'S mobile home.

(7) All notices by the TENANT to the LANDLORD shall be sent to _____ in care of the Park Manager, _____ .
All notices by the LANDLORD to the TENANT shall be delivered to the TENANT'S LOT NUMBER specified above, unless the TENANT specifies in writing another address.

(8) The TENANT may sell his mobile home to another prospective TENANT as set forth in the Rules and Regulations and upon approval of the LANDLORD which approval shall not be unreasonably withheld.

(9) Rules and Regulations of the _____
may be modified, amended, or added to by giving TENANT thirty (30) days' written notice of said changes, except in cases affecting health, life, and property damages.

(10) It is specifically understood and agreed by and between the parties hereto that the provisions of Part III, Chapter 83 of the Florida Mobile Home Landlord and Tenant Act, are made a part of this lease agreement and govern mobile home park tenancies.

(11) Underskirting and tie-down equipment and any other equipment required by law, local ordinance or regulation of mobile home park, or by this Lease, shall be the responsibility and expense of the TENANT. Cement block underskirting, raised enclosure where lot size permits, carport (eleven feet wide) with utility room, and tie-downs are all required equipment under this lease.

THIS AGREEMENT SHALL BE BINDING UPON THE HEIRS, ASSIGNS, AND REPRESENTATIVES OF THE RESPECTIVE PARTIES HERETO.

IN WITNESS WHEREOF, the parties hereto hereunto set their hands and seals this _____ day of _____, _____.

Signed, sealed, and delivered in the presence of:

BY:

_____   _____
(Witness)   LANDLORD

_____   _____
(Witness)   TENANT
                                                                        (SEAL)

                                                    _____
                                                    TENANT
                                                                        (SEAL)

TABLE 4–3

A Lot-Owned Park

RULES AND REGULATIONS

BREEZE HILL ESTATES

Lake Walk-in-Water, Florida

Breeze Hill is an adult park. It is in our mutual interest that we establish certain standards. To this end the following rules and regulations have been established. Your cooperation in carrying out these minimal regulations will be greatly appreciated. Reference to "Breeze Hill Management" (B.H.M.) shall mean that person or persons, designated by the Board of Directors of Breeze Hill Association to manage the operations and to enforce the Rules, Regulations and Restrictions of Breeze Hill Estates, Polk County, Florida.

1. Office hours Monday through Friday will be 9 A.M. to 5 P.M. Weekend hours, if required, will be posted. Emergencies should be reported to the Manager's residence or to the Lodge Office, if occuring after office hours.

2. Speed limit is 15 M.P.H. The use of horns is prohibited. Cars must be parked in driveways. *No parking in the roads.*

3. Each resident is required to keep his lot and driveway neat and orderly at all times. Storage under homes is prohibited unless completely screened from view. Type or method of screening must be approved by B.H.M. No storage is allowed on patio or under the carport.

4. No additions or alterations shall be made to homes or property without approval by the designated representative of B.H.M.

5. B.H.M. has authority to correct alterations made without express permission, to make any repairs or perform any needed maintenance to correct exterior defects and to charge homeowner costs incurred.

6. Because of underground utilities, it will be necessary to obtain permission from B.H.M. before planting any trees, shrubbery or any vegetation requiring digging.

7. All antennas must be located as near the rear of the home as is practicable. No electronic equipment will be allowed that causes interference in other resident's electronic equipment.

8. No extended repairing of cars, outboard motors, cycles, building or storage of boats or recreational vehicles or similar disturbing activities will be allowed on private premises.

9. Only umbrella-type clothes lines located behind homes will be allowed. These must be stored away when not in use.

10. Electricity is individually metered and payable directly by each individual resident to Peace River Cooperative.

11. Use of the recreation building, pool, pier, shuffleboard courts, etc., is subject to rules posted at the lodge. Breeze Hill Association assumes no responsibility for residents or their guests or for possessions of residents or their guests.

12. Children must be guests of residents for a maximum of 15 days in one vacation period, with a total allowable stay of 30 days in any calendar year. All guests are to abide by state law and register at the office of B.H.M.

13. In consideration of other residents you are asked to maintain the volume on radios and T.V. to a level that will not disturb others. If necessary volume is to be lowered after 10 P.M.

14. Children using recreational facilities must abide by posted rules and be strictly supervised by adults. Children not properly supervised will be requested to leave the areas.

15. Use of manual water sprinkler is permissible. Automatic sprinklers will not be allowed in order to conserve water. Under extreme drought conditions, watering of any kind may be prohibited.

16. Signs will be prohibited within the boundaries of Breeze Hill Estates. Homes for sale may be listed with the office or advertised through any broker or publication. One professional sign no larger than one square foot, and meeting Breeze Hill Management approval, will be allowed per lot.

17. Breeze Hill Estates is for single family purposes. It is hereby agreed that no home will be sold or subleased without first notifying B.H.M. Purchasers or Lessees must be approved by B.H.M. prior to consumation of any transaction to sell or lease.

18. Garbage containers, of a type approved by B.H.M., are to be kept at the rear of homes out of sight from streets. Containers are to be placed at curbside twice a week on days designated by Management.

19. No soliciting, peddling or commercial enterprises will be allowed in Breeze Hill Estates unless it is of mutual benefit to all residents. Any such activity must be approved by B.H.M.

20. No commercial trucks will be allowed in Breeze Hill Estates except for the purpose of picking up or delivering merchandise to residents, or on park business. This does not apply to pick up trucks which are hereby considered the same as passenger vehicles. All vehicles, including automobiles, trucks, motorcycles, mopeds, lawnmowers, etc. must have adequate mufflers and must be operated in a safe and orderly fashion, not annoying other residents.

21. Proper attire will be required at Breeze Hill Estates at all times. Specific requirements for Public Areas, such as Recreation Building, will be posted.

22. An extra charge will be made for residents using washing machines contained within their mobile homes. This charge is to defray the cost of the additional load on water and sewer systems. This charge will be $4.50 per month, per home. If costs indicate that an adjustment in this charge is in order, the rate may be adjusted by B.H.M.

23. B.H.M. absolves themselves of all liability or responsibility related to losses incurred by fire, theft, property damage, accidents, Act of God, or any causes, whatsoever.

24. B.H.M. reserves the right to institute legal action against any resident or guest who refuses to comply with all rules and regulations as herein provided. The Board of Directors of the Breeze Hill Association reserves the right to add or alter rules and regulations as circumstances require.

25. There will be a limit of two well mannered pets (dogs or cats) per residence. No pet shall weigh in excess of 30 pounds. The owner shall keep all pets tethered within the borders of his own property or in the owner's automobile, if not on the owner's property. Owners will be responsible to keep runs clean and odorless at all times and to see that their pets make no noise or perform any acts which may be annoying to management or other residents.

26. An area is provided at a nominal charge for storage of boats, trailers, recreational vehicles, etc. Every effort will be made to protect items stored in this area, however, Management will in no way be responsible for fire, theft, or other damage that may be incurred.

27. Approval of all plans for permanent or temporary structures or fences must be approved in writing by the appointed representative of the Board of Directors of B.H.M. Management reserves the right to refuse approval on any grounds including purely esthetic consideration which it shall in its discretion determine to be significant to preserve the environment and harmonious development of the subdivision.

28. Picnic tables, storage sheds, outdoor grills, and similar personal items must be approved by B.H.M. and kept in first class condition at all times.

29. No littering. This especially includes cigarette butts and other personal debris such as candy and gum wrappers. The management specifically asks that cigarette butts be held until a proper receptacle is reached and under no circumstances are they to be discarded on the ground in public areas or on private yards.

30. Regardless of lot location or configuration, residents are strictly forbidden to trespass on another person's lot without his permission.

31. The exterior of all structures must be completed within 60 calendar days from commencement except where completion is impossible because of strikes, fires, national emergencies, or Acts of God or would result in great hardship. Time extensions must be approved by B.H.M. All construction must comply with applicable codes and zoning regulations.

32. No noxious or offensive activity shall be carried on within Breeze Hill Estates nor shall anything be done to cause embarrassment, discomfort, annoyance or nuisance to other residents.

33. No structure of a temporary nature, travel trailer, tent, shack, garage, barn or other outbuilding shall be used at any time as a residence either temporarily or permanently.

34. These restrictions are for the protection of each person as a property owner. The intent is to provide a dignified, well kept residential development in which an enjoyable home can be maintained. We are delighted to have you join us at Breeze Hill and sincerely hope that your residence here will be one of the happiest periods of your life.

A COPY OF THESE RULES MUST BE REVIEWED AND DELIVERED TO ALL NEW RESIDENTS AT TIME OF CLOSING.

Witness As to Signature of Buyer   Above Offer Hereby Confirmed

_____   _____ (Seal)
                                                              Buyer

_____   _____ (Seal)
                                                              Buyer

TABLE 4–4

Approximate County Tax on a $20,000 Mobile Home
(1978 tax rates)

Tax ($)	State
50	Texas
75	West Virginia
100	Alabama, Louisiana, Pennsylvania, Tennessee
150	Georgia, Indiana, New Mexico
200	Florida, Illinois, Kentucky, Mississippi, Missouri, Virginia, Wyoming
250	Arkansas, Iowa, North Dakota, Oklahoma, South Carolina
300	Arizona, Arkansas, Idaho, Maine, Minnesota, Ohio, Utah
350	California, Colorado, Delaware, Montana
400	Connecticut, Idaho, Maryland
500	Massachusetts, Nebraska, Oregon, South Dakota
750	New Hampshire

Note: Some county taxes listed above are reduced in consideration of the following: (1) aged 65 or over; (2) homestead exemption; (3) veterans.

Some states set a limit on the maximum annual income one may receive in order to qualify for a tax reduction. See Table 4–5. Please remember that these figures are "for comparison only," and that real estate taxes can vary widely from one jurisdiction to another.

TABLE 4–5

Maximum Annual Income Limitations*

State	Dollars
Arkansas	7,500
California	12,000
Colorado	(Tax credit)
Connecticut	(Tax benefits)
Florida	(Homestead exemption on owned land)
Georgia	(Homestead exemption on owned land)
Idaho	7,500
Illinois	(20 percent discount)
Iowa	4,000
Montana	8,000
New Hampshire	5,000–20,000 (depending on age)
New York	6,500
North Dakota	6,500
Oklahoma	4,000
Oregon	7,500 (veterans)
South Carolina	12,000
Tennessee	4,800
Utah	4,500 (veterans)

*See explanatory note at bottom of Table 4–4.

CHAPTER 5

MOBILE HOME PARK SELECTION

Because the mobile home owner is likely to reside in a mobile home park for many years, he should exercise great care in selecting the park. As noted earlier, it is not easy to move if you find the park is not to your liking.

In the past, out of thousands in this country, only the better-grade parks were rated by Woodall. However, the one-to-five-star park classification system mentioned earlier is no longer being used by Woodall. Nonetheless, the star ratings have been retained by some parks, which continue to advertise their "five star rating" as an indication of their superiority (figure 5–1).

Woodall's has changed its directory to an annual entitled *Florida and Southern States Retirement and Resort Communities*. It lists rental and lot-owned mobile home parks; conventional home subdivisions; hotels; apartments; and multi-family dwellings. Because it is issued yearly the monthly rental fees of the parks are fairly up to date.

Several typical Woodall listings are shown in figure 5–2.

In effect, it is necessary to make up a list of desirable features and make your own park ratings.

Fig. 5-1. A five-star park entrance sign.

Fig. 5-2. Park listings by Woodall.

Fairway Village

FACILITY DESCRIPTION: mobile home park, 758 sites, rental park, lots 50' x 80' to 60' x 90', level/sandy, lakeside/Golf course; IMPROVEMENTS: water & sewer, electric, paved streets, curbs & gutters, street lights, sidewalks, coin-op laundry; SECURITY: manager lives on site, local police patrol; COMMUNITY SERVICES: fire, police, refuse collection, hospital, medical services, park, public transportation, golf course on site marina, churches, neighborhood shopping 1 block, regional shopping 1 mile, facility has own bus or taxi service, Courtesy Bus; ON-SITE RECREATION: instruction available in sewing, craft rooms for woodworking/pottery, clubs for cards/golf, 2 swim pools heated, jacuzzi, billiards, shuffleboard, fishing, golf course, putting green, recreation hall, square/ballroom dancing, bingo, potlucks; FEES: Rental Park — $91.50 to $106.50 per month, $91.50 typical monthly cost; ELIGIBILITY: minimum age 40, no children, pet section; ADDRESS: Dept. W, 1100 Belcher Rd., Largo, FL 33540.

Swan Lake Estates

FACILITY DESCRIPTION: mobile home park, 241 sites, rental park, lots 42' x 75' to 52' x 75', level/loam soil, mountain view, lakeside/wooded; IMPROVEMENTS: water & sewer, gas, electric, paved streets, curbs & gutters, street lights; SECURITY: restricted visitor parking area, internal security patrol, manager lives on site; COMMUNITY SERVICES: fire, police, refuse collection, hospital 2 miles, medical services, park, public transportation, golf course 2 miles, churches, neighborhood shopping 1 block, regional shopping 2 miles; ON-SITE RECREATION: instruction available in sewing/weaving/painting, clubs for travel/cards, swim pool heated, jacuzzi, billiards, shuffleboard, fishing, square dancing, bingo, potlucks; FEES: Rental Park — $95 per month, $95 typical monthly cost; BUSINESS HISTORY: facility has been operating for 5 years, corporation has been in business for 2 years, 10% vacancy rate; ELIGIBILITY: minimum age 18; ADDRESS: Dept. W, 4550 Flowing Wells Rd., Tucson, AZ 85705.

SEVEN HILLS MOBILE HOME ESTATES

FACILITY DESCRIPTION: mobile home park, development/subdivision, 300 sites, subdivision, land sale only, level, mountain view; IMPROVEMENTS: water & sewer, gas, electric, paved streets, curbs & gutters, street lights; SECURITY: local police patrol; COMMUNITY SERVICES: fire, police, refuse collection, hospital 2 miles, golf course next door, churches, neighborhood shopping 5 blocks, regional shopping 1 mile; ON-SITE RECREATION: instruction available in sewing/painting/jewelry making, Adult classes of Hemet Unified System: Spanish, dancing, many others, clubs for cards, swim pool heated, jacuzzi, billiards, shuffleboard, square/round/ballroom dancing, potlucks, full-time recreation director; FEES: Subdivisions — $10,000 to $14,000 purchase price lots; BUSINESS HISTORY: facility has been operating for 3 years, corporation has been in business for 3 years; ELIGIBILITY: minimum age 45, no children, pets, with restrictions; ADDRESS: Dept. W, 2516 Silver Oak Way, Hemet, CA 92343.

LAZY DAYS MOBILE VILLAGE

FACILITY DESCRIPTION: mobile home park, development/subdivision, 421 sites, subdivision, single-family homes purchased from development, lots 50' x 100' to 75' x 100', level, close to Gulf beaches-fishing; IMPROVEMENTS: water & sewer, gas, electric, paved streets; SECURITY: internal security patrol; COMMUNITY SERVICES: fire, police, refuse collection, hospital 5 miles, medical services, park, public transportation, golf course 2 miles, marina 2 miles, churches, neighborhood shopping 1 1/2 miles, regional shopping 3 miles; ON-SITE RECREATION: craft rooms for sewing, clubs for travel/cards/golf, bowling clubs, swim pool heated, billiards, shuffleboard, round/ballroom dancing, bingo, potlucks, sauna; FEES: Developments — $15,000 purchase price new, $13,000 purchase price resale, $4,000 purchase price lots only, $23 additional fees per month; BUSINESS HISTORY: facility has been operating for 4 years; ELIGIBILITY: minimum age 40, pets, with restrictions, Pets restricted to 15 lbs. (small) on leash.; ADDRESS: Dept. W, 2524 N. Tamiami Trail, N. Ft. Myers, FL 33903.

Park Location

One of the problems facing the prospective mobile home buyer is the selection of the area in which to settle. One obvious guideline is weather conditions. For example, the Southern states—Georgia, Alabama, Florida, Mississippi, and Texas—have the advantage of moderate winter temperatures but longer summers, with temperatures above the national average. The Western states—Arizona, New Mexico, and California (figure 5-3) attract many retirees whose friends located there earlier. Southern California has the advantage of moderate temperatures throughout the year.

Fig. 5-3. A Western mobile home park setting.

Geographical location. Caution should be exercised about locating in parks in certain areas. In Florida, for instance, much of the central interior area should be avoided because of the phosphate mining. This industry leaves tailings, or scrap, shown in figure 5-4, which covers many acres of ground, rising like mountains on the landscape, and producing radiation from the uranium by-products found in these tailings. The other unfortunate consequence of this industry has been its vast use of water, in hundreds of millions of gallons daily (from the aquifer that is the main source of water for all of Florida). This tremendous removal of water has given rise to intrusion of salt water from the western coast of the state into the wells which supply residents of mobile home parks along the coast.

Since salt water intrusion is irreversible, it creates a threat of water shortage in the affected area. No long range plans have been made to secure water from other sources when the wells become "salted." Licenses are still being issued to additional phosphate firms which will increase the water use in the future and worsen the salt water intrusion. A widely reported "sinkhole" also affected one Florida locality recently, as a result of ground water depletion.

Some states, particularly Arizona and California, have long-range water programs and are not likely to have shortages in the near future.

The section of California that lies along the earthquake fault should be avoided, for obvious reasons.

Thus no single section of the country can claim the perfect conditions for mobile home park living. In many instances, what may influence a person's selection is having a friend living in one—especially true in retirement parks.

Smaller parks. Medium-size parks of 200 to 300 mobile homes have advantages over the larger parks. Generally they have better management-resident relations and are less likely to be bought by large investment corporations, chiefly interested in making a profit.

Park ownership should be investigated at the outset to avoid moving into a park that is not locally owned. Woodall's does list the "Business History" of the park, identifying the ownership, but in the final analysis your own personal inspection is the best guide in choosing the park. A high vacancy rate is a warning of problems, while waiting lists indicate a desirable park.

Picking the Park

Once you have settled on the area where you would like to live, your next move is to select several parks you want to look at.

Fig. 5-4. Phosphate scrap or tailings.

First, call the parks to find out if there are lot vacancies and, if it is a rental park, the present monthly rate. While Woodall's and other park directories try to keep such information up to date, rentals change during the year.

The park's location is of utmost importance. Is it located directly on a heavily traveled highway, making entrance and exit difficult? Or is it set back some distance, thus helping to lessen the noise from highway traffic? Are there open areas around the park which possibly could be zoned for heavy industry in the future? Or is such industry already present within sight of the park? The park manager may be able to offer you answers to such questions, but you may want to check further.

Take a ride through the park to observe and make notes on the points discussed below.

Appearance. Start with the entrance. It should be attractive (figure 5-5), and have a sign with the park's name on it, illuminated throughout the night to provide a ready identification for emergency vehicles, which may not be familiar with the park's location.

Park roads should be checked for appearance and maintenance. Are they sufficiently wide? Do they have concrete gutters for quick water runoff and long life? To increase the number of mobile homes in a given area, some developers settle for narrow streets which can result in traffic congestion. However, narrower streets will suffice if there is no street parking allowed and emergency vehicles can get through. It is also easier to move cars in and out of carports if street parking is prohibited.

A feature best observed at night is the adequacy of the street lighting. Good lighting lends itself to better security. Lighting around such areas as visitor parking facilities, as well as around pool and clubhouse, should be high enough to illuminate a large area.

The park should have at least two entrances to provide an exit in an emergency. Large parks may require even more gateways to afford easy exit from the park onto the adjacent thoroughfare.

Poor grading or inadequate block footings at the mobile home (figure 7–28) may permit water to run beneath the home and cause the ground to settle. The mobile home itself then settles, creating further problems, as a consequence of poor setup practices in the park. If possible, select a lot on higher ground and insist on having at least two courses, layers, of blocks (used for skirting) cemented to avoid a pool developing beneath the mobile home in heavy rains.

Parking. There should be adequate parking provided for visitors, preferably near the clubhouse. Enough spaces should be provided, depending upon the park's size, to obviate casual parking on lawns and streets, a practice both unsightly and potentially dangerous in an emergency.

With the longer mobile homes, it is possible to park two cars in the carport, which is generally constructed of concrete to withstand the wear and tear. Thus one-car families have a convenient place for a visitor to park. Large parks may have several parking areas located throughout the grounds as an additional convenience for guests.

Fig. 5-5. This park entrance road is clearly marked and has a light for night illumination.

Park requirements. Many parks have numerous rules about carports, sheds, planters, porches, patios, fences, color of mobile homes, and other matters that affect the park's appearance. Most parks allow parking only of automobiles in the carport. Recreational vehicles, trucks, boats, and towed vehicles have to be parked in a restricted area in the park, often fenced in to avoid spoiling the overall appearance of the mobile home community.

Most parks also require that a shed, (figure 9–8), of a design and style approved by the management, be located on the carport area for storage and for such equipment as a washer and dryer. No outside storage is permitted in the majority of parks, again for the sake of appearance.

Most also specify concrete carports. Connected to the street by a concrete apron, carports must be at least 11 feet wide; a 12-foot apron and carport is preferable, especially for larger cars.

Planters are designed by the park management to provide a uniform appearance. Some parks even specify or supply the shrubbery for them. Parks also regulate the construction and appearance of porches and patios to be added by the residents.

Fences are permitted in some parks, especially in the pet section, but again they must conform to rules specifying their size, material, installation methods, and similar details.

In inspecting a prospective park one should note whether it has underground utility facilities and, if so, how they are metered. Some parks meter and bill the electricity provided for mobile home owners, sometimes at a considerable markup. In other parks, the home owners are billed directly by the power company which installs the meters.

Another item to investigate is TV antennas. In some parks individual antennas are not permitted because of their appearance, and the park requires that TV sets be connected to a central cable or antenna system (at a nominal charge).

Here are additional conditions to check:

1. What are street conditions after heavy rain or snow?

2. Check noise levels if the park is near an airfield, railroad, or an expressway likely to have 24-hour traffic. Pick the rush hour for such a check.

3. Is traffic speed controlled? Some parks have put in artificial "bumps" to slow down service trucks as well as residents.

4. Take a walk through the park and talk to the residents. Check the pet section if you expect to reside in or near it.

Parks may be classified as adult (no children), family, and retirement. Your age is likely to have a bearing on the type you select. People tend to congregate with others in their age group, who have similar tastes in entertainment and living requirements.

Observe, when going through the park, whether the rules—such as those forbidding children to swim in the pool at specified time—are being obeyed. Did they shower prior to entering the pool and observe all the pool rules posted nearby?

If there is a pet section in the park under consideration, find out the number of pets allowed, the rules governing their placement, and what behavior might be regarded as objectionable to other park residents. This is important to those prospective purchasers who expect to bring their pets to the park as well as to non-pet-owners who fear they may be annoyed by other folks' animals.

Check if the park has laundry facilities at the clubhouse or elsewhere for residents' use: whether only washers or dryers are available, or both, and the rates charged.

Some parks require home owners to have their own laundry facilities installed in the shed space, not within the mobile home itself. This may affect the mobile home that you will be buying.

Some parks are new; others may have existed for twenty years or more. Their age is important from the standpoint of having neighbors in your own age group, especially if it happens to be a retirement park. The size and types of mobile homes are clues to the age of the park (figure 5–6).

Fig. 5-6. An older mobile home.

Park rules It is vitally important to secure a copy of the park operating rules before signing any contract. I know of one park which has 113 pages of *do's* and *don't's,* primarily for the park's benefit. Too many *don't's* cause poor management-resident relations.

Such rules should be given a careful reading before making your park selection. One may find restrictions rather hard to accept after living many years in a conventional-home residential neighborhood. However, park rules are necessary to maintain a well-kept park, free of annoyances to the residents. A sample set of such rules was given in table 4-1.

The appearance of the clubhouse indicates good or poor management and is a good indication of overall park housekeeping. Check the floor for cleanliness.

One should also note the size of the clubhouse provided in relation to park size and number of residents. The size of that facility frequently does not keep pace with the park's expansion. Consequently, the clubhouse may be too small to provide enough card rooms or kitchen and workshop facilities to meet residents' needs.

For most gatherings that take place in the clubhouse, the kitchen is the focal point, handling food for the recreational programs. Kitchen facilities should include kitchen ranges and ovens, multiple cabinets, and work table, as well as sinks (figure 5-7). Cabinets should have locks.

Fig. 5-7. A clubhouse kitchen with plenty of storage and work space.

Many parks restrict the number of adult occupants of a home to the number of original purchasers and require additional rent if additional occupants become permanent residents in the mobile home.

Other parks limit the visitor's stay by charging extra weekly or monthly amounts if the specified limit is exceeded.

There are so many regulations imposed on the residents that many owners feel that they are being imposed on. While managements justify the rules on the ground they benefit the residents, some of them are questionable.

Park Details

While inspecting the park, attention should be directed to such questions as these: Are the floors in the recreation building kept clean? Are all the rooms separated from the main hall air conditioned? Are rest rooms and laundry facilities kept clean and dry? Are trash facilities located near the kitchen and kept emptied?

Waste disposal. In a park of several hundred homes, it is preferable to have the trash-garbage disposal system out of sight.

In some parks, the residents are required to have a partial enclosure at the end of carports for their trash cans. In others, the residents have to carry their waste to a central location, where "dumpsters" are placed for use of the residents. The latter are rather unsightly and may lead to infestation by rodents. This is also harder on older residents.

Mail. Mail delivery in parks varies. In some, individual mail boxes, set on a post by the curb, serve as receptacles. In others, mail is delivered to the door, either to mail boxes located on the mobile home or slots in the doors. It may also be delivered to a bank of locked boxes at a central point in the park (figure 5-8).

Fig. 5-8. Mailboxes at a central point.

Space rental. Most parks are rental parks. Their charge for ground space varies a great deal, depending upon the quality of the park, its location, and nearness to shopping centers, schools, and other facilities. Some parks make a practice of starting with low rental to attract buyers to fill the park as quickly as possible. Rent increases follow, even with the lease system. The leases are only for one year and thus the park management is free to boost the monthly rates since the residents are "locked in" once they've moved in.

To further aggravate the situation, parks are being bought by corporations for speculative investment. One such corporation owns over 6,000 spaces in twelve parks.

Additions. If you contemplate adding a patio to your mobile home after you have become a resident, make sure that park rules allow for such an addition and that space will be available.

Transportation. A park may be located some distance away from shopping centers, schools, and places of worship, thus requiring the use of public transportation or your own car. Proximity to these facilities is an advantage. Retirees should consider that they may be unable to drive their own car later, due to age, failing eyesight, or other infirmities.

Automotive restrictions. To keep down the level of noise, many parks do not allow motorcycles or other loud vehicles on the grounds; whether they are owned by residents or visitors.

Buying on a friend's advice. While a friend may extoll the virtues of the park in which he or she is a resident, care should be exercised in following such advice. What may suit him or her may not necessarily suit you, whether your differences are over location, rules, manager, or whatever. Independent judgment is not only desirable, it might prove to be a life saver. Once you are committed to a particular park, you become "captive" unless you are able to sell your mobile home readily.

"Package Deals." Many parks offer a package deal when you buy a space in the park. The salesman at the park not only handles the rental or sale of lots but also sells certain makes of mobile homes, "approved" by the park, and such items as the erection of the mobile home on its site, carport, shed, approach apron, and air-conditioning/heat unit. In other words, your mobile home will be ready to move into, once you have signed the contract. (Due allowance must be made, of course, for the time required to complete this work.)

Such parks are classified as "closed" parks (i.e., the buyer is limited in the make or makes of mobile homes that the park will allow to be brought in). Some states have outlawed this practice because of the many complaints made by prospective customers and by mobile home dealers. Some parks have tried to justify this practice, claiming that they want the park to have a uniform appearance. The Federal Trade Commission has instituted suits in some states to protect the buyers and to prevent collusion in these matters.

"Entrance" and "Exit" fees. Some parks charge additional sums called "entrance" and "exit" fees. An "entrance" fee applies if a lot renter brings in a mobile home, the purchase of which has not been handled by the park. Or an "exit" fee is charged if the resident decides to remove his mobile home from the park.

Although such fees are usually held unlawful, some parks find ways to evade the law. This practice has warranted continuing public condemnation.

Landscaping. There are wide variations among parks with regard to care of grounds and planters, and other landscaping services. Some parks mow the lawns and trim the grass; others only mow the lawns and leave the trimming to the residents. In parks where the lots are owned by the residents, grass cutting may be left to the individual residents.

Also, some parks provide and set the plants and bushes in the planters which are part of the mobile home. Others expect the new resident to do this on his own. Some parks provide some gardening tools to residents. Find out about these services from the salesman or park manager when negotiating the purchase of the mobile home.

Emergency equipment. Parks vary considerably in the equipment they have available for use in emergency, such as lengths of rope, lanterns, and saw horses to be used to block off an area in case of fire, windstorm, or other calamity. Some parks have very little indeed for these purposes (figure 5-9); their equipment may be limited to some fire extinguishers in the clubhouse.

Fig. 5-9. The only emergency equipment available in some parks.

Utilities. The better parks have the utility wiring for electrical service and telephone lines distributed underground to eliminate unsightly wires and poles. At each lot, there is a meter mounted on a service box which has an emergency cutoff switch to completely disconnect the mobile home from power service.

Access to the telephone wiring is via a terminal box on the back of the mobile home.

Mobile homes are vulnerable to accidental shorts and wire breakage caused by rodents and workmen making repairs to other equipment where such wiring is exposed under the home.

Park layouts. There are many park layout designs; it goes without saying that this is a prime factor in the park's appearance. Parks used to be laid out in straight rows of mobile homes, with little done to break up the monotony. All homes had to be white and of the same rectangular shape, varying only in length. The park area was stripped bare of any trees, compounding this basic poverty of appearance.

The newer parks include winding streets, with homes at varying angles, several parking areas distributed through the park, and trees, shrubbery, and flowers near the clubhouse to enhance the overall effect. An illuminated entrance sign, together with flowers and shrubs, adds to the park's desirability as a place to live.

Some states require that the guest parking area be based on at least one space for every four mobile homes in the park. Such regulations became necessary when some parks tried to cut such areas to a minimum to provide more mobile home lots.

From the foregoing, one can see that there are many factors to consider when trying to select a mobile home park. The rental vs. owned lot choice is also important when one considers the greater freedom and lower costs to their residents in the owned-lot parks.

Park elevation. An important final factor in your selection is finding out the park's elevation above sea level, especially in the coastal regions of Florida. Many of these areas are only 10 feet or so above sea level, are poorly drained; and should torrential rains occur, scenes such as those shown in figure 5–10 are likely to occur.

Fig. 5-10. Torrential rains and poor drainage are responsible for this flood.

The bottom of the floor assembly of a mobile home has only thin protection; it can suffer considerable damage if the rainwater rises and covers lots and streets.

Park Managers

A park manager may take you on a park tour if you appear to be interested in becoming a resident, or even help you get in touch with some residents. His initial contact with you will give you a chance to form an opinion about him. After all, he is the man with whom you will be dealing during your residence.

Check with the manager about the details of purchasing the mobile home if this happens to be a "closed" park, whether this would be a package deal, and so forth. He may refer you to a salesman who actually handles the sales of mobile homes, their selection, accessories, and take you to the model homes in the park.

In "open" parks, the manager may make arrangements with a local mobile home dealer for you to see models of various manufacturers which meet with his approval.

A park manager should be courteous, well liked by the residents, yet firm and impartial in enforcement of park rules. Unfortunately, many a mobile home park has a manager who is not interested in helping residents with their problems. This is a good reason why a prospective resident should, if possible, ask present park residents about the manager's qualities and responses to their needs. The treatment you receive from the manager when you make your inquiries about locating in the park can be an indication, though not always, of his attitude toward the residents. Even residents of a neighboring park may be able to give you an opinion of the manager of the park in which you expect to reside.

In the owned-lot parks the residents have control over their manager, as he is hired by the representatives of the residents (who own the park). In rental parks, the residents have no voice in manager selection and often have to make the best of it or move out.

Park Living

Once you have settled in the park, you will want to get acquainted with your neighbors. Many parks have associations which conduct monthly meetings. Such gatherings offer a chance to meet other residents who may offer to help you get settled.

It is a common practice in many parks to introduce the new residents and identify their mobile home so others will recognize them as their neighbors. New residents are encouraged to join the various recreational facilities, such as bridge clubs and bowling clubs. In this way the ice is broken for a new resident. Neighborliness prevails to a much greater extent than in apartment or condominium living.

Any early problems with your new mobile home should be taken up with the dealer or the park manager, if the home has been sold through the park office. Under the warranty, the necessary repairs have to be made within a specified period. If the dealer fails to correct the problem, contact the manufacturer or the consumer complaint office in your area.

Inquire about the course of rents in the park over the past few years. Yearly increases of 15 to 25 percent suggest that the park owner may be greedy and that continuing rent increases are to be expected.

Some parks even try to control the type of news that appears in park-industry newspapers, which print news from various parks in addition to advertisements. Park "tidbits" written occasionally by a park resident as a regular contributor to the paper have been known to be restricted by the park management, by its refusal to allow the newspaper (distributed free) to be brought into the park.

Park associations, composed of park residents in the rental park, are quite common. Some are set up strictly for entertainment purposes, while others try to protect tenants who become involved in controversy with management. Strong leadership will result in a strong association.

Should the park owner decide to sell the park, the residents can request that they be given the first chance to buy. Thus, the park will become a lot-owned park, of a condominium type, with the residents owning all of the recreational facilities and being charged a small monthly fee for maintenance. A board of governors or its counterpart is elected to run the park.

Recreation

One of the attractions of mobile home living is a well-run recreation program, promoted either by the park management or the residents themselves. Ask about the recreation facilities when shopping for a park.

The extent of the programs depends upon the residents—their willingness to support and develop a plan that provides entertainment for themselves and their neighbors. In retirement parks particular attention is given to having other facilities besides a clubhouse—a pool, heated in the winter (figure 5–11), shuffleboard courts (figure 5–12), and horseshoes.

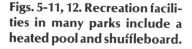
Figs. 5-11, 12. Recreation facilities in many parks include a heated pool and shuffleboard.

Many parks have facilities—guided either by a paid recreation director or by the residents themselves, organized in various committees—that sponsor dances, movies, bingo, kaffee-klatsches, potluck dinners, and the like. Outside entertainers may be invited to add to the interest in various park functions (figure 5-13).

Residents may collect money, sell tickets, or operate such functions as bazaars (figure 5-14) or horse races, where door prizes are won by lucky ticket holders. Food and other items are sold to raise money for a charity or other deserving causes.

A modern park will have a clubhouse, large enough to accommodate the greatest number of residents expected to attend such affairs as a New Year's Eve party, with space left for dancing and entertainers. A large kitchen is a must for the preparation of food for potlucks, dances, and other social affairs. Restrooms, card rooms, hobby rooms, and a pool room round out a well-designed clubhouse.

Figs. 5-13, 14. Park residents often enjoy events such as kitchen bands or raising funds at a bazaar.

Whether the recreational director works full- or part-time, his salary must be paid by residents through an additional levy per household. As a full-time employee, he can be expected to coordinate all activities, social as well as recreational. Only the largest parks can afford this amenity; more generally the task falls on volunteers from the park community. Volunteers may of course help the director in planning details as well.

Bingo is one of the widely supported, inside-the-park entertainments. It brings many residents together once or twice a week at a designated time. A special bingo board illuminates the figures to be played (figure 5-15) while another board has the numbers light up as they are called (figure 5-16).

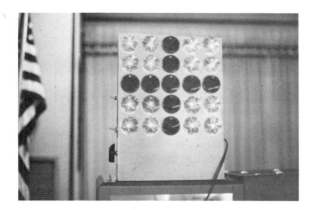

Figs. 5-15 (a, b), 16. Bingo is a favorite park entertainment. (Left to right) An illuminated bingo figure board, a side close-up of the board, and a large bingo numbers board.

A park of any size will have one or more pools, generally heated for use in the winter (if in the South) for the comfort of its users. Pool-side deck and furniture provide comfort for the sun bathers (figure 5–17). Pool rules require the use of conveniently located shower or showers.

Potlucks are generally held once a month, with residents bringing covered dishes or dessert. They serve as social gatherings for residents who may be unable to attend other park functions (figure 5–18). An entertainment may follow.

Parks may offer a variety of facilities:

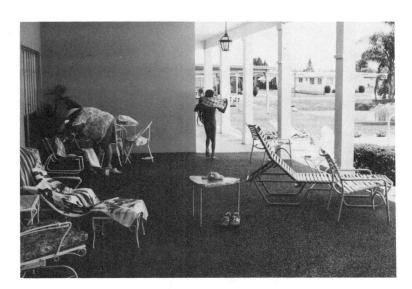

Fig. 5-17. A pool-side porch.

Fig. 5-18. A potluck gathering.

Picnics are another form of recreation, organized by the entertainment committee on such holidays as Memorial Day, Fourth of July, and Labor Day. Generally held within the park (figure 5–19), they may include a shuffleboard tournament, horseshoe contest, and other games. Food and drinks may be brought by the residents or the affair catered by an outside concern. Tickets, sold for the picnic, cover the cost of food if catered.

Other affairs include celebration of 50th wedding anniversaries of the residents and pool parties.

Card parties, bridge (figure 5–20), and pinochle are popular, and many clubhouses have card rooms available. Slides and movies are also shown here; residents often enjoy seeing themselves in movies taken at park affairs. Or they may show slides of trips

Fig. 5-19. A summer picnic.

Fig. 5-20. A bridge party at the clubhouse.

that they have taken before or since entering the park. The card room, when not occupied, may be used as a sewing room. There may be a pool and billiards room as well (figure 5–21).

Other recreation may consist of trips to local theaters or charter bus journeys to more distant places of entertainment. Plane trips may be arranged to places such as Las Vegas, Mexico, Hawaii, and Europe. These group trips require careful planning, not only by the recreational committee in the park, but by the sponsoring travel agencies.

Golf courses are featured in some deluxe parks; alternatively, the residents may become members of a nearby golf course. Bowling can be enjoyed by park residents as a group, on a weekly basis; it attracts both men and women.

Fishing is available to many park residents located near suitable waters. Trips in chartered or walk-on boats can be arranged for the residents by the park committee at a reasonable price.

These examples illustrate some of the entertainment which mobile home residents can enjoy, especially in retirement and adult parks where owners with time on their hands may want to compensate for having been unable to travel during their working lives.

Fig. 5-21. A game of pool.

CHAPTER 6

THE PURCHASE

You will have to decide on the maximum price you can afford to pay for your mobile home and what down payment you can handle. Remember that to the base price quoted by the dealer or park salesman must be added many other items, which may come to an additional 20 or 30 percent or more. Some salesmen may quote a total price, ready for you to move in, but be sure to get a complete breakdown of the various items included so you can compare it with those for other models and parks.

As with cars, you may find a list posted in many models, together with prices for extra items or options. The posted prices reflect only the cost of the mobile home and not the costs of completing its installation, unless so stated.

An Example

An illustration of prices quoted for a double-wide, 24-by-48 foot mobile home is given in table 6–1. These are early-1981 approximate prices, probably to be "shaved" somewhat once the dealer finds that the purchaser is serious about buying the mobile home.

Some saving can be made by not buying the furniture and by omitting the patio. But in the long run you will save if the items you want are installed at the time of your purchase rather than later. Substituting a heat pump for the conventional air conditioner will add several hundred dollars to the initial cost, but it will be a more desirable unit to have over a long period of time, especially in colder areas.

Should the transaction involve the house lot, it will be necessary to determine its exact price as lots can vary in price by several thousands of dollars, depending upon their size, location, surroundings, quality of park, and other factors. Financing your loans for the lot may also differ from that for your mobile home loan.

TABLE 6–1

Costs of Mobile Home and Basic Options

Facility	Cost
Base price (including setup and anchoring)	$21,000
Furniture	2,000
Carport	1,000
Shed, 8′ by 14′	1,100
Driveway	600
Skirting, planter, and steps	500
Sod	300
Air conditioner	1,000
Plumbing, electrical connections	500
Patio	1,000
Impact fee (permit for sewage and water connections)	700
Total	$29,700

Make explicit arrangement in your purchase agreement for chemical treatment of the lot to prevent termite infestation, a procedure often overlooked. While negotiating for the purchase of the mobile home you may inquire about such matters as the use of concrete as a base for the lot under the mobile home (described in Chapter 7), and also its cost.

Financing

The dealer or park salesman may try to arrange financing of the mobile home and the lot for you. However, since he will be the third party involved, his interest rate is likely to be higher than if you go to such conventional lenders as savings and loan associations, credit unions, commercial banks, finance companies, or other traditional sources for your loan.

Depending upon the size and type of loan, a certain minimum down payment is required on all of the types of loans outlined in this chapter. However, it is to your advantage to make the down payment as large as possible, and pay off the loan in as short a time as possible, to save interest charges.

Once you have decided on the mobile home you want, the dealer will have you sign a purchase-agreement form. It lists the cost of the mobile home, optional equipment, and accessories and their costs, and amounts for down payment, insurance, and finance charges.

Figure 6–1 shows a portion of a typical form used by dealers and mobile home park salesmen as a purchase agreement or contract for the purchase of a mobile home.

Sales tax. Some states impose a sales tax, basing it on price of the mobile home and its options. However, such additional matters as impact fee, carport, driveway, planter, and the like, which are site constructed, should be excluded from the total price on which the sales tax is paid. See Chapter 4 for details. Check this carefully, as it is a common practice to charge the sales tax on the total amount of transaction.

Hitch price. In reviewing your purchase agreement, make sure that you have not been charged for the running gear: the tow bar, hitch, and wheels used to transport your mobile home from dealer or factory to your site. They are removed by the contractor once the setup has been completed, and are taken away to be used over and over. Thus, there is no excuse for the dealer to charge you for them, except possibly a small fee for their use. Ask the dealer about the charge, if any, stipulated in the agreement for this item.

First step. Examine the purchase agreement for the list of all options that you have selected and their prices, and for the warranty covering the mobile home for a definite period. Do not accept any verbal promises. Strike out all blank lines to prevent future tampering with the agreement. If in doubt about handling the transaction yourself, have an attorney check the details. His fee is well worth paying if it avoids future complications.

Once the agreement has been signed, the dealer will request a deposit. This deposit is a legal way to protect you and the dealer. Should you fail to go through with the purchase, the dealer retains the deposit. The dealer is obligated to deliver your purchase (the mobile home) to you once he has accepted the deposit. You may now be reasonably sure about your purchase.

The purchaser of an item gets a three-day cooling-off period in some states. He can change his mind about going through with the transaction within that time.

To protect him, some states further require that the dealer place the money received as payment for the mobile home in an escrow account in a bank. This money is released later when the mobile home is delivered to its purchaser.

Title certificate. Once the mobile home is ready for occupancy, in many states it is legally transferred to the purchaser by a certificate of title, much like that for a car; it has the same provisions for later transfer of the mobile home to another purchaser, for instance. In the current transaction, it transfers the mobile home from the dealer or manufacturer to you.

After all concerned have signed the title, it is recorded with the registrar of motor vehicles, or other agency handling the titling or registration of motor vehicles. Not all states require registration of mobile homes by tags or titles. Some use decals, with a low, one-time-only fee. See table 6–2 for details.

TABLE 6–2

Procedures for Registration of Mobile Homes, by State

Note: States where *no* registration tag is required: Colorado, Delaware, Georgia, Illinois, Indiana, Kentucky, Massachusetts, Michigan, Mississippi, Missouri, New Jersey, New Hampshire, North Carolina, Ohio, Pennsylvania, Tennessee, Utah, Virginia, Washington.
States requiring labels: Idaho, Montana, New Mexico, North Dakota.

State	Requirement
Alabama	Registration
Arizona	Registration not required if over 8 by 40 feet
Arkansas	Certificate of title
California	Each section $11 (1980), no tags
Connecticut	Certificate of title
Florida	Annual registration label for each section
Iowa	One tag only
Kansas	Registration tags
Louisiana	House trailer plates, one per section
Maryland	Title optional
Minnesota	Title only
Nebraska	Tag $2.50
Oklahoma	Tag
Oregon	Registration tag $6
South Dakota	License $10
Texas	Car registration tag once
Wisconsin	License plate $18

The certificate of title (or other transferring certificate) records a description of the mobile home, manufacturer's name, year of manufacture, and serial number.

If you pay the purchase price of the mobile home in full, the dealer or salesman will give you the certificate of title (or similar paper), making the mobile home legally yours.

ORM 500

PURCHASE AGREEMENT
UCC § 2-201

PHONE:	
SOLD TO	DATE
ADDRESS	SALESMAN

SUBJECT TO THE TERMS AND CONDITIONS STATED ON BOTH SIDES OF THIS AGREEMENT SELLER AGREES TO SELL AND THE PURCHASER AGREES TO PURCHASE THE FOLLOWING DESCRIBED PROPERTY:

MAKE	MODEL	B. ROOMS	APPROX.	STOCK NUMBERS
			L. W.	
SERIAL NUMBER ☐ NEW COLOR ☐ USED	PROPOSED DELIVERY DATE	KEY NUMBERS	HUD label number	

OPTIONAL EQUIPMENT, LABOR AND ACCESSORIES				
		PRICE OF UNIT	$	
		OPTIONAL EQUIPMENT		
		COST OF SET-UP PARTS		
		SUB-TOTAL		
		SALES TAX		
		NON-TAXABLE ITEMS		
		VARIOUS FEES AND INSURANCE		
		1. CASH PRICE	$	
		TRADE-IN ALLOWANCE	$	
		LESS: BAL. DUE ON ABOVE	$	
		NET ALLOWANCE		
		CASH DOWN PAYMENT		
		CASH AS AGREED SEE "REMARKS"	$	
		2. LESS TOTAL CREDITS		
		3. UNPAID BALANCE OF CASH SALE PRICE	$	

Title to said equipment shall remain in the Seller until the agreed purchase price therefor is paid in full ☐ in cash or by the execution of a ☐ Retail Installment Contract, or a Security Agreement and its acceptance by a financing agency; thereupon title to the within described unit passes to the buyer as of the date of either full cash payment or on the signing of said credit instruments even though the actual physical delivery may not be made until a later date.

IT IS MUTUALLY UNDERSTOOD THAT THIS AGREEMENT IS SUBJECT TO NECESSARY CORRECTIONS, AND ADJUSTMENTS CONCERNING CHANGES IN NET PAYOFF ON TRADE-IN TO BE MADE AT THE TIME OF SETTLEMENT.

S.S.#   /   /   Name _____

S.S.#   /   /   Name _____

BALANCE CARRIED TO OPTIONAL EQUIPMENT $

Fig. 6-1. A portion of a sales form for a mobile home purchase.

If the mobile home is to be financed, the lender will hold the title certificate, giving you instead a copy to show that you have a conditional ownership of the mobile home. As part of this financing you have to sign a promissory note that binds you legally to repay the loan to the lender. The right financing arrangement will not only save you money but may make it possible for you to purchase a better or larger model, or order better accessories.

In the past, mobile homes were not considered the best collateral by lending institutions. They were regarded as temporary housing, purchased by persons who might not meet their obligations or who might abandon their property. This is no longer the case.

Another important change came when Congress passed the Consumer Credit Act of 1969, popularly known as the Truth-in-Lending Law. It defined many terms pertaining to financing. Banks, credit unions, finance companies, mobile home dealers—all financial sources—now have to quote financing charges in dollars and cents, and in terms of an annual percentage rate (APR) as well.

The financing of a mobile home is determined by the category into which the loan falls: (1) conventional; (2) HUD/FHA; (3) Veterans Administration (veterans only).

Conventional Loans

As noted above, banks and savings and loan associations have begun to welcome loan applications from prospective mobile home purchasers in recent years, reversing a far less receptive attitude that prevailed for decades. Improvements in construction and the entrance of large, nationally known corporations into the mobile home market have helped upgrade the image of mobile home life expectancy. The introduction of double- and other multi-wides, with prices ranging from $20,000 to $40,000 and even higher, has brought into this market people of sounder financial standing. Persons unable to purchase conventional housing but who need financing to cope with the higher prices of mobile homes have also entered this market.

Conventional mobile home loans still have some built-in limits. They range from 12 to 15 years in length, with a down payment of 25 to 30 percent. Thus a $20,000 loan will require a down payment of $5,000 or $6,000. Such an amount may be more than many people can afford to lay out. They are then likely to turn to other financing sources, such as the Federal Housing Administration Title 1 loans, or Veterans Administration (VA) loans, where lower down payments and longer repayment periods are the rule.

The first step in securing any type of loan is to fill out a credit application. This will furnish the lender the required information about your past and present employment, credit record, debts if any, your earning capacity, and other information which he has to consider to determine your credit worthiness.

HUD/FHA Insured Loans

Under Title 1 of the National Housing Act, the Department of Housing and Urban Development, through the Federal Housing Administration, insures approved lending institutions against loss on mobile home loans under the terms provided in that act.

Conditions. To qualify for a HUD/FHA insured mobile home loan, the loan must meet the following conditions:

1. The loan may be made to finance a new mobile home or a used mobile home that was previously financed under the same HUD/FHA insured mobile home loan.

2. The mobile home must be the purchaser's principal residence.

3. The mobile home must meet HUD's construction and safety standards.

4. A written warranty form, prescribed by HUD/FHA, must be delivered to the purchaser.

5. The mobile home must have a minimum size of 10 by 40 feet.

6. The mobile home must be placed in an approved mobile home park, meeting minimum standards relating to sanitation, lot location, vehicular access, landscaping, and any other requirements prescribed by FHA commission.

7. When the mobile home is placed on a lot owned by the borrower:
   a. The site must be at least a quarter-acre in size.
   b. The site must have adequate sanitary facilities.
   c. Present zoning must permit placement of the mobile home.

8. Flood insurance coverage to the amount of the loan is required in areas having special flood hazards and the community in which the mobile home is located must participate in the National Flood Insurance Program.

9. The maximum loan amount cannot be greater

than $18,000 for a single-wide, or $27,000 for a multi-wide, or 130 percent of the total home price.

Charges and fees. The following charges and fees are allowed:

1. Filing or recording fees.
2. Documentary stamp taxes.
3. State and local sales taxes.
4. Cost of comprehensive and extended coverage insurance for maximum of five years.
5. Itemized setup charges, including transportation charges and tie-downs by the dealer, not exceeding $500 for single- and $1,000 for multi-wides.
6. Skirting cost, the actual cost or $300, whichever is the lesser amount.
7. Central air-conditioning or heat-pump allowance, no greater than dealer's cost plus installation.

Borrower's minimum investment. The borrower must make a minimum down payment of at least 5 percent of the first $3,000 of the total cost, plus 10 percent of any amount in excess of $3,000, excluding charges and fees.

Financing charges. The maximum financing charge may not exceed 17 percent* simple interest per year. The only other charge may be a 1 percent origination fee collected from the borrower.

_____

*Subject to financial market interest changes.

Form Approved
OMB No. 76-RO371

VETERANS ADMINISTRATION
REQUEST FOR DETERMINATION OF ELIGIBILITY AND AVAILABLE LOAN GUARANTY ENTITLEMENT

TO

VETERANS ADMINISTRATION
ATTN: Loan Guaranty Division
P.O. BOX 505
JACKSONVILLE, FL 32201

NOTE: Please read instructions on reverse before completing this form. If additional space is required, attach separate sheet.

1. FIRST-MIDDLE-LAST NAME OF VETERAN

2. ADDRESS OF VETERAN (No., street or rural route, city or P.O., State and ZIP code)

3. DATE OF BIRTH

4. MILITARY SERVICE DATA—I request the Veterans Administration to determine my eligibility and the amount of entitlement based on the following period(s) of active military duty: (Start with latest period of service and list all periods of active duty since September 16, 1940.)

PERIOD OF ACTIVE SERVICE		NAME (Show your name exactly as it appears on your separation papers (DD Form 214) or statement of service)	SERVICE NUMBER	BRANCH OF SERVICE
DATE FROM	DATE TO			
4A.				
4B.				
4C.				
4D.				

5A. WERE YOU DISCHARGED, RETIRED, OR SEPARATED FROM SERVICE BECAUSE OF DISABILITY, OR DO YOU NOW HAVE ANY SERVICE-CONNECTED DISABILITIES? ☐ YES ☐ NO (If "Yes," complete Item 5B)

5B. VA FILE NUMBER C-

6. IS THERE A CERTIFICATE OF ELIGIBILITY FOR LOAN GUARANTY OR DIRECT LOAN PURPOSES ENCLOSED? ☐ YES ☐ NO (If "No," complete Items 7A and 7B)

7A. HAVE YOU PREVIOUSLY APPLIED FOR A CERTIFICATE OF ELIGIBILITY FOR LOAN GUARANTY OR DIRECT LOAN PURPOSES? ☐ YES ☐ NO (If "Yes," give location of VA office(s) involved)

7B. HAVE YOU PREVIOUSLY RECEIVED SUCH A CERTIFICATE OF ELIGIBILITY? ☐ YES ☐ NO (If "Yes," give location of VA office(s) involved)

8A. HAVE YOU PREVIOUSLY SECURED A VA DIRECT HOME LOAN? ☐ YES ☐ NO (If "Yes," give location of VA office(s) involved and complete Items 9 through 18)

8B. HAVE YOU PREVIOUSLY OBTAINED HOME, FARM, CONDOMINIUM OR BUSINESS LOAN(S) WHICH WERE GUARANTEED OR INSURED BY VA? ☐ YES ☐ NO (If "Yes," give location of VA office(s) involved and complete Items 9 through 18)

8C. HAVE YOU PREVIOUSLY OBTAINED A VA MOBILE HOME AND/OR LOT LOAN(S)? ☐ YES ☐ NO (If "Yes," give location of VA office(s) involved)

NOTE: Complete Items 9 through 18 only if you have previously acquired property with the assistance of a GI Loan.

9. ADDRESS OF PROPERTY PREVIOUSLY PURCHASED WITH GUARANTY ENTITLEMENT

10. DATE YOU PURCHASED PROPERTY

11. DO YOU NOW OWN THE REAL PROPERTY DESCRIBED IN ITEM 9? ☐ YES ☐ NO (If "Yes," do not complete Items 12 through 18)

Fig. 6-2. Part of a VA certificate of eligibility.

Loan requirements. The loan shall be payable either monthly or every two weeks, with the first payment due not later than two months from the loan date, or in equal installments quarterly, semiannually, or annually, with the first payment due one year from the loan date.

Maximum loan term is 15 years and 32 days for single-wides and 20 years and 32 days for multi-wides.

Dealer loans. Loans may be processed by the mobile home dealer if he meets the requirements specified by HUD/FHA.

Direct loans. The borrower may apply directly for a loan through the insured (the dealer), provided:

1. The insured obtains a placement certificate form which states that the mobile home has been placed on a site as in items 6 or 7 (page 86).
2. That the borrower has not offered a rebate.

Insurance charge requirements. The insured must pay the HUD/FHA commissioner an insurance charge equal to .54 percent annually on each loan; such charge cannot be passed on to the borrower.

Combination loans. Loans for the mobile home, including the lot, may not include furniture.

The maximum insurable loan amounts shall not exceed:

1. $35,000 for 20 years and 32 days for single-wide and a developed lot, with a $22,500 limit for the mobile home.
2. $47,500 for 25 years and 32 days for a multi-wide mobile home and a developed lot, and a maximum limit of $35,000 for the mobile home.
3. Maximum lot loan amounts: $12,500 for 15 years, 32 days on developed lot.
4. The borrower must agree that the mobile home will not be moved during the life of the loan.

Veterans Administration Loans

The Veterans' Housing Acts of 1970 and 1974 authorize the VA to guarantee loans made by private lenders to veterans for the purchase of new and used mobile homes. Such loans are available to veterans only.

The term "GI loan" refers to a loan made by a private institution to a veteran for any eligible purposes. The VA does not charge for guaranteeing or insuring a GI loan.

Lenders. There are two types of lenders acceptable to VA, supervised and nonsupervised.

The supervised lender is subject to an examination by a federal or state agency or has been approved as an FHA lender. He can make a GI loan without first receiving approval from VA.

The nonsupervised lender has not been examined or approved as a FHA lender. He is required first to file an application with VA, whereupon VA sends a commitment which allows the lender to close the loan.

Eligibility. All veterans with sufficient qualifying service after September 15, 1940, and service women who have maximum loan guarantee entitlement of up to $27,000 or 50 percent whichever is less, are eligible for mobile home loans. Veterans who enlisted after September 7, 1980 must complete at least 24 months of active duty to be eligible to secure VA loan benefits. "Entitlement" is the amount of loan value available to the veteran, based upon the type and length of service.

A certificate of eligibility, shown in part in figure 6–2, must be filled out by veterans when applying for a loan. Application should be made to the nearest VA office.

Maximum loan amounts and terms. The following are the restrictions:

1. No maximum loan amount is now specified but the sum is determined by the invoice for the mobile home, plus the cost of the lot, and necessary fees.
2. The maximum term of the loan for a single-wide is 15 years, and 20 years for a double-wide. The veteran must locate the lender himself, and that lender may offer the loan for a shorter period of time.

Obtaining a loan. To obtain the loan the veteran must:

1. get a certificate of eligibility.
2. locate a mobile home which meets VA standards.
3. arrange for a rental or purchase a mobile home lot.
4. apply to a lender for a loan.
5. be a satisfactory credit risk.
6. have income in line with amount of loan and replayment terms.

Selling the mobile home. If the mobile home is sold, the GI loan can be assumed by the new purchaser, provided that the veteran gets a written release from VA from loan liability.

The veteran may be released from liability to the government if the purchaser of his mobile home has the sales contract state that the purchaser assumes all of the veteran's liabilities covering the loan guarantee and that the purchaser is a good credit risk. A written request to the VA office that originated the loan is required.

Insurance

If your mobile home is financed, the lender will require that it be covered by insurance to the amount of the loan. The basic coverage required is for loss from fire and theft. Additional insurance may be required, depending upon the lender.

Complete coverage. Since you may want to have complete coverage, beyond that required by the lender, you should consider what is known as the comprehensive mobile home policy. It covers fire, flood, theft of mobile home, earthquake, windstorm, landslide, and lightning. In addition, there is adjacent-structure coverage: awnings, steps, utility shed, carport, cabana, porch, skirting, and air-conditioning unit. Personal-effects coverage includes their damage or loss, both inside and outside the mobile home—from robbery and burglary. They are also covered, inside, for damage due to flood, fire, lightning, explosion, windstorm, earthquake, vandalism, and other perils.

Special valuable-item coverage extends to stamp and coin collections, jewelry, art, antiques, cameras, and the like. Valuable stamp and coin collections can be covered by a separate supplemental policy, a very desirable option, as the normal coverage on such items is limited to $500, or as low as $100 with some companies.

Additional living-expense coverage is included in the policy, as well as antennas and tie-down equipment.

Most policies carry a $100-deductible clause for the mobile home, adjacent structures, and personal effects. This amount can be reduced for an additional premium.

Some companies will not write flood and windstorm coverage in specific coastal areas or any policies at all in certain areas of the country. Inquire about such limitations before you sign the contract for the mobile home.

Replacement value. One of the items to consider is the replacement-value coverage of the mobile home. This is generally written as a separate binder, for a small additional cost. Such coverage will give you a replacement home of the same vintage that you purchased, or the value of the destroyed home in cash. This is a very important additional coverage, well worth its cost, as it will protect you against the ever-increasing cost of mobile homes, should you become the victim of such a calamity.

Shopping for insurance. Your mobile home dealer will probably ask you to let him secure you an insurance policy to cover the newly purchased home. However, this may not be your best option.

Before you sign for an insurance policy you should inquire about the ratings of the various insurance companies. One firm that specializes in insurance companies' ratings is A. M. Best & Company. Its publication, "Best's Key Rating Guide—Property Casualty," is comparable to Standard and Poor's ratings of stocks and bonds. Check the company rating, office locations, and check with the state insurance department, which will be able to advise you of the insurer's past record.

Don't buy insurance solely on the basis of price. A cheap policy may omit certain coverages that are important to you. Your mobile home investment is large enough to warrant the best protection possible; hence, the company should be known for settling its claims quickly and equitably.

You may also want to satisfy yourself that your insurer is not over-exposed in those areas of the country subject to hurricanes, tornadoes, or other natural disasters. A small insurance company can fail when faced with a large number of claims from such a calamity, resulting in staggering financial losses to its insured.

To avoid such risks, some companies write policies that cover only a part of a mobile home park or an area, so that their losses would not be catastrophic. Or they may select only certain mobile homes in a predetermined pattern rather than insuring all adjacent homes in a park.

In a rental park, your mobile home will have to be insured as soon as it has been readied for your occupancy, even though you have purchased it with cash.

Insurance costs. Many a new mobile home owner will discover that his insurance premium is considerably higher than he was accustomed to paying for conventional house insurance, even though the house had a much higher valuation. This is because mobile homes are susceptable to greater damage from high winds, and because of greater fire risks.

Combination fire insurance. Many insurance companies now offer so called "combination-plan" insurance, which combines mobile home insurance with coverage of the motor vehicles owned by the mobile home owner.

The rate for such insurance is likely to be lower than individual coverage. However, there may be an age factor that will prevent you from acquiring this type of insurance. Persons more than 65 or 70 years old may find that they are unable to change from their existing motor vehicle policy to the combination package due to age restrictions imposed by the insurance company.

When inquiring about mobile home insurance, check on the availability of a combination package that includes all members of the family.

Special insurance. Many persons, during their lifetimes, have acquired valuable articles, before moving into a mobile home. These may be stamp or coin collections, valuable jewelry, and the like.

Since practically every mobile home insurance policy specifies a value limit of $500 or less for such valuables, two or three choices exist. One is keeping them in a safe deposit box, if they are not too bulky. Another is to take out a special insurance policy, the so-called "floater policy," at an additional cost to cover loss due to theft, fire, or other hazards. You may also be able to broaden the coverage specified in a comprehensive policy.

For a valuable stamp collection, you may be required by some insurance companies to submit a complete inventory rather than only a statement of total worth. Also, some companies require that the amount of insurance policy taken should be at least 80 to 100 percent of the value of the collection and its worth checked periodically to maintain such a percentage. An association, the American Philatelic Society (APS) is recommended for such theft insurance as they appear to settle theft claims fairly and rapidly.

Some insurance companies limit the amount of insurance available for a single stamp or a plate block and this should be taken into consideration when insuring very valuable stamps.

Park inspection. The insurance premium that you are likely to pay may depend to a degree on the park where you are establishing your new residence. Some companies inspect the parks and classify them in accordance with conditions prevailing both inside and outside the park.

They may classify on the basis of general park appearance, security as exemplified by control of entrance to the park by nonresidents, percentage of tied down mobile homes, age of the park, type (family or adult), prevalence of crime in the surrounding area, and other factors.

Credit life insurance. This is another desirable coverage for an additional charge. Should the head of the household die, the mobile home loan will be paid off, as with conventional housing. It is preferable to buy this insurance from the bank or lending institution that furnished the loan.

Taxes

Despite wide publicity to the contrary, mobile homes are not exempt from state, county, or city taxes. One's taxes depend upon whether the home is on rental land or on a lot owned by the resident.

In lot-owned parks, some states collect taxes on land and home, just as with conventional housing. However, the taxes paid are lower than for conventional housing, since the assessed valuation may be less than one half.

In addition, states such as Florida and California offer a "homestead" exemption after residence of at least five years in the state, and an added exemption for owners over 65 years of age. Florida, however, makes up for the lost revenue by taxing the mobile home owners in rental parks, charging them high renewal fees for their yearly registration labels, and by basing these fees on mobile home length (including tow bars).

Finally, of 38 states responding to a survey, only 4 said they did not collect taxes on mobile home accessories. These states are Illinois, Iowa, Kentucky, and Michigan.

California's New Mobile Home Laws

The California legislature passed some important laws in 1979 relating to mobile homes, implemented on January 1, 1980, and July 1, 1980.

The first law allows mobile homes to be installed on permanent foundations and makes them subject to local property taxes. The second law provides that any *new* mobile home installed for residential purposes becomes subject to local property taxes.

Thus, these laws make mobile homes equivalent to conventional housing in the matter of their taxation. They no longer require registration plates to be issued by the Department of Motor Vehicles.

A fee of $11 for each home section is still retained but is to be paid to the Department of Housing and Community Development instead of the Department of Motor Vehicles. The first-named department issues a building permit to the mobile home applicant, and the mobile home becomes subject to the local or county tax if it passes the required inspections.

Such property tax on a $20,000 mobile home, for example (less $7,000 homeowner's exemption), at an approximate rate of 1.25 percent gives a tax bill of $162.00 in Sonoma County. Similarly, the property tax on a $20,000 mobile home, placed on a $8,000 lot, would result, on the same basis, in a tax bill of $262.50.

Helpful Guidelines

The California Department of Consumer Affairs (Box 310, Sacramento, California) offers a series of guides helpful in purchasing a mobile home or any other product or service. While they relate primarily to California residents such guidelines would be helpful in any other state.

When buying.

1. Shop around and compare costs of the product or service. Ask about fees and specific services of doctors, lawyers, and other professionals. Use the Yellow Pages.
2. Check consumer publications for useful cost and quality comparisons of similar products.
3. Many of the advertisers listed in the Yellow Pages must be licensed or registered by the state department of consumer affairs. Look for licensing notices when you use the Yellow Pages.
4. When dealing with a licensed professional, ask to see a valid license or proof of registration. If in doubt, contact the appropriate licensing agency (see "State Government Offices" in the White pages).
5. Look for "Consumer Tips" scattered throughout the Yellow Pages; they may save you time and money.

If a problem arises.

1. First, take your complaint to the manager or owner of the company where you bought your product or service. Save copies of all letters, receipts, cancelled checks, and warranties. If, after a reasonable length of time, you have not received satisfaction from the company, gather up the facts and seek outside assistance.
2. If you have a local county or city consumer protection agency, contact it for advice on your complaint (see "City or County Government Offices" in the White Pages).
3. Some communities have private consumer groups that are very successful in helping consumers resolve their problems. Ask your local consumer agency.
4. Look under "Consumer: Consumer and Protection Coordinators" in the White Pages for a number to call about your complaint.
5. Use the small claims court. Consumer agencies can give advice on its use.

See the addresses of the various state departments of consumer affairs in the Appendix.

CHAPTER 7

MOBILE HOME SETUP

When selecting a lot in a mobile home park, many people have definite preferences about the directional orientation of their mobile home. Some prefer an east-west orientation, with the carport on the south side. To others, a corner lot is desirable, so as not to be close to neighbors on adjacent sides.

In the 1950s, mobile home setup was very simple. The home itself was a single-wide structure, 8 feet wide and 24 or more feet long. The only requirement was to locate it on a fairly level ground surface and block it up to perfect level. This was done by the owner himself or a hired person.

Setting Up

Today, setting up a mobile home is beyond the capabilities of the buyer. Many homes are now double- or triple-wide, and getting them joined together requires considerable experience, plus trucking facilities, and a crew of men equipped with suitable tools.

Preliminary steps. The ground on which the home will rest must be leveled and all grass removed. This eliminates any possible fire danger when the grass dries out. The lot area should not be freshly filled ground, or there will be considerable settling.

If no concrete pad is to be installed, an agreement should be made to have the home re-leveled after about six months to avoid having problems with doors, appliances, and such, to say nothing of the inconvenience of having to walk on a tilted floor.

Concrete pad. Good site preparation entails pouring a concrete pad of the same size as the mobile home, just as is done for conventional homes. Using gravel and tar paper to reduce moisture penetration, reenforcing mesh should be supported about one inch above the gravel surface over the whole area. This is standard procedure in pouring a concrete slab for a conventional home.

An even better way is to pour a footing, 6 to 8 inches deep and about a foot wide, around the perimeter of the pad prior to pouring the pad itself (figure 7–1).

Such a pad will prevent the mobile home from settling later, after the furniture has been installed and the residents have moved in. Otherwise, gradual settling will occur, especially if the land is sandy or water collects under the home due to poor drainage.

Piers. Concrete piers, that support the mobile home above the ground, are constructed of standard 8 by 8 by 16 inches celled (hollow) concrete blocks,

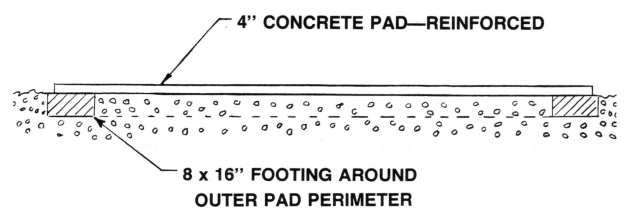

4" CONCRETE PAD—REINFORCED

8 x 16" FOOTING AROUND OUTER PAD PERIMETER

Fig. 7-1. Diagram of a concrete pad with footings for a mobile home.

placed on top of a base of solid concrete, with minimum dimensions of 16 by 16 by 4 inches. A cap of solid concrete 8 by 8 by 4 inches completes the assembly. Two pressure-treated beveled wooden wedges are placed on top of the cap next to the frame of the mobile home. When driven together toward each other, they fill the space between the cap and the frame (figure 7–2). This arrangement is suitable for piers not exceeding 40 inches in height. Double tiers of interlocking concrete blocks are used to provide stability for piers up to 80 inches in height.

Fig. 7-2. Wedges between the footing and the frame are supposed to be facing toward each other, not as shown here.

Joining Mobile Home Sections

Individual mobile home sections are trucked to the site from the dealer or the mobile home manufacturer. Each section is attached to the truck by a hitch bolted to the mobile home frame (figure 7–3).

Fig. 7-3. A hitch is bolted to the frame for moving the home.

Removable axles and tires support it during its journey (figure 7–4). The section placement is handled for the dealer or park by a special setup crew, who have facilities to move, level, and join the sections, and install supporting piers, anchoring, and skirting.

Fig. 7-4. The axle is removed from the frame at its destination.

Assembly. The initial step is moving the first section, generally the appliance side, to a marked area on the site, jacking it up at each end, and temporarily blocking it to support the entire length (figure 7–5).

Fig. 7-5. The first section ready for its counterpart.

Piers are set up at the approximate locations of the over-the-roof anchoring straps, installed by the manufacturer. Pier height is determined by the predetermined mobile home height above the site. Treated-wood beveled wedges, about ⅜ inch thick by 6 inches wide and 16 inches long, are used to finally level the mobile home at each pier (figure 7–6).

Then the second section is moved up near the first (figure 7–7), jacked up to approximately the same height as the first (figure 7–8), and then slid over to the first section (figure 7–9). Installing concrete piers and leveling the second section with the help of the wooden beveled wedges, so it matches the first-section floor level, follow. The spaces left between the two sections (figures 7–10 and 11) have to be filled to bar outside air and insects.

The two sections may be tied together at their junctions by brackets installed along the section edge by the manufacturer. The walls, roof, and floor edges are nailed together, using spikes (driven in diagonally), or other means supplied by the manufacturer.

Fig. 7-6. A close-up of the wooden wedges for leveling the home. Note that the wedges should be in line, not 90° to each other, as shown.

Fig. 7-7. Assembling the sections. A second section is lined up.

Fig. 7-8. The second section is jacked up.

Fig. 7-9. The second section is slid next to the first.

Fig. 7-10. The wall junction space in a double-wide.

Fig. 7-11. The ceiling junction space in a double-wide.

Setup personnel. Many states require that a permit be issued, licensed personnel set up the mobile home, and a qualified person such as a park manager oversee the work being done. Yet poor workmanship is the rule in far too many cases with no final examination being made by anyone. Your own presence on the site at the time may inspire more care from the work crew.

There are two sources of setup personnel. They may be supplied by the dealer who sold you the mobile home. The contract often specifies that he handle all the details, from setting up the mobile home to having it cleaned inside and out, windows and doors washed, property sodded, carport and shed added, carport apron poured, and the like.

The other source is the park itself, if it handled the sale of the mobile home. Then the park manager usually oversees the work and is responsible for it. A well-managed park will have regulations governing the setup work and will hire responsible help to do it.

My own recent examination of several typical setups disclosed many poor jobs, with no follow-up check by the dealer who supplied the crew. An even

better solution, then, would be to have a local inspector actually inspect the setup before it is enclosed by skirting.

One of the requirements for leveling a mobile home is the use of beveled wooden wedges, of specified size. These are driven, in turn, one over the other on each support pier to level the mobile home throughout its entire length (figure 7–12). Yet, many setup jobs use a number of any convenient pieces of lumber to take up several inches of space (figure 7–13) rather than use the two wooden wedges as required by many states. As the piers consist of a number of concrete blocks, available in different heights, the approximately correct height can be readily determined and the wedges used to get it exactly right. Sloppy crews have been known to drive wedges at right angles to each other.

The restriction to treated wooden wedges is directly related to the termite problem. Termites build their tunnels upward on the support piers. Once they get into the untreated pieces of lumber, stacked 2 or more inches high, they can rapidly destroy the infested supports.

Figs. 7-12, 13. Tapered wooden wedges should be used for leveling, but some unscrupulous setup companies will use any old lumber pieces (right).

Leveling. Poor leveling of a mobile home, single- or multi-wide, can usually be traced to too hasty an effort by the setup crew, who are generally paid a fixed amount for each job. On a long double-wide, there may be six or more piers in each four rows (figure 7–14) to be checked for proper level height at each support pier.

Poor leveling produces many problems: stress on the whole structure; uneven floor throughout its whole length; squeaky floors; buckling of paneling; doors of appliances (such as a refrigerator) swinging shut instead of remaining open in the desired posi-tion; and many other similar defects.

You should check the setup installation on your own for faulty leveling and insist that the dealer or park, as the case may be, take any corrective action needed.

The setup crew know that once the skirting has been set up in place, their work, good or bad, is hidden from the purchaser. It is a simple matter to forget to add the wooden wedges on top of a pier or to use only one wedge so it bears against the frame member along a line, and not against the whole wedge surface.

Fig. 7-14. Piers are placed in four rows.

Leveling checkup. For a simple check of the leveling, stretch a long, heavy string or cord taut along the bottom edge of the mobile home (figure 7–15). The string should follow the edge of the mobile home. Variations in the bottom edge relative to the string indicate improper leveling.

Mark a spot on the string halfway between the string ends and hang an ordinary string level at that point (figure 7–16). Observe if it shows a true horizontal bubble reading. The reading will be an accurate indication that the entire mobile home is or is not set up horizontally. The string level can be used to check leveling across the width of the mobile home in the same way. A good setup and leveling job will pass these tests.

Figs. 7-15, 16. Leveling is very important. A string (left) and a string level.

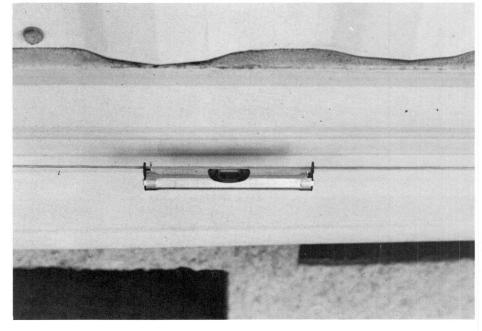

Leveling in both directions, lengthwise and cross-wise, can also be checked inside with the help of a 4- or 6-foot mason's level. It should show a practically level reading as you move it progressively along the carpeting. Large deviations from the true horizontal are basic indications of a bad leveling job, and it should be brought to the attention of the dealer or mobile home park if the work was done by their contractor.

Sealing. When mobile home sections are brought together (see figures 7–8 and 9) a small gap will remain between them (see figures 7–10 and 11). This gap is supposed to be filled with material furnished by the manufacturer or provided by the setup man. It should close the ceiling, wall, and floor junctions.

One creative solution might be to nail or bond a narrow strip of hardboard or other material along the bottom covering of the mobile home to completely seal the junction. Or, if the gap is narrow, elastic mastic material could be brushed into the gap. Otherwise if left open, this gap can invite termites or other insects.

The junction areas on ceiling and walls are covered with raised strips of matching paneling and trim to make these areas less conspicuous (figure 7–17). The floor junction is covered by the carpeting, which initially extends beyond the junction in each section. The ends are glued together to conceal the carpeting junction.

Fig. 7-17. Ceiling trim covers the junction in a double-wide.

Roof assembly. Roofs of the adjoining mobile home sections are joined with either a flat piece of metal or a specially shaped cap (figure 7–18). To prevent leaks, caulking compound is placed under the joining piece and the sheet metal screws that attach it to the roof sections.

Front end support. In some parks, the back end of the planter is built up to support the front end of the mobile home. Since such planters may be built on substantial footings, they do not tend to sink down into the soil. Thus supported, the front end of the mobile home may stay at its original level while the remainder of the structure settles with its supporting piers. The remedy is to eliminate such support at the planter and use thinner blocks between the planter and the front end of the mobile home. The whole mobile home can then settle evenly.

Anchoring

Initially, mobile homes depended upon their weight alone to remain in place when set up level on the concrete piers.

Fig. 7-18. (Top) Two sections ready to join. (Right) The roof cap in place.

As mobile homes increased in number and size, state laws came to require that they be anchored on their site.

Federal regulations. HUD requires manufacturers to install over-the-roof straps or cables at specific intervals of length. HUD also requires that an anchoring system diagram be supplied by the manufacturer with each mobile home to indicate the proper method of anchoring. The HUD mobile home construction standard includes wind-zone maps, which divide the country into belts according to the prevalence of winds, particularly tornadoes and hurricanes. For these areas, mobile homes and their anchoring systems must be able to meet some of the higher stresses imposed by all but the worst of these natural forces.

Should you anchor? The anchoring expense may be as much as 1 or 2 percent of your total cost, but it may save your home and its occupants in a windstorm. Moreover, the insurance rate may be lower if it is anchored. Unanchored, a mobile home (especially the single-wide) is distinctly at risk in high winds. Even a wind velocity of about fifty miles an hour may move a single-wide off its supporting piers if not screened by trees or other structures. The resulting structural damage may amount to many thousands of dollars in repair bills.

Tornadoes have been experienced all over the country; although damage to conventional homes has been largely confined to lost roofs, unanchored mobile homes in the same areas have generally sustained much greater damage (figure 7–19). The damage was generally total when they were lifted off their support piers and deposited some distance away.

A mobile home park on level ground, unprotected by ground cover such as trees, is an easy target for destruction not only by hurricanes and tornadoes but by thunderstorms of moderate intensity. The mobile homes that have not been properly anchored are prime sources for destruction of other nearby homes, with possible loss of life. Cars, carports, sheds, and other structures too may be damaged.

Present support setups. Placing the mobile home on piers, with space below it, provides additional lift in high winds and adds to the instability.

The problem that exists even with anchored homes is the variation in types of soils and the reduced capability of anchors in poor soils. Anchors should be imbedded in concrete, or longer anchors used where tests indicate poor soil.

The basic problem, of course, is the present method of supporting the mobile home. In conventional housing, the foundation blocks the entrance of wind under the house, and is by far a better anchoring means for the house itself. When mobile homes adopt this system of anchoring, much of the damage that now results will be eliminated, as will most of the settling problem.

Fig. 7-19. Tornado damage.

Anchoring Systems

There are several methods of installing anchoring, depending upon whether the mobile home is single- or multi-wide.

Single-wides. Because of the greater vulnerability of single-wides to high winds, installation of over-the-top straps or cables is required of the mobile home manufacturers. Such straps must be at least 1¼ inches wide and .035 inch thick and made from galvanized steel of a specified strength.

Multi-wides. Some manufacturers do not supply the over-the-roof straps for multi-wides but depend upon the anchoring contractor to install only frame ties.

Do-your-own. For the do-it-yourselfer, anchor manufacturers supply kits that contain the necessary anchors, straps, clips, and anchor bolts, as well as a complete set of instructions (figure 7–20). Tell the supplier the type of soil in which the anchors will be installed so that he can provide anchors suitable for that soil.

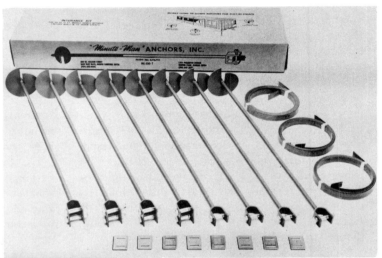

Fig. 7-20. An anchoring kit.

Fig. 7-21. A double anchor tie.

Anchors. Anchors have special brackets (figure 7–21) in which special high-strength slotted bolts, capable of accepting the ends of anchoring straps, are inserted. These bolts are then rotated to wind the end of the strap around the bolt. This eliminates the use of turnbuckles to tighten the straps. Figure 7–22 shows the frame tie secured to the mobile home frame.

Anchors (figure 7–23) have an auger-type end. They are installed in the ground at an angle just inside the mobile home perimeter (figure 7–24) so they do not interfere with the installation of skirting later.

Fig. 7-22. A frame tie.

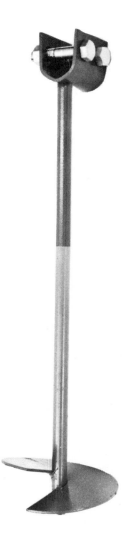

Fig. 7-23. A double-strap anchor.

Fig. 7-24. An anchor in place.

Installation. Anchors may be installed by rotating them into the soil with a special machine (a preferred method), or by digging a hole with a post digger (to a depth of 2 feet, for a 3-foot anchor). The anchor is then rotated into the soil with the aid of a piece of pipe (figure 7–25) until it is seated with the bracket almost flush with the surface of the soil. The hole should be refilled with the soil, a half a foot at a time, and tamped each time to solidify it. Proper tamping is important to get a solid installation.

When only frame ties are used, a preferred method is to dig a hole about 1 foot in diameter and 1½ feet deep, insert the anchor as before, and pour concrete around the top end of each anchor. The purpose of this anchor support is to prevent the wind from bending the top section of the anchor. Such bending would allow the mobile home to shift sideways and possibly slide off its piers.

The combination of over-the-roof ties (installed by the mobile home manufacturer) and frame ties, both tied to each anchor, is desirable for increased safety in high winds (figure 7–26).

Fig. 7-25. A pipe helps rotate anchor into place.

Fig. 7-26. An anchor with frame and overhead straps.

The number of over-the-roof ties built in by the manufacturer determines the number and location of anchors. If only frame ties are installed, however, they should be placed next to the support piers, using the special clips provided for this purpose. Piers are generally placed a maximum of 5 feet from each end of the mobile home and 10 feet apart.

Skirting

A mobile home installation is not complete until it is protected with skirting installed between the mobile home and the ground. The home then takes on a look of considerable permanence.

Concrete blocks. Many mobile home parks started out with skirting composed of concrete blocks. They may measure about 16 inches long and 4 inches square, with one of the 4-inch faces left rough, to be used as the outside surface. A space of about 8 inches is left between adjoining blocks (figure 7–27).

A one- or two-block course is laid around the periphery of the mobile home, in line or just inside its outside surface. Mortar should be used to tie the rows together and in between the blocks to form a sealed wall to prevent water from seeping under the mobile home. These two rows are laid to leave a vertical space of 4, 8, 12, or more inches, in multiples of four, so additional rows of blocks can be laid above the initial course. It might prevent the condition shown in figure 7–28, where water from a downspout is able to flow under the mobile home.

Block advantages. The use of blocks conveys two advantages. First, they serve as indicators of mobile home settlement. They cannot be removed because the weight of the mobile home will rest on them instead of the supporting piers. The other advantage is that they will temporarily support the weight of the home.

When the blocks in the top row look as though they cannot be moved, whether in particular spots or over the whole perimeter, re-leveling is called for. If the beveled wooden wedges have been properly installed, they can be used to raise the frame where necessary at the various piers.

Remember that installation of all of the blocks cannot be completed until workmen have completed water and sewage lines, electrical service, and air conditioning.

Figs. 7-27, 28. (Top) Concrete block skirting. (Right) Care should be taken so that water from a downspout cannot flow under the home.

The concrete block skirting provides ventilation under the mobile home; that's especially desirable with wet soil conditions. However, the openings in the skirting invite many other problems.

Block disadvantages. Although blocks can be readily removed at any point at which you may need to crawl under the home, this is also convenient for other crawling things such as insects, rodents, snakes, black widow spiders, tarantulas, and the like. One precaution should be always followed. *Never* crawl under a mobile home unless you have a long stick with you to explore the area ahead. Too many people have been surprised by, or surprised a snake which has found a cool sanctuary there. Air-conditioning service men, plumbers, and others have had such experiences while doing their work under mobile homes.

Mildew, rusting, and odors underneath the mobile home will result from insufficient ventilation. The proponents of concrete block skirting say that extensive ventilation is necessary, which the blocks do provide; others deny that more than 5 percent open space is needed to secure adequate ventilation. If a concrete pad has been properly installed beneath the mobile home the arrangement is more than adequate.

Other types of skirting. If metal or vinyl solid skirting is used to enclose the area, it should have several vents, or doors, around the periphery of the home to provide access as well as ventilation. Vinyl skirting does not dent as easily as metal skirting and is available in kit form for do-it-yourself installation. The skirting should be installed against a course of bricks or blocks to close possible gaps created by soil irregularity, thereby preventing the entrance of rodents or snakes.

Vinyl skirting of a ventilated type is illustrated in figure 7–29. Complete installation instructions are provided in the do-it-yourself kit. Read the instructions before you buy, however, to see if you have the necessary experience for the task.

Access to the underside of the mobile home is available by lifting the top rails and sliding the chosen panel upward.

For horizontal metal skirting, ventilation is achieved by overlap of the horizontal panels.

In the northern part of the country insulated skirting helps keep the underside of the mobile home warm in the winter and cool in the summer.

Before installing any special type of skirting, get permission to use it from the park manager. Many parks require the same type of skirting throughout the park.

Fig. 7-29. Vinyl skirting on a mobile home.

CHAPTER 8

MOBILE HOME COOLING AND HEATING

A mobile home, like a conventional house, requires provision for heating and cooling. The practical answer to both needs is to install a central cooling/heating unit capable of maintaining proper indoor temperature, summer or winter.

Mobile homes, which must now meet HUD standards, require adequate insulation throughout the entire structure to satisfy government requirements. Part of the HUD construction standards for mobile homes are given below.

Energy Efficiency Ratio (EER)

Mechanical air conditioners below 65,000 BTU (British Thermal Units) capacity (or 5½ tons), manufactured after June 1, 1977, are required to have an energy efficiency ratio (EER) of at least 6.5, while for units manufactured after January 1, 1980, the efficiency ratio is to be at least 7.2.

The energy efficiency ratio is the capacity of the air-conditioner unit in BTUs, divided by the power used in watts. Thus a 42,000-BTU air conditioner, requiring a power input of 6,000 watts (6 kilowatts) has an energy ratio of 7.0. The higher the EER ratio, the more efficient the air-conditioner is; and the less it costs to operate. You understand, of course, that even a very efficient large capacity model can be more expensive to operate than less efficient smaller capacity machine.

Heating and Cooling Certificates

From the point of view of prevailing temperatures, the Department of Housing and Urban Development (HUD) has designated various areas of the country as either Zones I, II, or III (III is Alaska) (see figure 2–12B). Mobile home manufacturers have to supply storm doors and windows for mobile homes sold in Zones II and III. They also provide a heating certificate, kept readily visible within the home.

This certificate specifies the temperature zone in which the home's heating will be able to maintain 70° F. for a given range of outdoor temperature (at a maximum wind velocity of 15 miles per hour).

A comfort cooling certificate may be combined with the heating certificate, specifying, for a home equipped with a central duct system, the capacity of the cooling unit (in BTUs) needed to maintain 75° F. temperature for a specified range of outdoor temperature.

Adequate insulation must be installed within the roof, walls, and floor assembly to achieve the inside temperature limits specified on the certificates.

Window Units

Window air-conditioning units are not, as a rule, satisfactory because of their limited ability to distribute air. Neither can any current models of which I am aware be satisfactorily installed in mobile home windows, which are not strong enough to support their weight. The use of several window air conditioners would also obstruct the windows as exits in case of fire.

Another argument against their use is the probability that existing electrical circuits may not be adequate to handle the electrical load of several window units.

Size Requirements

The size of the central air-conditioning unit is determined by several factors:

1. The temperature extremes for both cooling and heating.
2. The length of the air ducts and their size, which determine the airflow resistance that dissipates the efficiency of the air conditioner.
3. The cubic feet of airspace inside the mobile home.
4. The amount of insulation in the roof, walls, and floor assembly needed to retain the internal heated or cooled air.

One will have to rely on the calculations made by the manufacturer or the contractor, who installs the central air-conditioning/heating unit or heat pump.

Such units are generally specified as "2-ton" or "3-ton," or, converted to BTUs, 24,000 and 36,000 BTUs, respectively. Several factors affect the size of the unit needed for cooling or heating: the number and size of windows; the type of windows, whether plain, thermopane glass, or storm; insulation; and the wind and sun protection afforded by trees, other mobile homes, awnings, and glass coatings such as Solar X.

Types of Cooling/Heating Units

There are two major types of combined cooling/heating units for use with a central duct system. One is the conventional air-conditioner unit, which also includes heat strips. It connects to the central duct system by means of two large diameter, plastic, flexible ducts (figure 8–1), one from the output of the air conditioner and the other from the return air duct. The ducts are insulated on the outside and use coiled wire to maintain their round shape. This installation is all on the outside except for the cooling or evaporator section and the heat strips, which are placed within the air conditioner unit.

The other system employs the heat pump. This new development heats the home interior by extracting heat from the air; it cools with the same unit in a conventional manner. Auxiliary electric heat strips provide extra heat should the outside air temperature fall below 40° F. This is a combined external and internal installation.

In addition, there is the separate furnace-type heating unit that burns oil or gas for use in Northern climates, where electric heat is too expensive to use. It is installed inside the mobile home in accordance with HUD regulations.

Humidifiers

One accessory that seems to have been overlooked in mobile home heating systems is a humidifier. Many persons find that they are able to withstand lower temperatures when humidity has been added to the normally dry air present in mobile homes in the Northern winter. The addition of moisture has been a standard practice in conventional homes, but it is absent in mobile home installations. The reason for this neglect is unknown; but a humidifier would be helpful from the standpoint of energy conservation.

Fig. 8-1. Air-conditioner ducts.

Conventional Air-Conditioning/ Heating Unit

A typical unit (figure 8–2) consists of a compressor assembly, cooling coils, evaporator unit, and an exhaust fan for cooling, as well as a separate blower for the heat cycle, which includes resistance wire coils, the so-called "heat strips." A system of relays converts the signal from the thermostat inside the mobile home to provide either cooling or heating. All items are contained within a round unit (figure 8–3) or units of other shapes (figure 8–4).

Figs. 8-2, 3, 4. There is a variety of air conditioner types.

Base

One requisite for installing such a unit is a concrete base, which supports it outside the mobile home.

The use of such equipment as power grass mowers by the park maintenance crews makes it necessary to protect the unit against accidental contact with such machinery. It is, therefore, imperative to have the concrete base extend about 6 inches beyond the perimeter of the unit to protect it. The base also should be several inches high to raise the unit above the soil level to prevent premature rusting of the outer case and the equipment within. These specifications should be spelled out when you sign your contract for the mobile home. The tendency otherwise is to make the base as small as possible, without regard to protecting the unit. The larger base also allows some leeway in positioning the air conditioner relative to the mobile home. Figure 8–5 illustrates a smaller-than-required base size.

Fig. 8-5. This air conditioner's base is too small.

Thermostats

A thermostat is needed to automatically control the cooling or heating cycle to keep the temperature at a chosen level. Ideally, it should be located in a hallway or some place where it is away from air circulating from the floor or ceiling registers of the central duct system. It should also be positioned about 5 feet above the floor level.

Thermostat Types

There are two types of thermostats that can be furnished by the air-conditioning contractor: magnetic or mercury.

The first, being cheaper, is more likely to be installed by the contractor if you raise no objection. But if you know how both types work, you will be quite definite about your preference for the second.

The magnetic type requires a certain minimum spacing between the contacts to operate properly. It requires wider changes in temperature to operate than the mercury type and thus gives poor control. Its other inherent disadvantage is electrical arcing across the contacts when they open. Just like the points under the distributor cap of an automobile, they wear out and must be replaced.

The mercury type uses a tiltable tube (figure 8–6), containing mercury in a vacuum. Tilting of this tube is controlled by a spiral spring which expands or contracts in length in conformance with temperature changes. The mercury acts as a set of contacts, which open or close in accordance with the motion of the spiral spring. This in turn operates the control relays in the air conditioner. Thus, this type of thermostat is more sensitive to smaller temperature changes than the magnetic type. It also has a longer life span and thus less maintenance expense. You should ask for the mercury thermostat at the time of purchase and include the requirement as part of the contract.

Both thermostat types have two switches, located at either the top or bottom part of the thermostat. One switches from air conditioning to heat (figure 8–6). The other controls the circulating fan in the air-conditioning unit. In one position, it is ON when you want to move the air within the mobile home continuously. In the other, AUTO controls the circulating fan automatically, turning it on and off as controlled by the air-conditioner unit.

Fig. 8-6. A thermostat's interior view—note mercury switch.

Heat Strips

Heat strips are actually coils of resistance wire, mounted within an insulated box inside the air-conditioner unit. They generally have a 5-kilowatt capacity per strip. The number of strips used depends on how many the mobile home requires to keep it at 70° F. for a given outside temperature and wind velocity.

In Southern areas, where the temperature seldom drops to the freezing point, three 5-kilowatt strips will generally suffice to keep a 24 by 60 foot mobile home comfortable.

Safety devices. In an air-conditioner unit, the heat strips are turned on sequentially, one at a time, by electrical circuitry, to give the circulating blower time to start moving the heated air in the central duct system. As a safety device, there is a thermal cutout. This is preset to a specified temperature limit at which the heat strips cut off if the blower fails. In addition, fusible wire links are sometimes inserted in each strip connection as an additional safeguard. However, there have been some cases where a cutout has failed to function and the plastic air-conditioning ducts have caught fire, setting the mobile home itself on fire (figure 8–7).

Fig. 8-7. An air-conditioner cutout failure caused this fire.

An inexpensive way to guard against such a failure is to have an additional thermal cutout connected in the circuit, in series with the first. Failure of one cutout to operate would still leave the other free to cut off the heat strips. The additional cutout would have to be installed by the manufacturer of the air conditioner as part of original equipment.

For additional protection against a possible fire, a short length of round metal duct, extending from the air-conditioner output opening, should be used to connect to the plastic duct.

Low-Voltage Control

Areas such as that around Tampa, Florida (which has the highest number of thunderstorms in the country), are likely to experience low-voltage conditions as a result of the numerous storms. These "brown-outs" may also occur in other areas, where the utilities have difficulties maintaining constant line voltages.

Some makers of air-conditioning equipment will supply as an additional safeguard in their equipment a low-voltage cutout unit. This is a small, self-contained unit (figure 8–8) which is connected to the compressor assembly to safeguard its operation. If the line voltage falls below a predetermined limit, this cutout unit will prevent the compressor unit from starting. This device prevents a possible burnout of the compressor should it attempt to start with the line voltage low. As compressor assemblies cost several hundred dollars to replace, this protection is well worth the extra cost.

Fig. 8-8. A low-voltage cutout.

If you specify this unit in the contract, make sure that it is actually installed in the air conditioner by the manufacturer.

Split Air Conditioner

In new air-conditioner design, part of the equipment is placed under the mobile home. This contains the A coil, or cooling section, while the outside part contains the compressor and controls.

The shorter plastic pipes need extend only from the A-coil unit to the registers within, resulting in greater efficiency and cost reduction. Two small insulated pipes lead from the compressor unit to the A-coil unit. The compressor unit size is much smaller than that of a conventional air conditioner.

Figures 8–9, 10, and 11 show both of these units as well as the schematic of the installation.

Figs. 8-9, 10, 11. A split air conditioner: (left) air handler, (right) the condensing unit, installation diagram.

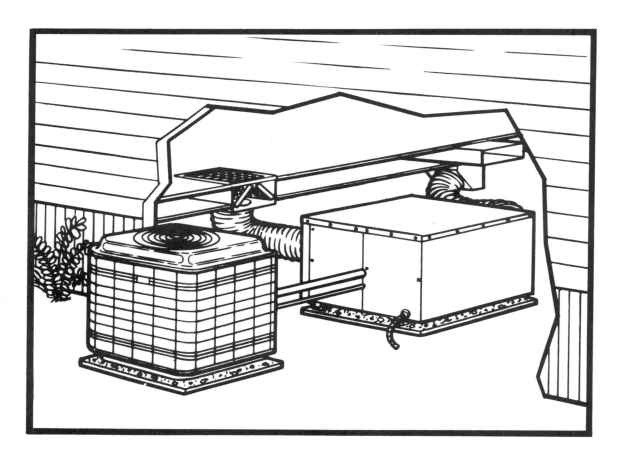

Duct Installation

Manufacturers of air-conditioning/heating equipment provide openings at the back of the units (figure 8–1) to connect the flexible plastic ducts to the mobile home's central duct system. They ascertain, through tests, the proper required diameter for the ducts connecting up with the air-conditioning unit to provide adequate cooling and heating airflow. The diameters of these output and return duct connections on the unit are supposed to determine the sizes of the connecting plastic ducts used by the air-conditioning contractor. In many cases, however, the contractor may attach adapters (size reducers) to the air conditioner openings, allowing him to use, say 10- or 12-inch diameter plastic ducts where 14-inch diameter ducts are called for by the manufacturer.

Since the purchaser of the mobile home cannot readily see the size of the plastic ducts, the air-conditioning contractor can get away with such a substitution, saving money for himself by using the smaller ducts. The mobile home owner loses because, with the smaller ducts, the air conditioner has to operate for longer periods to maintain the desired temperature, whether for the cooling or heating cycle.

Smaller ducts offer greater resistance to airflow. For example, substitution of a 10-inch duct for the required 14-inch duct reduces duct area from 154 square inches to 79 inches, just about half.

The only satisfactory method of protecting yourself against such a practice is to specify in your contract that external duct work must be of the diameter determined by the openings on the air conditioner and that no reducers be used. If this clause is included, you will have a case for redress if you discover later that smaller ducts have been used.

Heat Pumps

This is a newer version of the air-conditioning/heating unit (figure 8–12) that is able to provide heating from the outside air unless the temperature falls below 40° F. An auxiliary electric heat unit is provided, which automatically turns on when the outside temperature falls to that limit.

Figs. 8-12. A heat pump. Note the size of the base.

The operation cycles of the heat pump are charted in figures 8–13 and 14 for heating and cooling, respectively.

Heat Cycle. In the winter, the heat pump works like an air conditioner in reverse, extracting the heat that is present even in the cold winter air. The heat is

Figs. 8-13, 14. A heat pump's heating cycle (top) and cooling cycle.

absorbed by refrigerant in the outdoor coils *A* in figure 8-13. The compressor *B* pressurizes the refrigerant and sends it to the indoor coils *C*, where it gives up its heat to the air, circulated through the mobile home by a fan *D*. The refrigerant then flows outside and the cycle repeats.

Cooling cycle. In the summer, the heat pump works like a conventional air conditioner. The refrigerant in the indoor coils *A* absorbs heat from the air inside the mobile home and the fan *B* circulates the cooled air. The compressor *C* then pressurizes the refrigerant and sends it to the outdoor coils *D* where it gives up its heat to the surrounding air; the cycle then repeats.

As with conventional air-conditioning units, a concrete base should be provided for the external heat pump unit, extending several inches beyond its periphery and several inches high, to protect the unit against lawn mowers and rust.

Indoor installation. The indoor coils and their blower are mounted in a special enclosure in the mobile home, in a closet or in other available space. The auxiliary electric heating unit may be mounted in a separate insulated cabinet within the enclosure rather than in the external heat-pump unit. The refrigerant from the compressor unit in the heat pump is circulated through insulated piping to the indoor coils in the enclosure.

Cost. The heat pump, although initially more expensive, costs less to operate during cold-season heating than does the conventional air conditioner, which depends solely on electrical heat strips for heating.

A single thermostat setting controls the living space temperature for the heat pump. It operates automatically, either on heating or cooling cycle, depending upon external temperature; no manual switching from heat to cool is required.

Heat Reclaim Device

A recent development helps to reduce the cost of heating the hot water in your mobile home. This is the heat-reclaim device, which attaches to the air conditioner or heat pump. An example is shown in figure 8-15. It takes the indoor heat before it is dispersed into the outside air and uses it to heat the hot water whenever the air-conditioning system is in operation.

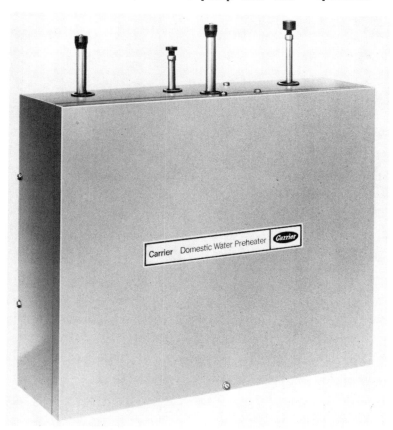

Fig. 8-15. A heat-reclaim device.

The device mounts on a ceiling or a wall and takes only a short time to install, especially at the initial installation of the air-conditioning unit. Two of its outside lines connect to the air conditioner or heat pump and the other two to the hot water heater.

Heat

In the North, where electric heat has become too expensive, gas or oil furnaces are used in its place.

Gas furnaces. Mobile home gas furnaces can be operated on either LPG or natural gas. LPG is lique-fied petroleum gas stored in steel bottles; it is also referred to as "bottled gas." HUD states that the term LPG refers to such gases as: propane, propylene, butane, and butylene. However, it is more expensive to use than natural gas which, in some areas, can be piped directly to the mobile home.

The HUD standard specifies that LPG containers or bottles must be stored outside the mobile home, and gives mounting and venting details for safety control devices required in installation.

A typical natural gas—LPG furnace is shown in figure 8-16. At the bottom is an A-coil (evaporator coil) used with an external air-conditioning unit to provide cooling within the mobile home through refrigeration lines brought in from the air condi-tioner. A special dual flue assembly handles both the exhaust and combustion air to the furnace.

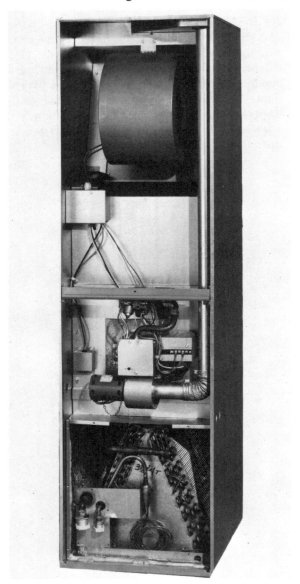

Fig. 8-16. A gas furnace and evaporator coils.

Oil furnaces. These are more complex than the LPG—natural gas type, and are apt to bring in oil odors. To the uncertainty about supplies of fuel oil you should add the greater furnace complexity, periodic maintenance requirements and storage-plus-pump cost.

A HUD standard lists various details of oil tanks and pumps in relation to their height above the furnace and other appliance installations.

Central Duct Systems

For input, there are two types of central duct systems in use—floor register and overhead register. Each has its proponents; the selection depends upon the region where the mobile home is located.

Overhead registers. In the South, where the use of air conditioning extends well over half the year, the overhead type is preferable because of its greater efficiency. Cold air falls down naturally from the registers—in addition to being propelled by the air pressure of the air-conditioning system—to floor level, and returns to separate return air registers in each room, except the bathrooms.

To cut costs, most mobile homes have instead a single return opening near the center of the mobile home. With this arrangement, doors are cut off 1 or 2 inches above floor level to allow air return even when the doors are closed; or there may be screened openings in the space above each door for the same purpose.

In selecting the location of your mobile home registers, specify the ceiling-register type if it is available as an option and the mobile home is to be located in an area with a warm climate.

Floor registers. The floor-register type of central air conditioning is not efficient for the cooling cycle because the cold air leaving the ducts must be driven upward at increased velocity in order to displace the existing warm air near the ceiling. The main return register may be found either on the floor or near it, sometimes only 2 or 3 feet away from one of the registers supplying the cold air. Thus, part of the cold air being fed from the air conditioner is lost and efficiency lowered.

In the colder regions of the country, with cooling required for shorter periods, the floor-register type is more efficient, as the warm air for heating rises naturally out of the floor registers. However, the main return should be near the ceiling level.

Duct construction. Two types of ducts are used in the central air-conditioning systems within the mobile home.

One is the metallic-duct type, of aluminum or galvanized steel, which must be well insulated to reduce losses, especially in the longer mobile homes. A particular disadvantage with aluminum ducting is that, with its large expansion factor, the ducts are apt to "crackle" on the heat cycle.

Solid molded plastic ducts, while more expensive to start with, do not need insulation. Besides saving materials they may save labor and do not make annoying noises on the heat cycle.

Flexible plastic ducts connect the duct system to the air-conditioning unit outside. A cross-over duct must be installed between sections of a multiwide, using flexible plastic duct for that purpose. In heat-pump installations, both ends of the central duct system terminate at the cabinet containing the coils and blower unit (figure 8–17) in a closet in the mobile home.

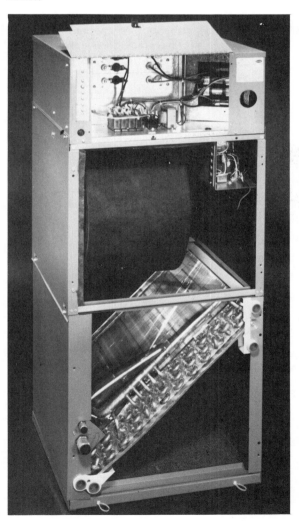

Fig. 8-17. Evaporator coils and blower assembly in the heat pump's cabinet.

Filters

All duct systems for central air conditioning/ heating units require periodic replacement of dust filters. These filters may be installed on the return side of the system. Be sure to replace the filters with identical size units.

Dirty filters cut down the air conditioner air flow, which increases the load and decreases the efficiency of the whole operation.

Air-Conditioner Life Expenctancy

In the South, the life of an air-conditioner compressor unit may be shorter than in the North. Seven or eight years is average. In heat pumps, the compressor operates on both the heating and cooling cycles and thus its life may be somewhat shorter.

In many instances, Southern mobile home owners, who go north for the summer, leave their air conditioners off for the several month period of the absence. It would be advisable to have a neighbor start and run the unit for a short period of time every couple of weeks. This is the same practice as is recommended for car air conditioners. When the unit is started after a long shutdown, the compressor lacks lubrication for a while and its seals harden— factors which shorten the unit's life expectancy.

Service Contracts

Most air-conditioning/heating units and heat pumps come with a one-year guarantee for the basic unit, and a five-year warranty on the compressor assembly. Some companies offer a service contract for a period of one or more years to take effect when the initial warranty runs out. *Do not take long service contracts.*

These contracts vary in their coverage. They may for example have three plans, and the purchaser of the service selects one of the options. A sample of such a contract is presented below.

AIR CONDITIONER SERVICE CONTRACT

PLAN I

(A) Labor required for two complete inspections of the equipment.
(B) Repairs for the equipment to be performed at a labor rate not to exceed _____ per hour.
(C) Parts and material to be furnished at list price.

Price per year _____

PLAN II

(A) Same as above (A).
(B) Labor required to maintain the equipment in working order.
(C) Same as above (C).

Price per year _____

PLAN III

(A) Same as above (A).
(B) Same as (B) in Plan II.
(C) Parts and material to maintain the equipment in working order with exception of (D).
(D) The cost of a replacement compressor will be borne by the owner at his expense after expiration of five year warranty.

Price per year _____

The price per year of these options may vary considerably. Many service companies solicit such business in the mobile home parks, initially offering low rates to get as many contracts as possible. Very few service companies will accept more than a one-year renewal after the first five years.

Summation

Here, in outline form, are the key points regarding air-conditioner or heat-pump installation to be kept in mind in signing your mobile home purchase contract:

1. Conventional air-conditioning/heating unit vs. heat pump:
    a. Brand name
    b. Ratings in BTUs
    c. Relative costs
    d. Energy efficiency ratios (EER)
2. Internal ducts:
    a. Ceiling or floor?
    b. Metal or molded plastic?
3. Exterior air-conditioner ducts:
    a. Size to match the output and return connections on the air conditioner
    b. To be supported off the ground (a HUD requirement)
    c. Cost included in the contract
4. If heat pump: home manufacturer to install evaporator-blower cabinet and other equipment in mobile home
5. If heat pump: manufacturer to install refrigeration lines to outside of mobile home to connect to heat pump
6. Concrete base: to extend beyond bottom surface of air conditioner or heat pump
7. Thermostat: mercury type.

CHAPTER 9

THE ACCESSORIES

Purchasing the mobile home itself is only the beginning. Many mobile home parks are located in southern California and in Texas, Florida, and other Southern states where the emphasis is on outdoor living throughout the year. You're likely to enjoy that lifestyle more if you add certain accessories to your mobile home.

You may decide that you'd like such additions as a patio and/or a screened porch. Before you can add them to your mobile home, however, you must obtain approval from the park management; their appearance, location, and size, must conform to park standards.

Many accessories are available to the mobile home owner: some of them are even mandatory in some parks where these items help preserve a uniform appearance. You will have to purchase these when you sign the contract.

More and more mobile homes are now sold with various accessories added to make a package deal. These features are offered by the park salesman or the dealer at the time of purchase. If you're buying through the park, you can expect to be offered accessories that are approved by the park management.

If you hire an outside contractor, be sure to specify in writing all construction instructions that you expect him to follow, and you may insist upon a written guarantee from him setting a deadline for completion of the work. Also, you will generally need from the park management approval of the contractor who is to do the job.

The Accessories

Basic accessories include such items as carport roof and driveway, awnings, steps, overhangs, stor-

age shed, planter, patio, and gutters and downspouts. Most parks require that, except for awnings and a patio, they be installed prior to occupancy. (Required items such as the air-conditioning/heating unit or heat pump, skirting, and anchoring have been described in Chapters 7 and 8).

If the dealer offers to arrange for the required accessories, it may be wise to contact other companies for a competitive price. Many dealers and parks operate on a referral basis. Companies engaged in sheet metal and concrete work, or who sell air conditioners and other items, may have under-the-table arrangements for such referrals. These referrals may not always be based on product quality or price.

Your contractor should be licensed, insured, and bonded—a requirement for all accessory contractors. He should be a member of the contractors' association in the area. Check the company with the Better Business Bureau, and request references from other persons in the park who can vouch for the quality of the company's work. Their praise or condemnation will make it easier for you to decide whether to accept or reject the company's bid.

The importance of quality work should not be overlooked. Obtain several bids, and when an item is priced substantially lower than the other bids, try to find out the reason. The materials to be furnished may be shoddy, the labor inexperienced, or the work may extend beyond the specified completion date. Or, instead of supplying sheet metal finished in baked enamel, the contractor may supply sheet metal sprayed with just a coat of lacquer, whose protection is short lived.

Some companies employ a "quality control" man to oversee the finished work. He inspects the work that has been done and reports any deficiencies to the company, which undertakes to correct any faulty workmanship or parts found by his inspection. The benefits of such arrangements are self-evident.

Awnings

They protect the windows of your home from sun or rain, can be lowered to protect them from high winds or flying objects in bad weather, and add to the home's attractiveness. They are made in solid (figure 9-1) or slat types. To have them serve as window protectors they should have side members, extending 8 to 10 inches on each side, have adjustable arms to regulate their angular position in respect to the home, and clips to lock them in place when lowered.

Awnings should also have cross-members for

strength in high winds. They are generally made of aluminum inter-locking channel sections (figure 9–2). A smooth, painted aluminum sheet on the inside of the awning, if used, eliminates the tedious job of washing each individual channel section.

Many persons, to break up the monotony of solid-color, wide awnings, request that some of the color sections match the mobile home trim (figure 9–1). To meet such a request, many companies take unpainted sections and spray them with lacquer, although the other sections have been finished in baked enamel. After a few years of sun and salt in coastal areas, the lacquer will wash off and you will be faced with a refinishing job.

To avoid this specify that such color striping be done with enamel, not lacquer. It may cost a little more but you will not have bare awning sections after a short period of time. Only enamel should be used to repaint them.

Awnings should be free of dents or marks. The awning dealer should do the installation. Caulking compound should be used at the top of the awning, between its mounting strip and the wall. It should also be used in installing all mounting screws to prevent leakage of water into the mobile home wall.

Figs. 9-1, 2. Awnings add to the appearance of a mobile home. (Right) Inside view of an awning.

Roof Overhangs

One problem with many a mobile home is its appearance, with the roof ending at the wall (figure 9–3). A roof overhang (figure 9–4), extending 18 to 24 inches and supported by suitable brackets (figure 9–5), makes for a more pleasant appearance, eliminates possible water leakage, and serves as a support for gutters and downspouts. It also keeps roof water from running over the edge and down the wall, perhaps staining it.

It is important that a seal be provided where wall and overhang section join. This is done either with a piece of aluminum extending the length of the joint, and sealed with mastic, or with fiberglass cloth, imbedded in sealing material.

Figs. 9-3, 4, 5. (Above) No overhang here. (Left) An overhang adds to the appearance. (Right) A built-on overhang and gutter.

Carports

Carports are required in practically all parks to keep cars off the streets. Some parks allow a soil or gravel surface, but the vast majority require concrete or macadam.

When a concrete carport driveway is required, it is important that it be constructed to obtain a lasting surface, free of cracks, especially in the colder climates. The water from the downspouts should drain away from the carport to prevent frost heaving and surface cracks. Further details were given on page 93. A concrete top surface should be finished smooth for easier cleaning.

The carport driveway and apron installation may be done by the park as part of the package deal of installing the mobile home. Although the park generally contracts this work out, you should insist that the concrete work be done in accordance with your wishes. You are the one who is paying for it.

Carport Roofs

The roofs consist, in many instances, of flat aluminum pans, with raised sides, that interlock to form a slanted roof over the driveway. They shade parked cars and the adjacent side of the mobile home.

Since this roof is a continuation of the mobile home roof, a gutter and downspouts are generally mounted along its outer edge. Proper interlocking of the two roofs and sealing of their junction are both important.

Carport roofs are supported on the outer roof edge by aluminum columns or fabricated shapes (figure 9–6) between the carport roof and the concrete driveway.

Fig. 9-6. Carport roof supports.

It is important that the carport roof have enough slope to facilitate fast water runoff, about an inch of drop for every 18 inches of roof width. Otherwise, the roof could collapse under the weight of water in a heavy storm.

To reduce the carport temperature in the summer, many owners install, or have a contractor install, styrofoam slabs or other lightweight insulating material inside the aluminum pans forming the roof. It is important that the top surface of these slabs be covered with a thin aluminum sheet or other material. Otherwise, birds and the weather will reduce the thickness of the insulating material in a short time.

A problem that arises with carport roofs that are not insulated is condensation of moisture on their underside. This results in water dripping on the car until the sun is able to dry out the roof. This dripping is likely to cause spots on the car's finish. A solution to this problem is given in Chapter 11.

Gutters and Downspouts

Too many contractors install the gutters with no concern for making them self-cleaning or for allowing them to empty rapidly. A gutter 50 to 60 feet long, hung level on the bottom edge of the carport roof, will not drain quickly in a driving rainstorm. For proper operation, it should have a drop of several inches from one end to the other, where the downspout is located. Many installers hang it perfectly level, or seem to try to. This results in a low spot in the middle if the gutter is in two sections. Water and dirt collect there. If a gutter has such a joint, a leak will develop because the gutter will tend to sag at the joint.

On the conventional houses, a facia board, 8 to 10 inches wide and mounted just below the roof edge, serves as the mounting surface for the gutter, which can be sloped down toward the downspout. This feature can also be achieved by installing a metal strip below the outer carport edge and slanting the gutter downward to the downspout to let the water out quickly.

Another good solution is to have the contractor install a third downspout at the junction of the two gutter sections. A seamless gutter will eliminate the leakage problem but it still will have to be mounted with a slight slope toward the downspout for quick water drainage.

Front Trim

Many mobile homes have trim installed across the front edge of the carport, the home itself, and the edge of the overhang (figure 9–1). This enhances the overall look of the mobile home. Again, this trim should be enamel-finished, not sprayed with lacquer that will fade and discolor in a few years. As such trim is frequently installed by the contractor who installs the carport roof, the enamel finish should be specified by the purchaser. It is customary to have the gutters finished in the same color, continuing the color scheme around the mobile home.

The trim should be securely fastened to prevent noise in high winds.

Garages

The latest trend is to replace the carport with a garage, similar to those for conventional housing. It may be a separate structure or the equivalent of a carport with one side and the back enclosed, and a three-section garage door at the front, opened manually or remotely controlled. This is one further step toward the look of the conventional house, with the car hidden from street view. The overall appearance is greatly improved, and the car is protected from the elements.

Insulation of the roof is a must to keep the garage interior cool.

Steps

Since practically all mobile homes are some distance above ground level, steps are required. Three or four steps should keep their riser heights to 8 or 9 inches, which is generally accepted as standard.

The step width should be at least 12 inches; the length should be about 12 inches longer than the door width. Steps can be of cast concrete, brick, steel, or aluminum. Aluminum or concrete steps will last much longer than steel or brick, the last named acting as a dirt catcher. For safety, they should be bonded to the mobile home by mortar if made of concrete or brick. A handrail, preferably of aluminum should be installed for the same reason. Usually it can be obtained in a design that will match the supports for your carport roof. The steps should be attractive, since persons entering your home gain their first impressions here (figure 9–7).

For additional safety, they can be covered with carpeting to provide a nonslippery surface. Wooden steps should be avoided as they attract termites and

Fig. 9-7. Attractive steps add to appearance.

have a relatively short life when exposed to the weather.

Storage Sheds

People just beginning mobile home living usually find that the many material things they have accumulated in the attics and basements of conventional homes must now find a place in their new mobile homes. They may find it necessary to store bicycles, tricycles, garden tools, tools, a workbench, washer and dryer, and the like. Since most mobile homes lack garage space for storage, the need for additional storage area becomes evident. Without it, the carport is apt to become cluttered with equipment.

Practically every mobile home park requires that a storage shed be installed when a mobile home is purchased, to avoid just such a problem. These sheds are required to harmonize in appearance with the mobile home, structurally and in color. Often, the shed acts as an additional support for the carport roof and is placed at the rear of the carport (figure 9–8). In some installations, the shed stands alone as an independent structure. In this case it should be tied down just like the mobile home with overhead cables or straps to the driveway which extends under it and forms its floor. The tie-down protects the shed against high winds.

Shed sizes. The shed is generally constructed 8-feet wide for a 12-foot driveway, leaving ample passageway between it and the mobile home. The length or depth of the shed can be varied to suit the purchaser's desires. A standard depth is 8 feet.

Shed details. If a washer and a dryer, plus a small sink are to be installed in the shed (figure 9–9), and perhaps a workbench, a minimum depth of 10 feet is likely to be more useful.

Fig. 9-8. The shed helps to support the carport roof.

Fig. 9-9. A washer and dryer plus a sink requires a large shed.

Also, arrangements should be made with the park to have 220-volt electrical service brought from a circuit breaker in the circuit breaker box within the mobile home for the dryer. A 110-volt service has to be provided for the washer and lights within the shed. The connections have to be made before the driveway is poured if the shed is located on it.

The cold and hot water piping, together with the drain pipe for the washer, must also be extended into the shed at the same time (figure 9-10). Hot water piping should be insulated to prevent heat loss.

Shelves are generally installed by the contractor who builds the shed; make sure to specify the arrangement that suits your needs. The shed structure

Fig. 9-10. The piping and electrical service for the washer and dryer in a shed.

itself may consist of narrow aluminum pans (figure 9–11) tied together with self-tapping screws. A door and a window are generally included.

To prevent water seepage underneath the walls of the shed, the space should be sealed with caulking compound, both inside and outside.

Besides serving as a storage space, a shed can double as a workroom if you install a workbench and such electric tools as a grinder and a drill press (figure 9–12). Do-it-yourselfers will find the details given in Chapter 13 a considerable help in improving their sheds.

Fig. 9-11. The shed's internal construction.

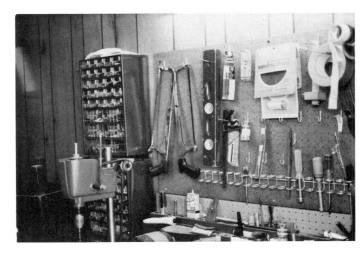

Fig. 9-12. A finished shed workshop.

Screen Rooms and Porches

In the South especially, the screen room is a popular feature. It can be built on the carport area (figure 9–13), but this cuts down the area available for parking the car if the mobile home is 40 to 45 feet long, and there is only a short apron from the street.

The screen room will require indoor-outdoor type carpeting to withstand the weather. Furniture ought to be of the outdoor nonrusting type, plastic coated for ease of cleaning.

Porches. A porch is a part of the mobile home itself, with a separate concrete floor and a foundation made of concrete or other material matching the mobile home. Access from the mobile home is provided through large sliding glass doors. A separate roof has to be provided as well as a kick plate around the lower perimeter of the porch.

Fig. 9-13. An enclosed screen porch.

After a period of time, however, many persons have found that enclosing the porch with glass windows or panels is a practical solution to escape wind-driven rains (figure 9–14).

Glass windows and individual screens still allow plenty of air to enter, but they protect the interior in bad weather. One important concern is the roof construction, especially its junction with the mobile home. Leaks will develop unless adequate joint construction and sealing are employed by an experienced installer.

The roof must be insulated to help the porch stay cool in the summer and retain heat in the winter. Some people install a separate air-conditioner to make the porch habitable on hot summer days (figure 9–15). The unit should be placed as high as practicable for maximum efficiency.

A final caution about porches: some contractors use the space within the porch foundation walls as a receptacle for rubbish and scraps of wood during construction. If this trash is not removed, termites may move in.

Figs. 9-14, 15. An enclosed porch. (Right) A porch air conditioner (which should be placed higher).

"Florida rooms." The so-called "Florida rooms," popular in that state, are nothing but an extension of the mobile home itself. Several large windows, of either plain or bay type, provide plenty of light (figure 9–16). The room itself may be separated from the basic home by sliding glass doors or a large opening. Its advantage is that the room is an integral part of the mobile home, and not an "add-on"; heating and cooling are provided by the central duct system. Chances of settling and leaks are greatly reduced.

Fig. 9-16. A "Florida room" with bay windows.

Planters

To improve appearance, many parks require the addition of a planter in front of the home. The planter may contain shrubs, flowers, small palm trees, or other decorative greenery. Many parks put shrubs into the planters when you move in but expect you to add other plants or flowers later.

Planters are built with solid walls of concrete blocks, bricks, or other material. If supported by footings, they create a problem: When the front of the mobile home rests on the back wall of the planter, its footings keep the front of the house from settling, but the remainder of the home can sink, resulting in a tilt toward the rear. The only remedy is to re-level, and re-leveling may be required more than once as the mobile home continues to settle in the rear.

The problem can be relieved by removing the blocks between the mobile home and the planter, and replacing them with half blocks—slightly less than half the thickness of conventional blocks (figure

9–17). The mobile home can then settle uniformly, with the load being carried only by the piers under the mobile home.

Do-It-Yourself Projects

In some areas of the country, it is possible to obtain materials (lumber and metal) in bulk or cut-to-size to build your own screen room (page 131) or other additions. But first check with the park man-

Fig. 9-17. Half-blocks replace regular-size blocks.

ager and get approval before you purchase the materials and start construction. Appearance, location, and other factors are certain to influence his decision on such a project.

Patios

If you want to add a patio area next to your mobile home, permission will have to be obtained from the park management beforehand. The concrete surface should slope slightly downward from the center to the outer perimeter for quick drainage and drying after a rainstorm.

CHAPTER 10

LANDSCAPING AND INTERIOR DECORATING

Landscaping

Even the new multi-wides with their low-angled roofs continue to look like boxes. However, the sterile appearance, the absence of finished foundations, and absence of a chimney or two can be softened by appropriate choice of shrubbery and trees where they are permitted. Trees serve a secondary purpose; they help shield the home from the effects of high winds and thus reduce stress on the structure. They also act as noise barriers.

Another reason some people find mobile homes unattractive is that unlike conventional houses, which are on larger lots parallel to the street, mobile homes are usually placed lengthwise on narrow lots. This close parallel spacing, limited only by the fire laws in many instances, conveys a cramped, monotonous picture. The increasing number of mobile homes that are being placed close to the curb line, approaching the so-called zero placement is also unattractive. Compare this to conventional houses, which are normally set back 25 to 50 feet from the curb. Crowding the mobile homes to generate more lots also makes park streets appear narrower than they actually are.

Each of the three basic mobile home locations—in a mobile home rental park, on your own lot in a park, and in the suburbs on your own lot—has its individual landscaping opportunities. The lot-owned sites permit you greater latitude in your landscaping designs than do rental sites.

Rental parks may prohibit any trees or shrubbery beyond those present when you move in. The principal reason is that bushes interfere with the operation of the large mowers used to cut the grass. And the mowers seem to get larger every year in order to speed up the cutting operation and save money.

A park bereft of trees or shrubbery frequently becomes a source of resentment to neighboring home owners who take pride in a well-developed and landscaped subdivision, not limited to one planter and two bushes per home.

Getting started. Landscaping helps to overcome deficiencies in appearance. Grasses, trees, shrubbery, and flowers create pleasant surroundings for your mobile home within the limits of park rules and regulations.

Nurseries, county extension services, and how-to-do-it books are excellent sources of information when you start making landscaping plans. Observe what other residents have already done with the land around their mobile home. Some of their ideas may prove adaptable for your own lot.

But, by all means secure the approval of the park management. Make a detailed plan on paper so it can be readily visualized.

Planters. In many mobile home parks planters are mandatory. They may be made of brick, stone, or concrete blocks—the same blocks used for skirting (figure 10–1).

The shrubs and flowers grown in planters should be slow-growing varieties to prevent overcrowding.

But the sides and rear of mobile homes still present a stark appearance, barely relieved by an occasional awning or two, and perhaps some shutters. The latter, for some unknown reason, have remained narrow (figure 10–2), probably a carryover from recreational vehicles. They do not compare in size or attractiveness to conventional home shutters. Lack of overhangs also detracts from mobile homes' appearance.

Fig. 10-1. Some flowers will add to the appearance of this concrete block planter.

Fig. 10-2. Shutters would look better if they were wider.

Grasses. You may find it useful to know about the various grasses, especially if you own your own land.

There are two basic varieties that we need to consider—the cool-season grasses and the warm-region grasses. Both types are subject to damage from various types of insects, above and below the ground level.

The cool-season grasses are the Kentucky bluegrasses, found in the varieties: Merion, Fylking, Pennstar, Adelphia, and Baron; they should be blended in a mix. If the mixture is planted in a light shade, red fescue should be added to bluegrass. Fertilizer should be applied in spring and fall. The growing period is April through October.

Some of the warm-season grasses are: St. Augustine; Floratam, a variety of St. Augustine; Zoysia; Bahia; and Centipede. Annual rye grass should be used for winter crop.

There is also Dichondra, actually a ground cover that grows slightly more than 2 inches in height. It consists of small round leaves that spread by vinelike propagation. It gives a good appearance where adequate watering is available and requires infrequent mowing because it grows slowly.

Centipede grass likes very little fertilizer, grows in sunny areas, and prefers acid soil.

Grass distribution in states with many mobile homes:

Alabama	St. Augustine in the south; Bermuda, Zoysia, Centipede elsewhere
Arizona	Cool season grasses in the north; Bermuda elsewhere
California	Bluegrass, bent grass, perennial rye in the north; Bermuda, St. Augustine, Zoysia, Dichondra elsewhere
Florida	St. Augustine in the north; Bahia in central and southern areas
Georgia	Bermuda in the north; Centipede and Zoysia elsewhere
Oklahoma	Bermuda
Texas	Bermuda in the north; St. Augustine elsewhere
Virginia	Bermuda and Zoysia

Grass enemies. Several types of insects attack various grasses and require control. You can do it yourself or hire professional help. Chinch bugs attack St. Augustine grass by sucking plant juices at the base. Floratam is not bothered by them. Sod worms feed on grass blades and leave large brown spots.

The Bahia grass is subject to attack by mole crickets, relatives of the conventional cricket, growing to 1½ inches in length. They subsist on the grass roots, chewing on them until the grass dies. They are most active in the spring when insecticides are most effective. They can be controlled by spraying the lawn with a special assortment of chemicals every other month. Your local garden supply shop will be happy to tell you the ingredients. A home remedy applies diluted kitchen detergent to the lawn, forcing the mole crickets to the surface.

In many rental mobile home parks, even though the residents do not own the lots, they are expected to take care of their lawn and keep the grass growing regardless of such problems as insect infestation.

Since insect-control service is expensive on an individual-lot basis, many park residents band together and have the whole park sprayed in one operation, at a sharp reduction in cost per lot (figure 10–3). Such a wholesale operation also prevents the pests from moving to an unsprayed area.

Fig. 10-3. Spraying for mole crickets.

Shrubs. There are many types of shrubs that can be planted; their selection depends upon the climate and soil of the mobile home park. In central and southern Florida, for example, the high summer temperature limits the number of types of shrubs that are appropriate for those conditions. The milder climate of southern California allows one to grow many more varieties of shrubs and flowers.

Roses. In sandy soil it is necessary to add heavy clay below roses and to their plantings to maintain the "wet feet" that roses like. Otherwise, the rapid drainage of rain or sprinkled water through the surrounding soil will leave the roses very little moisture to sustain them. One way to maintain needed moisture is to place 10 to 20 pounds of heavy clay in the bottom of the hole dug for planting. The clay is placed directly below the other planting material so that the rose roots will eventually reach the clay and its retained moisture.

Another problem with roses in the South is their long blooming period during the continuing long warm weather. They do not have a resting period during the winter months as do those in the North. As a consequence, rose bushes in the South do not last for 10 to 15 years, but are likely to "burn" themselves out in 6 to 8 years. Replacement will be necessary as they dwindle in size and produce fewer blooms.

During the cool weather in December and January, when their blooming period is at a low ebb, rose bushes should be cut back to 8 to 12 inches from the ground. Climbers should not be cut back as much since their older canes develop blooms the following year.

Only rose types native to the area and developed from a particular stock should be planted. For example, Chrysler Imperial and Peace roses, and the climber Don Juan, do well in Florida. Other rose types are suitable in other areas. McFarland and Pyle's *How to Grow Roses,* published by Macmillan, will help you make a selection.

A special fertilizer, Fertilome, a combination of fertilizer and systemic insecticide—the latter spreading through the root system—has been found to be effective against aphids which attack rose buds and leaves. This fertilizer reduces the need for spraying to a minimum.

Hibiscus. This popular bush grows well in southern California and Florida. It has to be trimmed occasionally since it grows fast. It requires adequate watering to bloom freely and to prevent bud drop. The latter may be caused by deficiencies in trace elements in the fertilizer.

Flowers. It always comes as a surprise to some folks that certain flowers do not do as well as in the South as in the North. For example, planting of pansies, tulips, and crocuses, should be avoided if you make your home in an area with a warm climate. Consult your local agricultural agent for a recommendation on which flowers or plants will do well in your area.

Bird of Paradise. This favorite flower of California and Florida requires considerable moisture and fertilizer for good growth. It should have at least one bloom showing when you purchase it. Otherwise, you may have to wait as long as three to four years before it blooms.

Trees. Care should be exercised in planting trees (if permitted by the management), considering the limited ground area available at a mobile home site.

A citrus tree may appear small when sold in its tin one-gallon or five-gallon container. But over a period of six to eight years, under good growing conditions, it may grow 8 to 10 feet high and 8 feet in diameter. If planted too close to a mobile home, it will require continuing trimming and may also present a mowing problem.

Another favorite, the Norfolk Island pine, will grow to a height of 16 feet, and 8 feet in diameter in the same period of time, starting as a 3-foot tree in a 5-gallon container. And it will keep growing until it reaches 30 or 40 feet high with a correspondingly large diameter.

A good guide that will help you care for all the plants listed above is Tom Riker's *The Healthy Garden Book.*

Landscaping on private lots. Mobile homes on private land in suburban areas do not face the restrictions one encounters in rental parks. Their lot size is likely to be considerably larger, making it possible to develop large plantings of flowers and shrubs. Neither are there likely to be restrictions on their placement or number (figure 10–4).

Fig. 10-4. A decorative corner planting.

Even parks where the lots are owned by the mobile home residents are more lenient about adding shrubs and trees. This is largely because the owner is responsible for cutting his own lawn.

Some states, such as Vermont, require that a minimum of two trees be planted at each mobile home, to be replaced immediately should they die.

Containers. In recent years we have witnessed more and more plants in containers suspended in macrame holders within carports, patios, and other areas (figure 10–5). This keeps them out of the way while enhancing the appearance of the mobile home. It also helps keep such sensative plants as cascading begonias out of the sun's scorching rays, allowing them to be protected by the carport roof or other overhang.

Fig. 10-5. An orchid plant in a macrame holder.

Scheduling. To take care of plants you must establish a definite schedule for their watering. The same applies to shrubs and flowers in your planter.

If you own your own lot you will probably have to cut the grass. In rental parks you will have to trim it at the curb and around the carport area. All these tasks will require some of your time and scheduling, cutting the grass weekly and watering it.

Decorating

In the process of buying a mobile home you will be faced with decisions about its interior decoration. Many mobile home manufacturers offer choices such as these: color and type of paneling; built-ins; type and color of tiles or other covering in bathrooms and kitchens; draperies, color and type; and other options.

Some even offer a choice in structural features: particle board or plywood; 5/32-inch luan or ¼-inch-thick wall paneling; overhead or floor duct work; and shingled or metal roofs.

Color. This is an important decision; you'll have to live with your choice for years to come.

The choice of paneling color determines whether your interior will be light or not. Consider that if you add awnings later they will tend to darken the interior, by cutting off some of the light coming through the windows. The installation of a carport roof, or even a mobile home moving into the lot next door can block out some of your light, too.

Thus, most people prefer light-color paneling, which also tends to make each room look larger. The same applies to ceilings, which generally are white or buff. With ceilings only 7 to 7½ feet high, you will welcome any strategy that creates the illusion of height. Should you wish to repaint a ceiling later, you may want to retain its original color to maintain this appearance. One wall could be an accent wall, by having the manufacturer use a dark paneling on it (figure 10–6).

Size, doors, windows, and draperies—all contribute to the appearance of a room and together determine the amount of light within it.

Draperies. Used as attractive fabrics in combination with sheer curtains, drapes enhance a room by reducing or covering the windows' sharp outlines. And of course, they provide privacy (figure 10–7). Valances add to the appearance, hiding the traverse rods for draperies and creating a richer-looking window treatment (figure 10–8).

Wall coverings. For many years, the prevailing practice was to use luan paneling in bathroom and kitchen. The trend now is to wallpaper one or both, to break up the monotony of paneling extending throughout the mobile home (figure 10–9). You may have a choice of patterns when you order your mobile home. Vinyl wallpaper is preferable since it is washable. Other rooms, such as a dining room, may also be papered (figure 10–10).

If you are offered a choice of 5/32-inch-thick luan paneling vs. conventional ¼-inch-thick paneling, by all means select the latter, even at additional cost. It stiffens the mobile home walls and has greater fire resistance.

Floor coverings. The carpet color, which you choose, should be in harmony with your wall coverings.

Select, if possible, a better-grade carpet than generally comes as standard with mobile homes. High traffic density, confined to a narrow path, tends to mat down sculptured carpeting. The earlier replacement will eventually cost you more than if you had ordered better-grade carpeting initially. Also remember that once your carpeting has been cleaned it will start showing soil in a shorter period of time. Never have the carpeting steam-cleaned if the floor is particle board.

The more common covering for kitchen and bathroom floors is linoleum or cheaper grades of vinyl tile. If replacing them with a high-grade covering is an expensive option, consider covering the bathroom floor with washable bathroom carpeting. It is available in various sizes and types that can be cut to fit the bathroom floor, and replaced when you get tired of the color. Special kitchen carpeting is available and can be installed later. It will give your

Fig. 10-6. An accent wall.

Figs. 10-7, 8. Drapes add to a room's appearance and (right) valances complement drapes.

Figs. 10-9, 10. A wallpapered bathroom and (below) a dining room with a wallpapered accent wall.

floor long-term protection, is cleanable, and is easy underfoot (figure 10–11).

Furniture. A problem in many mobile homes is that the location of windows and doors limits the furniture arrangement and prevents moving furniture around to create a new look.

A visit to model rooms in furniture or department stores will help you to develop a furniture arrangement that creates a restful atmosphere. Avoid overcrowding and the blocking of passageways. Many of the illustrations of mobile homes, with expensive dramatic-looking interiors, are of large multi-wides, not the run-of-the-mill smaller mobile homes, with smaller rooms which are designed for smaller pocketbooks.

Redecorating. There are certain improvements that will add to the appearance of a mobile home after you have lived in it a few years. Some, described in Chapter 13, list in detail the steps to be followed in making improvements.

One of the obvious areas to update is the dining room lighting. In a majority of mobile homes the

Fig. 10-11. A kitchen carpet is attractive and practical.

original light fixture (figure 10–12) leaves much to be desired. It does not add to the appearance and replacing it with a new, better fixture will give the room a new look. Another popular improvement is the addition of a dimmer control (figure 10–13) in place of the conventional on-off switch. This control is stepless and provides any degree of illumination desired.

If there is no built-in cabinet in the dining room (see figure 1–14) to store dishes, silverware, and similar items, that addition by the handy man is also popular.

The so-called shelter magazines, such as *Better Homes and Gardens,* can provide inspiration for redecorating your mobile home.

Remember that, due to their structural design,

mobile homes cannot be radically altered. One cannot relocate a major bearing wall without encountering support problems, nor can you add a conventional brick fireplace; its weight would cause an excessive load on the frame's outriggers.

Carpeting. Many mobile homes, modestly priced and built years ago, may not have wall-to-wall carpeting in every room. Replacing area carpeting with carpeting over the whole floor area will not only cut down the noise level but also make your home look better. A good, thick pad, plus a good carpet, will substantially increase your home's value. Your selection of carpeting color and quality depends only on your pocketbook and taste.

Figs. 10-12, 13. A dining room 5-bulb fixture and (right) its dimmer control.

CHAPTER 11

MOBILE HOME MAINTENANCE

Mobile home maintenance has been described as minimal compared to conventional housing. This depends upon who is doing the selling. Some of the maintenance can be avoided if you reside in a rental mobile home park. Your grass is cut and trimming will be done, in some parks. However, you are paying for this service as part of your rent.

However, the fact remains, as indicated by the many service trucks, that service is needed, either by yourself or a contractor, to keep your home in shape. The mobile home industry is gradually changing basic construction to eliminate some of the existing maintenance problems.

Exterior Maintenance

The owner's manual will provide you with suggestions on maintaining the exterior of your mobile home. It may have baked-on enamel on aluminum, vinyl, or even wood siding.

Washing. When your new mobile home is set up on its site it is likely to be grimy from its travels. One of the written requirements in your contract should be that the home be completely cleaned and washed prior to your acceptance.

Homes finished in baked enamel on aluminum can be washed and waxed at the same time by using special preparations available for this purpose. Purchase the commercial-type preparation containing water-soluble wax, and add water in the proportion specified on the container. The combined cleaner-wax product eliminates a separate waxing job as well as possible spotting during drying. Washing the mobile home twice a year is better than waiting longer periods when it becomes more difficult to remove the accumulated grime or salt.

Washing your mobile home is bound to take some time, if—for example—you have a number of large awnings to wash as well. Their construction will determine the speed with which they can be washed. Select a morning or evening to do the actual washing to avoid quick drying during the heat of the day. Spring and fall are the best times of the year for this task.

Use a long-handled brush and rinse with cold water. The resultant thin wax coating will help to prevent dirt and grime from collecting on the surface. A harder way is to wax the entire mobile home after you wash it. A different sort of wax is better if you elect this course. You'll find many brands in hardware and automotive supply outlets.

If you are unable to do this job yourself, you can hire a commercial service company. Caution: Do *not* hire a company that advertises that it uses high pressure for washing the mobile homes. Dirt will be driven into the finish with this method, instead of removing it. This method can also remove caulking.

Leveling. Your home, especially a multi-wide, must be properly leveled when it is set up. Squeaky floors, windows, and doors that are hard to open, and refrigerator doors that refuse to stay open are some of the symptoms of a bad leveling job. Other symptoms that are less apparent but may show up later are cracked seams between the mobile home sections and buckled roof and interior paneling.

If such signs appear within the warranty period the dealer should be notified and asked to re-level the mobile home. In some instances, a re-leveling is done six months after purchase as part of the contract. In many cases the soil on which a mobile home lot is situated is not sufficiently rolled or tamped to provide a lasting foundation for the piers. Thus settlement may occur with the first heavy rains. In the North, frost heaving may cause uneven settling.

If re-leveling is not in your contract, make a few checks yourself after you have been in your mobile home a month or more. Unless your home is on a concrete slab, settlement will occur. If it is uniform, though, you have no problem.

Your concrete skirting blocks will indicate if there is uneven settlement. The outer edge of the mobile home will settle on all or part of them. If you have solid skirting extending to the soil, some buckling will show up there if the mobile home settles unevenly.

You can check the leveling with a 4- or 6-foot carpenter's level, and in addition you will need a 3- to 5-ton hydraulic jack to do the adjusting. Start at the middle of one side of the mobile home and check crosswise with the level to determine if the home is level along its width moving from the center. (This procedure has already been sketched on page 101.)

Then proceed along the length of the mobile home, checking first in the lengthwise direction, and then crosswise. When you find a low spot, jack up the frame and adjust the wedges that support the frame on top of each pier. Since they are tapered, they can be used to adjust to the required distance between frame and ground, either more or less.

One word of warning: Do not use a standard automobile jack for this purpose. It does not have sufficient capacity for such heavy loading. Also, select a heavy board or a solid concrete block as a base on which to rest the jack.

Unless you have the proper tools available, this leveling is best left to the dealer's service department.

Painting the roof. If you have a metal or galvanized steel roof, this job will have to be done about every three years. Neglect will result in leaks with subsequent damage to your walls and ceilings. Rust will develop at the seams if they are not painted within that period. (A mobile home owner with an asphalt- or fiberglass-shingled roof is spared this chore as is the conventional-home owner.)

First, the roof should be washed down with a hose, to remove any accumulated dirt and dust. Use a broom to sweep the heavier accumulation of debris, such as tree leaves and branches. Any dirt accumulated in the gutters should also be removed.

You will need the following: (1) a 4-inch paint brush; (2) a wide roller, special for this work; (3) a clean bucket; (4) a long extension handle; (5) a roller dish; (6) a bucket of roof paint, 2- or 5-gallon size; (7) a plywood board, 4 by 6 feet; (8) wiping rags. The dealer who sells you the special roof paint will have items 1 through 6.

Wait until the roof has dried after washing it. Start with the outer roof edges and paint, with the 4-inch brush, all the edges, around any stacks, vents, and any other irregularities (figure 11-1). Be sure to use the plywood as a platform to stand on, moving it as you go along. Its area distributes your weight and thereby keeps the roof seams from opening. A platform should be required for the same reason if you have a contractor paint your roof. It is preferable to paint your roof early in the morning or late in the day.

Once you have painted the outer perimeter with the brush, you can proceed to paint the remaining surfaces with the roller. Start at the end farthest away from your ladder and work toward it, so you do not paint yourself in (figure 11-2). Again, be sure to use the plywood board as your working platform.

It is best to wait until the next day to put on the second coat, repeating the procedure. The use of special roof paints is recommended to secure a satisfactory painting job.

One word of caution: As you paint backward,

Fig. 11-1. Touch up any irregularities on the roof with a brush.

Fig. 11-2. Coat the roof with a roller.

away from your starting point, be careful as you approach completion at the other end. There is nothing to prevent you from falling off the roof.

Sealing joints. Leaks frequently develop at the junction of the mobile home's roof to the carport, shed, or other appended structures.

Most mobile homes lack the short overhangs that would allow the contractor who builds the additions to provide a permanent water seal at that critical seam. Also, because roofs flex in the wind, that junction will often develop a leak even if it has been well sealed initially.

Fiberglass cloth, several inches wide, extended over the full length of the junction, will correct this problem (figure 11-3). It is flexible and allows the junction to move. It should be lapped over the junction and held in place with special mastic. The cloth is available at the supply store that sells the roof paint. It should be painted over with a special paint, also available from the same supplier, for this purpose.

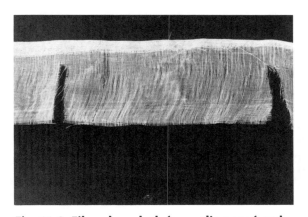

Fig. 11-3. Fiberglass cloth for sealing roof and carport junction.

Painting underside of carport roof. At certain times of the year, when high humidity develops at night, the carport roof may collect water on its underside through condensation. It may collect in large droplets that eventually fall onto the car parked below.

Two defects may result: The roof surface may develop mildew and spots, and the car finish may develop spots from these droplets.

A lacquer-like finish, heavier in substance than conventional lacquer, has been developed to eliminate this problem. It can be applied by brush, roller, or spray. The first two methods of application are more likely to be used by the mobile home owner since spraying requires special equipment. The finish

dries rapidly; that keeps dust from sticking to it. Brushing will produce overlaps that will be visible when it dries. The same is true of rollers. However, either of these methods can be used successfully if you take the time to do it properly.

First, the surface should be washed to remove all spots and left to dry thoroughly before applying this finish. Use a 3-inch brush or larger to get a wide coverage with one pass. Since the finish dries very quickly, do not attempt to cover a long distance at each pass. Work across so you can start overlapping as soon as possible. Continue this until you have covered the entire surface. Overlaps are bound to show, more so if the temperature is warm or hot. If possible, select a cool day (but above 50° F.) to do this job. Roller application is similar, except that you will be able to cover a longer and wider distance with each pass. Overlaps will still show to some extent.

If you are able to rent spraying equipment and use it correctly, coverage with it will be so rapid that no overlaps will appear (figure 11-4).

Caulking. Awnings, shaken by the wind, will often develop leaks at their mounting screws. This can be detected by drops of water appearing on the window panes under an awning during rain. To prevent greater damage later, such as water entering outside walls, the individual screws should be removed, one at a time, and the space filled with fresh caulking compound before replacing the screws.

Since caulking may dry out and crack after a few years, it also should be removed in such areas as the bottom of the shed next to the concrete driveway and replaced with fresh caulking. This will eliminate the possibility of water seepage into the shed during heavy rains.

Fig. 11-4. The underside of this carport roof was sprayed with a special lacquer.

Roof stacks or vents should be recaulked prior to roof painting if they show evidence of cracks.

Replacing outside fastening screws. In mobile home manufacture, the outer aluminum skin of the mobile home is secured by steel, cadmium-plated self-tapping screws. They are driven in place by power screwdrivers with a hexagon-head drive at-

drill. It consists of a dual-drive assembly, forward and reverse, and has attachments for driving conventional screws or nuts, in or out. Two cylindrical housings, one on the front end for forward drive and one at the rear for reverse drive, control the direction of motion. Press your fingers against either one to determine the rotation direction (figure 11–6).

Figs. 11-5, 6. A forward-reverse drill attachment is a great convenience.

tachment to match the screw heads. The steel screws allow fast assembly but result in corrosion later. The corrosion is due to galvanic action—the aluminum skin touching the steel fasteners, which have only a thin cadmium plating. All-aluminum screws cannot be driven at the factory's production pace, and therefore the plated screws are used instead. In a few years these steel screws begin to rust. In extreme cases, the fastener heads can snap off when an attempt is made to replace them.

To eliminate this continuing problem, these steel screws should be replaced with all-aluminum, self-tapping hexagon head screws available in hardware stores for this very purpose. Common sizes available are #8, in ½-, ¾-, and 1-inch lengths. Replacement screws should be of the same length as the original fasteners.

Door frame and awning fastening screws are likely to be the slightly larger #9 size and 1 inch and 1¼ inch in length. They should also be replaced. Do not use #8 screws to replace them. If the longer length is not available, use some caulking compound on the replacement screws as a filler.

The steel cadmium-plated screws are also likely to be used to support the gutters from the carport roofs or overhangs. These are subject to even greater corrosion because they're so often wet.

To replace screws quickly throughout the exterior of the mobile home, shed, and gutters, it is advisable to purchase a special tool available in hardware stores (figure 11–5). Known as a speed-reducer screwdriver, it fits into an ordinary ¼-inch power

By pressing your fingers on the rear housing you can remove the old screw. When you press your fingers around the front housing you can drive in the replacement screw. *Do not* drive the replacement screw completely in. Use a ¼ inch hexagon hand tool to complete the process. This will preclude the possibility of breaking off the head of the new fastener. Also, use a hand tool to start the old screws if they are rusted in.

Replacing hundreds of these screws will take time, but you will be rewarded with permanent fasteners that will not corrode or stain the outer skin. The new ones will last as long as your mobile home. Do not just replace a few here and there, since the remaining old screws will continue to corrode and their heads may snap off when you attempt to remove them later.

Heat tapes or cables. One of the vulnerable spots of a mobile home in a cold climate is its cold water supply pipe, extending from below the soil level to the mobile home floor assembly. This pipe may be subjected to temperatures below zero, and unless suitably protected the water in it will freeze.

To eliminate this possibility, heat cables (figure 11-7) have been developed that are capable of han-

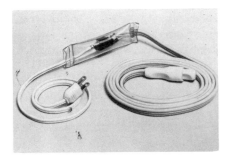

Fig. 11-7. A typical heat cable.

dling temperatures down to —50° F. Automatic thermostats are available that will turn the cable on when the temperature falls below +40° F. and shut it off when the outside temperature rises to that level.

These cables can be laid straight along the pipe or spiraled three turns per foot of pipe. The straight-laid cable will protect ¾-inch pipe down to —55° F., with one foot of cable required per foot of pipe. The spiraled cable, three turns per foot, will require 1½ feet of cable per foot of ¾-inch pipe, and will protect down to —65° F. To insulate the cable against cold exterior temperatures a fiberglass wrap, ½ inch thick, should be used. An outer wrap is placed over it. Heat cables are available in lengths from 6 to 200 feet.

To protect the pipe below the surface, dig down about 3 feet around the pipe. Start by securing the end of the cable at the pipe's lowest point and lay it straight along the pipe. Anchor the cable to the pipe with friction tape. Be sure that the thermostat is securely anchored to the surface of the pipe.

Extend the cable past the shut-off valve upward to the floor assembly. The fiberglass covering should then be wrapped around the pipe-cable assembly, followed by the outer wrap. To protect the cable and fiberglass wrap, split a 3-inch plastic pipe in half and fit it around them, using duct tape to hold them together. Cut out the pipe to fit around the shut-off valve, and fill the space around the plastic pipe with dirt. Plug the top of the plastic pipe with a split cork plug to prevent rodents from entering the pipe. Connect the lead cord to a 110-volt outlet located on the outside of the mobile home.

As an additional precaution in cold climates, the waste water line can be protected in the same fashion as the supply pipe.

Fire protection. Safety fire escape windows are required in all mobile home bedrooms, in accordance with HUD regulations. As we have already seen, the mandated windows are a less than perfect exit for a rapid escape in case of fire. However, you should familiarize yourself and your family with their use. Also, a family gathering spot should be designated, outside your mobile home. That way a quick check can be made to account for every member of the family. Lives have been lost when family members have reentered a burning mobile home, looking for children who were already safe outside. Instruct any guests about the special escape windows in their bedroom. They may not be familiar with their use.

Long extension cords, which are sometimes run under the carpeting, are one possible source of fire. This is a dangerous practice because the cord may develop a hot spot and ignite the carpeting. Extension cords should be replaced every ten years or so as the insulation tends to dry out and may crack.

Smoke detectors did not become mandatory until 1976. If your mobile home does not have them, it's a good idea to install them, one near each bedroom if those rooms are far apart.

The instruction booklet that comes with this unit tells how it should be tested and maintained. If it is battery-powered, the battery should be checked at least once a year.

Never empty ash trays into a waste basket or allow smoking in bed. A fire may smolder for a long while before flames erupt. Oily rags should not be stored in your home or under it. When stored they should be kept in air-right, metal containers.

The fire escape door, described in Chapter 13, can be readily installed and will prove to be far more satisfactory for escape purposes than the mandatory safety windows.

Another potential source of fire is the (LP) bottled gas container, which should be checked periodically. Apply a soapy water solution over such areas as pipe connections. Bubbling indicates a leak, which should be attended to immediately. The same procedure can be applied to natural gas lines. Check all pipe joints for leaks if you smell gas. *Don't* use a match or a lighter.

Commercial service firms. One quickly becomes accustomed to seeing many service trucks in mobile home parks. These firms perform such services as window and mobile home washing, carpet cleaning, roof painting, spraying the underside of carport roofs, termite protection, lawn cutting and trimming, installation of awnings and shutters, insulation, painting carport driveways, air conditioning and appliance service, remodeling, adding on extra rooms, and many others—even poodle hair trimming.

The fly-by-night nature of some of these companies makes it necessary to select carefully any company you want to do any of these jobs. Any guarantee or warranty they offer will be worth nothing if they have left for parts unknown.

Base your choice on the success that your neighbors have had with the company, or contact the Better Business Bureau. Determine if they are a member of a trade group in their specialty. Request the names of past customers whom you may contact for reference. By all means, do not pay for the job until it has been completed to your satisfaction.

It is a common practice for companies to ask the president of the park association for permission to present their wares or service to residents at a park gathering, such as a kaffee-klatsch or a potluck dinner. This acquaints many residents with the product or service with a single presentation. The addresses of residents are readily obtained for further solicitation by giving a door prize as a reward for attendance. A special cut-rate offer may be made to induce the residents to sign up for the company's service. The only problem is that, in many instances, the rates go up after the initial offer has expired.

In Florida, which has poor consumer protection laws, it is advisable to limit the extent of service agreements that require substantial advance payments to a maximum period of one year. As a rule, offers of reduced rates for two-or three-year contracts should be avoided.

A progressive payment arrangement should be made on remodeling or other work that calls for a considerable outlay of money. Any contractor who refuses to be a party to such an agreement should be viewed with suspicion. You will probably be better served if you find someone else.

Florida is one state that has poor or nonexistent laws to protect mobile home owners against disreputable remodeling contractors and air-conditioning services; these organizations can operate without posting a bond or securing a license. They are not required to put into an escrow account money that they collect as prepayment for service to be done two or three years later. Thus, it becomes simple for them to go out of business and start operating elsewhere. One such well-known franchiser went bankrupt in 1979, leaving thousands of customers stranded, with tens of thousands of dollars collected on future air conditioning contracts.

Ask for a written guarantee or a specific contract for any work or service that is likely to cost you a considerable amount of money. Oral agreements are very hard to prove in court if you find that you have to seek redress there later on.

Interior Maintenance

Interior maintenance poses a whole range of problems, some of them simple, some of them complex.

Kitchen. Read and save all the booklets that come with your kitchen appliances for future reference. Don't just presume that you know all about how to operate and maintain your appliance. A little extra care at the beginning can save you needless heartache later.

Kitchen cabinet shelves should be covered with paper, such as Contact, for easier cleaning. The doors should be cleaned with soap and water to remove any grease from cooking. An exhaust fan and hood on the kitchen range will prevent a lot of grease from being dissipated within the kitchen and will get rid of unwanted odors. The fan should be used whenever you're cooking. The filter should be washed frequently in soapy water.

Use plenty of water to flush the disposal unit and clean out its drain line which extends to the main sewer connection. In most mobile homes this line is almost horizontal; at a minimum it should slope ⅛-inch per foot.

Should your frost-free refrigerator give you trouble, check for possible freezing in the drain line that extends from the freezer to the evaporation tray beneath the refrigerator. A water purifier in the refrigerator water supply line will produce ice cubes free of contaminants.

Air-conditioning/heating units. These units are too complex for the average mobile home owner to repair or even to check their operation. Test equipment is required to check the Freon pressure, power and sequence of operation of the electrical heater system, and similar factors; an experienced service man should be used. About the only job that the owner can do is to replace the return air filter periodically. If clogged with dirt, it will reduce the efficiency of the system materially, and thus increase operating cost.

After the initial installation, the air-conditioning contractor is likely to offer a service contract for a period of one or more years. Since the initial installation has a one-year warranty, the service contract can be delayed until the second year. When signing a service maintenance contract insist on twice-yearly inspections of the whole unit. This will reduce the possibility of a breakdown during the summer or possible failure to get heat in the winter.

The newer compressors and fans within the unit do not require any periodic oiling as they have self-lubricating bearings.

Walls. While paneled walls help to keep maintenance down, they do require an occasional cleaning with a light application of detergent, followed by waxing. Be careful to use the detergent sparingly because the paneling surface is actually printed paper glued to a wood backing.

Floors. Some mobile homes' kitchen floors employ tile that's not of high quality; because the tile extends over a large area, the manufacturers use a cheaper grade to keep costs down. This tile is unlikely to last very long unless it is washed and waxed frequently. When it starts to show severe wear, a popular solution is to cover it with a good grade of carpet. The carpet is cemented over the tiled floor and can be kept clean by vacuuming. It can be cleaned at the same time as the rest of the carpeting.

Other manufacturers use a good grade of vinyl tile that requires no waxing at all if kept properly cleaned. It has a built-in wax finish and will far outlast the cheaper grade.

Carpeting. The particle-board flooring used in most mobile homes presents a carpet-cleaning problem. Any unnecessary moisture increases the possibility of buckling flooring. For that reason, whether you do it yourself or have it done, avoid cleaning equipment advertised as "deep penetration" or steam cleaning and keep the amount of moisture used to a minimum.

Washer and dryer. Your washer and dryer must be level to operate properly and without excessive vibration. A particle board floor will almost always vibrate a great deal if washer and dryer units are installed on it. A simple and effective remedy is to remove the appliances temporarily and to place a ¾ inch thick plywood board over the area allocated to the washer and dryer. Fasten the board to the flooring with #10 flat head screws, 1½ inches long, every 6 to 9 inches, to secure good bonding to the floor surface; the screws must be flush in the plywood board. Cover the plywood with a piece of sheet vinyl and cement it to the surface. This will prevent any spilled water from getting into the plywood.

Bathrooms. Tubs and showers in many bathrooms are now made of molded plastic or fiberglass. They should not be cleaned with abrasive cleaners.

Papered walls in the bathrooms may be washed down with detergent solution if you're sure that your wallpaper is washable; most of them are.

Cutting down heat gain and loss. There are several ways to reduce warm weather heat inside the mobile home. These suggestions can cut the cost of operating your air-conditioning system.

As simple a proposition as it sounds, many people actually forget that the sun streaming in their windows. produces a greenhouse effect that requires additional cooling. The heat and glare can be eliminated simply by installing awnings that will protect your windows from the sun and rain. Another tack is the application of very thin plastic material, specifically made for this purpose, to the window panes. The storm windows that HUD now requires will help hold the heat in during the winter, and their insulating effect will help reduce the load on your air conditioner during warm weather.

One of the principal functions of the air conditioner is to keep the humidity low. Showers, baths, and wet clothing hanging in the bathrooms all increase humidity thereby adding to discomfort within the home and adding to the cost of operating the air conditioner.

The size of the air-conditioning unit is important for comfort and economy. An oversize unit will operate less often, and thus allow greater temperature variations than the smaller unit. Selection of the correct size should be left to an air-conditioning expert or to the manufacturer of the mobile home.

Little can be done to correct the amount of insulation in various areas of the mobile home after it has been built and delivered. Make sure that it complies with the latest HUD regulations in this regard at the time of purchase.

Electrical systems. Most mobile homes have an adequate supply of electricity available from the park mains. It is primarily a 110/220-volt system, which will allow operation of an air conditioner equipped with heat strips. The latter may require as much as 15 kilowatts, a considerable load for heat purposes alone. For this reason, it is desirable to have electrical service of at least 150 amperes available to take care of all requirements of the mobile home.

The power within the mobile home is distributed from the distribution panel, which contains a number of circuit breakers of various capacities, depending upon their anticipated load. They should be marked, either at the factory or by the dealer, to indicate which circuits they control. In an emergency, the main circuit breaker will cut off all power within the mobile home.

Any additions or modification to the system should be made by a licensed electrician. Otherwise, you not only risk trouble, you also risk having your insurance canceled.

The electrical system should be checked after the mobile home has been readied for your occupancy. Continuous tripping of a circuit breaker indicates trouble in the circuit, and an electrician should be called.

The size of light bulbs used should be limited to that specified in the fixture.

Replacing faucet washers. Bathroom faucets of the replaceable-washer type can be readily repaired without recourse to a plumber. The only tools required are an adjustable wrench, opening up to at least 1½ inches, and one or two screwdrivers.

Shut off the water, either directly at the fixture, or at the main shut-off valve outside. Cover the drain to prevent parts being removed from falling in. Using the screwdriver, remove the faucet handle if the fastening screw can be seen. Otherwise, remove the covering cap and then the screw below it.

You will find a double nut assembly. The inner nut assembly or cartridge has to be removed; using the wrench, turn it counterclockwise. The lower end of this cartridge assembly has a rubber washer held by a screw. Take out the screw and washer and replace them both with replacement parts from a hardware store. Reverse the procedure to assemble.

For a kitchen sink or bathtub faucet that has a cartridge unit, you will probably need to replace the whole cartridge, not just a washer. In this case, you may have to go to a plumbing supply house to get the replacement parts.

Your maintenance. Keep a few tools handy: screwdrivers of various sizes, a hammer, an assortment of nails and screws, a step ladder, and a can or two of oil. You will be able to make many minor repairs without having to call professional help. Mobile homes do require maintenance, and probably to a larger extent than the conventional house. When the tasks are identical to those you would encounter in a conventional home you can find expert do-it-yourself guidance in a number of excellent paperback books, among them Hubbard Cobb's *Money-Saving Home Maintenance* and Charles Neal's *Do-It-Yourself Housebuilding: Step-by-Step.*

CHAPTER 12

MOBILE HOME PROBLEMS

In spite of the industry's claims to the contrary, mobile home living is not a panacea for our housing shortage. Here are some common problems:

1. Industry's desire to cut costs
2. The present method of supporting mobile homes on piers instead of a permanent foundation
3. Lack of a concrete base under the mobile home
4. Poor construction practices
5. Skimping on sizes and materials
6. Lack of inspection of multi-wides on site assembly
7. High insurance, financing, and maintenance costs

Some of these problems could be avoided, and a better product offered, with only a small increase in price. Others, such as zoning problems, will disappear once appearance of the homes has been upgraded, overcoming the basic contention by many that mobile home parks look like low-income housing. Most buyers would welcome a better-looking, long-lasting investment, and a more desirable place to live.

Many persons have returned to conventional housing after a try at mobile home living, as some new conventional-housing subdivisions are starting to offer the amenities commonly associated with mobile home living, e.g., recreational facilities, pools, and planned activities for the subdivision residents.

This chapter presents some of the problems that a new mobile home owner may be expected to encounter or that may develop over a period of time.

Roofs

Roof design hasn't changed much for many years. The cost factor has resulted in continuing use of thin-gauge galvanized sheet metal for this purpose. With many soldered-together panels and lengthy joints forming each side of the roof, leaks are almost inevitable; but even that is only one factor in poor roof design. Many manufacturers do not even give the roof an initial coating before the mobile home is delivered to the purchaser.

Reducing the roof slope angle also reduces the amount of roof material required. While conventional-housing roofs have a rise of 4 or more inches per foot, the rise on many mobile home roofs is only ¾-inch per foot. Not only is the builder saving on the cost of the roof material, but also on the smaller roof trusses.

By eliminating the roof overhangs the builders are cutting costs, but they introduce the problem of water leakage into the interior.

Unless the mobile home manufacturer "stretches" each roof side prior to assembly, a roof rumble develops in high winds, with the air entering under the roof surface through poorly sealed wall-to-roof corners. The end result is the "oil-can" effect— similar to the snapping noise when the bottom of an oil can is pressed.

In hot climates, the metal roof absorbs heat from the sun, and when adequate insulation is not installed, the heat is transmitted to the thin plastic ceiling. This is common because the low roof slope limits the space available for insulation.

The mobile home roof requires painting with special white paint at approximately 3-year intervals, a real expense if done by a roofing contractor. Walking on the metal to paint or make other repairs can cause open seams and leaks. This concern and how to avoid it have been dealt with in greater detail earlier.

Some manufacturers have developed fiberglass roofs which are free of many of the above problems, especially since they have an underlying wood base to strengthen the roof. Painting is eliminated but the extra cost of one thousand dollars or more may keep you from selecting that option.

Another choice fast gaining popularity is the shingled roof, with a greater rise angle, using asphalt or fiberglass shingles.

Floors

Mobile home floors cannot be compared to floors in conventional housing. The two-layer floor in conventional housing is unquestionably superior to the single thickness in mobile homes. Instead of hardwood lumber, the single-layer floor uses particle board, a material subject to warping from moisture; it also lacks the stiffness of plywood. Plywood, consisting of three or more layers of wood fibers, will displace or "sag" far less under a load, such as persons walking on it.

Particle floors, nailed and glued to the floor joists, are of the tongue-and-groove type. Individual sheets require approximately 1/16-inch separation for expansion due to changes in humidity. Even though these sheets are nailed to the floor joists, the softer texture of the particle board eventually allows it to loosen, resulting in squeaky floors. These floors are likely to develop a "spongy" feeling underfoot.

Mobile home manufacturers, who originally used plywood floors, changed to particle board because of its lower cost. Adding to the problem of too resilient flooring is the prevalent use of 2 by 6 inch floor joists, instead of 2 by 8 inch joists, a conventional housing industry standard for a given floor span.

Such construction practices contribute to a shorter mobile home life expectancy and ultimately require floor repairs that will cost more than if the floor had been constructed with better and stronger materials in the first place.

Insulation

The entrance of the Department of Housing and Urban Development into the mobile home home field, with its construction standards defining the ratings of insulation to be used for the various areas in the mobile home, has largely eliminated manufacturers' tendency to skimp on insulation, a practice all too common in the past. But a new problem has arisen. In today's construction, the outer skin of a mobile home consists of aluminum panels, inter-

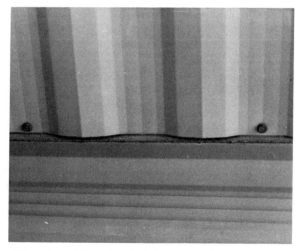

Fig. 12-1. The aluminum outer skin is corrugated to secure stiffness.

locked with each other. Their corrugated shape (figure 12-1), required for stiffness, allows outside air to enter under the skin through the corrugations, which extend from top to bottom. It has been found that this air, entering into the wall insulation, reduces its effectiveness and lowers its R value. (The higher the R rating the greater is its resistance to the flow of heat.) Insulation batts do not provide an air tight seal when nailed at random spaces along the 2 by 4-inch wall framing members.

The only practical solution is to securely nail insulation board, edge to edge, completely sealing the wall area from air penetrating the insulation, a manufacturing change of small additional cost but of great benefit to the consumer.

Paneling

For economy and ease of manufacturing, the industry has continued to use inferior paneling as standard for interior walls. We have detailed its characteristics and deficiencies earlier. You can easily check the type of paneling in your mobile home or in a model by simple tests. Press on the paneling between the wall framing members; if it gives, it is the imitation. Or observe the wood grain pattern on the wall; if it repeats, it is of low quality.

We have already learned that the luan paneling has a tendency to burn rapidly in a mobile home fire. The conventional 1/4-inch paneling is safer, and its use may add only about $200 to manufacturer's total cost.

Formaldehyde

Particle board flooring and luan paneling produce formaldehyde vapors in new mobile homes which can irritate your eyes. This irritation remains with some persons for many months after moving into the home. Their eyes persist in watering, even with frequent airing of the home by natural or forced circulation.

Some manufacturers and dealers have sought to provide relief from this condition by using products available on the market—products which will supposedly cure this problem in a matter of a few hours. However, the only thing that these products seem to do is mask the formaldehyde smell with oil of spearmint or wintergreen; they neither remove nor neutralize the irritant. Persons with very sensitive eyes have found that the problem is aggravated when they have been in smoke-filled surroundings before returning to their mobile home. Tests conducted by the University of Washington have found no reduction of formaldehyde irritation when so-called "miracle" cures were used.

The mobile home buyer who anticipates this problem can reduce it somewhat if he orders plywood floors and paneling instead of the cheaper standard offerings.

An additional factor contributing to the formaldehyde problem is the increasing use of urea formaldehyde (U.F.) foam insulation in mobile homes, both during their construction or as an extra insulation in existing homes. This type of insulation releases formaldehyde gas after its installation, adding to the gas problems from particle board floor and wall paneling. Also, this insulation, when used in roof assemblies and subjected to high roof temperatures, gradually shrinks in size over a period of time, reducing its effectiveness as an insulator.

Doors and Hinges

Cabinet doors, varying in width and length, often warp. This occurs over a period of time, primarily because of poor construction practices. The front face and door edges are covered with a plastic material, but the back surface often has only paint for protection. Thus, with the absorption of moisture and the force of surface tension caused by the plastic on the front face, the doors tend to warp outward as much as $\frac{1}{8}$-inch or more, depending upon the door length.

To eliminate the noise of doors closing, felt bumpers are put on backs of doors. For some reason, some manufacturers leave off the bumper that should be at the center of a wide door. Consequently, the doors lack evenly applied support and tend to warp.

Door warpage also puts pressure on the small door hinges that are usually used. They first begin to squeak and finally fail after a few years. The replacement expense will be yours to bear.

The solution to these problems is to use a door that has a plastic covering on both its front and back faces.

Curtains, Draperies, and Valances

Although the mobile home industry advertises that mobile homes come furnished with these items, do not plan to avoid this expense. Too many of the curtains supplied will be found to have a short life. When they are dry cleaned (never wash them), they are apt to tear or fall out of shape, so they cannot be rehung and must be replaced.

To save the cost of hardware, many manufacturers simply nail the valances to the ceiling with painted house laths instead of using valance rods. Valances cannot be removed except by removing the laths. Such construction also cuts off a part of the ceiling area, which will remain white while the surrounding area may darken from age.

Showers

Many mobile homes have built-in showers with plastic material protecting the walls, and aluminum shower doors.

The prefabricated showers are sealed in the corners with vertical and horizontal aluminum strips. The assembly screws constitute a real problem. These are generally plated steel. When inserted into the aluminum strips, they rapidly corrode due to the galvanic action between the two metals in the presence of soapy water, an alkali. The use of stainless steel screws would solve this problem, at very little additional expense, and eliminate one troubling maintenance problem.

Another simple shower stall improvement manufacturers should make is to switch from the thin shower doors in common use to thicker doors, which overhang the guide channels. This would divert the water, instead of leading it inside the shower door guide tracks (figure 12–2).

Fig. 12-2. Narrow shower doors trap the water in the guide channels.

Closets

Many closets, some of them as long as 8 feet, have only a single bracket at the center to support the clothes rod and the shelf across the closet. The bracket is secured with only a small woodscrew and will pull away eventually because of the strain of clothes continually being put on and taken off the rod. You can remedy this situation by using a machine screw to hold the bracket to the shelf (figure 12-3).

Fig. 12-3. A machine screw is best for securing a bracket to a shelf.

Kitchen Floors

For many years it has been a standard practice to allow a 4-inch space between the bottom of kitchen cabinets and the floor for ease of cleaning. That space will accommodate most vacuum cleaners.

Since many persons cover their kitchen floors with carpet, however, the space is reduced to 3 or 3½ inches and becomes inaccessible for cleaning. A slight increase in the toe space height by the manufacturers would correct this.

Cabinet Shelving

Many housewives like to cover the shelves in the kitchen cabinets with Contact paper or similar material. Some mobile home manufacturers, or their suppliers, leave these surfaces rough and spray-paint them. Most of the commonly used shelf coverings will not stick to the rough surface. The remedy is to specify in your purchase contract that all of the cabinet shelving is to be smoothly finished.

Support Piers

Outriggers are the tapered steel members extending from the main steel channel members in the floor assembly; they serve as supports. At the center of a double-wide mobile home, however, they are the weakest part of the floor assembly. Placing a heavy object, such as piano or an organ, in that area exerts a load for which the outriggers have not been designed.

To keep your floor from sagging under those circumstances, you should place, or have placed, an additional pier directly underneath. If the location of this heavy load is known in advance, the extra pier can be placed when the mobile home is being erected on its site.

Termites

Termites are encountered in a mobile home more often than in a conventional home. They can cause a considerable expense since a professional termite-control firm is needed. If you're not constantly on guard they may destroy your mobile home.

There are two types of termites, the subterranean or soil type, and the fly-in or drywood type.

Subterranean termites. The subterranean type strikes most heavily in California, eastern Texas, Alabama, Mississippi, Louisiana, Georgia, South Carolina, and Florida. It extends north of these states to a line from the northern border of California to southern New York State and Massachusetts, but wreaking less havoc. They cause damage of one-half billion dollars yearly, attacking every type of residential and commercial structure containing cellulose (lumber) materials. They infest as many as 2 million homes yearly, and yet very little thought has been given to prevention of their damage in mobile homes, where lumber, in various forms, represents probably 90 percent of the structure, much of it inaccessible for inspection.

One common problem encountered in mobile homes is that when the contractor's employees build a porch adjacent to the mobile home, they often discard garbage and scrap lumber in the space within the porch foundation. This is an almost irresistible invitation to termites.

Termites find it easy to tunnel into your property because they have to penetrate only the top of the soil. This is one reason why the soil should be treated, if possible, prior to setting up the mobile home. They'll not get in so easily if a concrete slab covers the ground beneath the mobile home.

Some of the termite problems, from both subterranean and drywood type, are caused by the indiscriminate use of wood scrap atop the supporting piers, instead of the required treated tapered wood wedges (see figure 7–13). The use of scrap lumber on piers as spacers, beneath the mobile home frames, is more dangerous than one would imagine. As the spacers are eaten away, they become unable to hold up the mobile home on the pier.

Subterranean termites require moisture to thrive; their presence can be detected by mud-like tunnels (figure 12–4) extending from the ground along the

Fig. 12-4. A mud-type termite tunnel.

mobile home piers, or from pipes extending into the floor assembly of the mobile home. They can also build their tunnels upward on the inside of the skirting around the mobile home. They are able to get through cracks in the concrete as small as 1/64-inch.

Treatment for subterranean termites consists of digging a trench around the periphery of the mobile home and saturating the earth with a chemical solution deadly to these insects. The same solution is used to saturate the space within a porch, steps, and the area beneath the mobile home. It can establish a

continuous termite-proof barrier for as much as five years, claim the manufacturers and exterminators.

Drywood-type termites. This type of termite does not depend upon access to moisture from the soil but upon moisture found within the wood itself. This insect is found along both coasts as far north as San Francisco and Virginia. Because they do not bore tunnels from the soil surface to the mobile home, they are harder to detect in the early stages of infestation.

The flying, or drywood-type, termites can readily enter the wood floor assembly through the space below the mobile home. Open skirting provides an easy entry. Their presence can be readily ascertained by examining the wall molding next to the floor area. Fine particles will be found, resembling brown coffee grounds, in the area they happen to be working. An exterminating company should be called at once to poison them by a gas process described below.

If flying swarmers are observed in the spring and fall, alighting on the nearest wood, they are starting a new colony. Clusters of their wings are a warning that termites have landed nearby and have started their destruction. The flying termites, when their presence is detected, may be destroyed by a gas that penetrates completely throughout the mobile home after a tentlike cocoon has been draped over it (figure 12–5). The structure retains the gas for a number of hours. After it is removed, the mobile home is again habitable after two or three days.

Fig. 12-5. A tented mobile home ready for a gas treatment for drywood termites.

Roaches and Similar Pests

One industry practice that contributes to this problem is that openings are left in the floors and walls.

Figure 12–6 shows an opening left in the wall for the drain and rubber hose connections for a washer installed within a mobile home. The opening measured 10 by 10 inches and had to be closed. The cutout section of the wall paneling was left nearby for the buyer. The only remedy was to notch this section to clear the pipes and then secure it with duct tape as a seal around pipes and the wall opening. Packaged steel wool is helpful in blocking large openings in the wall prior to using the duct tape.

Figs. 12-7, 8. Large pipe and tubing openings left under the sink and for the hot water heater can allow pests to enter if not properly sealed.

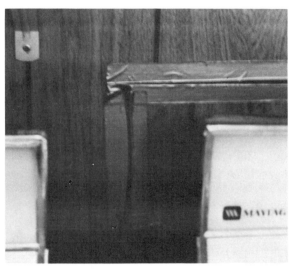

Fig. 12-6. The wall opening left for the washer piping connections had to be sealed up.

Another example is the large cutouts often left around the drain and water pipes under the sink, a perfect entrance for roaches, which require only a $1/32$-inch space to crawl through. Again, such openings had to be blocked with steel wool, followed by duct tape (figure 12–7). As a final precaution an occasional treatment with any of the sprays commercially available will help keep your home free of these pests.

Another insect entrance is the area around the hot water heater, where the main cold water pipe enters the mobile home. In many instances, a hole several inches in diameter is cut into the floor area, beneath the heater, unscreened or left otherwise unprotected, allowing bugs to enter (figure 12–8). In figure 3–8 is shown a wall opening, measuring 18 by 26 inches, left open by the manufacturer, located directly in back of the hot water heater. The opening was in the built-in cabinet in the bathroom.

Air duct problem. A defect that can "pave the way" for the entrance of roaches into the interior of a

mobile home is a carelessly installed air-conditioning duct system. In one instance, where floor openings were made for duct registers, the duct-opening lips were nailed to the sides of the floor openings. With space left between these duct lips and the floor, any crawling thing in the floor assembly could find its way into the mobile home through the floor register.

A simple solution was completely sealing the space between the metal lips and the floor register opening (figure 12-9) around the edges with caulking cord weatherstripping. This flexible material, available in hardware stores, must form a perfect seal between the metal lips and the edge of the floor register opening to be effective.

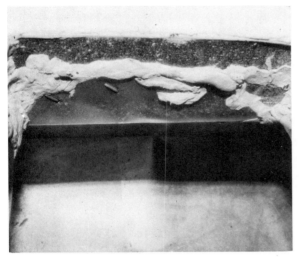

Fig. 12-9. Caulking between the duct ends and the floor register opening.

Another area, frequently overlooked, is the space between the bottom edge of the toilet bowl and the floor (figure 12-10). Any such space should be closed off with the same caulking material as above, otherwise you'll be maintaining an ideal hiding place for roaches.

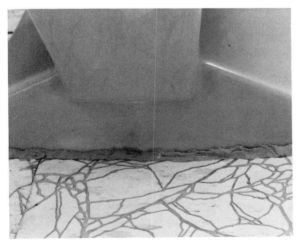

Fig. 12-10. Caulking seal between the toilet bowl and the floor.

Hot Water Heaters

Although necessary in every mobile home, their installation is often thoughtlessly carried out by the manufacturer.

Many heaters will be found with their piping, mostly galvanized steel, in the way when replacement becomes necessary. Or they may be turned around in such a way that the long electric heater element cannot be removed unless the pipes are disconnected first. To save money, many mobile home manufacturers omit the cold and hot water shut-off valves. In case of a leak, the main water shut-off valve has to be closed, cutting off the water supply to the entire home.

Also, in many instances, instead of having the heater rest on the floor, the heater pipes seem to be its only support, almost inevitably causing leaks to develop at the pipe joints. A leaky water heater creates problems rarely encountered in conventional housing. Any leak that develops is apt to have the water enter the mobile home floor in the heater area. If not detected immediately, water is absorbed by the particle board or carpeting. The size of the affected area depends upon how soon the leak is discovered.

Since particle board, when subjected to water, will expand rapidly, the ultimate result is usually a buckled floor which will probably require replacement. Light-colored carpeting could also become stained by the water and by the gluing materials used to bond the particle board to the floor joists.

Mobile Home Settlement

The pier method of supporting the mobile home, in use for many years, leaves much to be desired. From the standpoint of safety, the construction of a conventional concrete floor and solid foundation walls to which the mobile home could be tied seems to be the answer to the need for re-leveling, the possibility of shifting in high winds so the piers come through the floor, termite damage, and hazards from rodents and snakes. While some mobile home manufacturers have started to move in that direction, most of them adhere to the old method and seem likely to continue to do so as long as the customers will accept it. Unfortunately, many buyers assume that it is the best or only method available. Too much emphasis is placed on the initial lower cost of the product, with increased maintenance and safety overlooked or ignored.

Mobile Home Fasteners

The method of fastening the outer aluminum skin to the wall studs in most mobile homes is often inadequate, as has been pointed out in Chapter 11 and elsewhere.

To fasten the vertical, interlocking outer panels quickly, the common practice is to use cadmium-plated steel self-tapping screws for all assembly work. They can be driven in fast by power-driven socket-head screwdrivers on the assembly line. However, the galvanic action between aluminum and steel, especially if the cadmium plating is very thin or damaged during the assembly, results in these screws rusting rapidly; this is especially true in the coastal areas. The heads of the screws may even break off when an attempt is made to replace them.

The use of power-driven tools also can result in screwheads being broken off during the initial assembly and not being replaced as on the door frame shown in figure 3–4. This is one of the primary factors in the depreciation of mobile homes. If replacement of these screws is delayed, hundreds of rusty screws will appear over the exterior of a mobile home after a few years.

An even greater problem arises as contractors, who install such accessories as gutters and sheds, use the same type of screws, with the same power tools, where the screws may be exposed to water and the weather. They may use even less care in installing them, stripping off the cadmium plating from the screw heads.

Unfinished Doors and Windows

In many instances, the aluminum doors and window frames used on mobile homes may have no protective finish. They are thus subject to deterioration from the weather, especially in coastal regions, where there is salt in the air. "Pock"marks or whitish spots will begin appearing on their surfaces over a period of time (figure 12–11). While the addition of a protective finish, such as anodizing, would result in a higher price tag, the resulting longer life of the mobile home would justify it.

You should inquire about the finish when negotiating the purchase of a mobile home. The salesman should be specific and not give evasive answers or deny that protective finish is necessary.

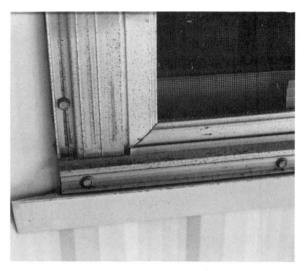

Fig. 12-11. A corroded window frame.

Waste Line Problems

Some mobile home manufacturers install the kitchen-sink drain line within the 2 by 6 inch floor joists. This plastic drain line, approximately 2½ inches in diameter and perhaps as long as 20 feet, may not be supported well enough to provide a uniform drop of at least ⅛-inch per foot. That much slope is needed, especially with garbage disposals, to keep the line clear. Unless the heavy waste matter that it carries is completely flushed down the waste line, gradual accumulation begins. It may take three or four years before it suddenly blocks and requires the services of a plumber to open it, but it is likely to plug again because the cause has not been removed.

The only permanent remedy is to have the plumber install a new drain line below the mobile home floor assembly (figures 12–12, 13). Sufficient slope for rapid drainage can then be secured, and the new line tapped into the original waste line extending from the bathrooms to the ground waste connection.

Some manufacturers now install the kitchen waste line below the floor assembly. But there are many thousands of mobile homes already built, or being built, with this design deficiency, a problem which will manifest itself only after years of use, and after any warranty has expired.

Figs. 12-12, 13. Two views of an outside kitchen drain line.

Made Easy for the Burglars

Most mobile homes have another basic disadvantage compared with conventional homes. Their exterior door construction provides far easier access to the inside by burglars, primarily due to basic door design and easily-picked locks. As characterized by one sheriff's department, the locks are only good to keep these doors from flapping in strong winds.

Exterior mobile home doors come as a complete frame-door assembly, ready to be inserted into the door opening. To eliminate the screen door, as used on conventional homes, and thus reduce cost, they are constructed with a center glass louvered section (figure 12–14), the so-called jalousie type. This is a built-in feature that allows the burglars to get into the mobile home by simply removing several glass sections near the door lock, and reaching the door latch on the inside.

Or the burglar can force the door lock from the outside without much trouble. The locks on most mobile homes have a short latch bolt that projects out only about ½-inch in locked position (figure 12–15). As the door's front edge is made square with

Fig. 12-15. The latch bolt projects only ½ inch.

Fig. 12-14. A jalousie-type exterior door.

the door, it becomes necessary to reduce the door's width so that the front edge will clear the door frame (figure 12–16). Thus, a gap is introduced which reduces the engaged length of the latch to 5/16- or ⅜-inch.

By bending the strike plate back, the above dimension can be reduced further. The strike plate can be easily bent because there is space available behind it as clearance between the door frame and the door frame opening.

Fig. 12-16. Door clearance in its frame leaves a gap.

Two types of dead bolt locks are available: a single cylinder dead bolt, opened by a latch from the inside, and the double cylinder dead bolt which requires a key to open it, from either the outside or inside.

Fig. 12-17. The single cylinder dead-bolt lock (above) is not as good as the double cylinder variety.

Thus even an amateur burglar can circumvent the lock very easily. Blocking the space behind the strike plate would help keep it from being bent.

Installation of an additional lock, a dead-bolt lock (figure 12–17), can give you a great deal more protection. The dead bolt lock latch is about 1 inch in size, and it engages at least 1 inch inside the door frame.

The single cylinder model isn't nearly as effective as one would like, because the burglar can reach its latch by removing the glass door louvres.

The double dead-bolt lock eliminates this problem as it requires the use of a key, but it does present a fire escape problem. The key should be stored near the door, readily available, but out of reach of the burglar trying to get in through the door louvres. Identical keys are available to unlock either of the two exterior doors, from inside or outside.

So long as mobile home manufacturers continue to install combination doors, with a center glass insert, owners will continue to suffer losses unless they install the dead-bolt locks.

Under-Home Hazards

Open skirting, such as spaced concrete blocks, invites rodents, rabbits, snakes, tarantulas, black widow spiders, lizards, mice, and insects. Snakes such as Florida pigmy rattlers have been known to place themselves just inside the spaced concrete blocks and strike at anything that moves by. The pigmy rattler can be particularly dangerous because its few rattles give insufficient noise to warn its target. You should not crawl beneath a mobile home, whether equipped with open-block or any other type of skirting, unless you have a flashlight and a long stick to prevent a sudden unpleasant encounter with a rodent or reptile.

The bottom of the mobile home may have openings left by workmen installing air conditioning, plumbing, electrical wiring, and telephone connections, all of which require access inside the floor assembly. We have already discussed at length elsewhere the insect infestation problems this can invite. The solution is to have the floor assembly completely sealed after the necessary alterations and connections have been made by requesting that this be done by the contractor.

Closed, ventilated skirting, with openings protected by screens, would go a long way in avoiding many of the problems outlined above.

High Maintenance Costs

Despite public relations programs to the contrary in newspapers and on TV, maintenance costs are higher for mobile homes than for conventional housing. Whenever you eliminate such an item as a foun-

dation, you create some of the problems just described.

The mobile home manufacturer, in expanding to multi-wide mobile homes, has in large measure lost control of the quality of his finished product. Subcontractors, who complete the erection of multi-wides, determine whether the purchaser will have satisfactory housing or not. Mobile home park management, too, plays a role because of often inadequate control of park appearance (figure 12-18), and inadequate screening of potential residents.

Fig. 12-18. Your neighbor?

We need not list again the infirmities to which mobile homes are liable. Suffice it to say that if you are not equipped to do much of the work yourself, or if you are not prepared to cope with maintenance costs higher than you would have expected in conventional single-family housing, you are likely to be disappointed with mobile home living. Moreover, the value of your investment is then likely to depreciate over the years.

High Insurance Costs

A mobile home buyer is generally surprised to find that his insurance premiums are considerably higher than those he paid for his conventional home. There are several reasons for this, although those reasons are small consolation when it comes time to pay the bill.

Mobile homes are generally a total loss in case of a fire; they are more subject to damage from high winds, and a total loss in most tornadoes; termites infest them more easily; and other factors make them a higher risk for insurance companies.

High Financing Costs

A person accustomed to 30- or even 40-year loans on conventional housing is surprised to find that loans on mobile homes (depending upon the loan type) may be limited to only 15 or 20 years. Banks, savings and loan associations, and other lenders may require a substantial down payment—greater than that for conventional housing—and yet consider mobile homes as a greater risk. The better-constructed mobile homes have not been around long enough to prove or disprove this theory.

Some mobile home purchasers slash the longevity even further by getting by with little maintenance or none (figure 12-19), arousing the ire of their neighbors and the anxiety of lenders who use the poor behavior of these mortgagees as a rationale for charging higher interest to all mobile home purchasers.

Fig. 12-19. No sign of any maintenance here.

Taxes

Many states levy a sales tax upon the purchase of a mobile home. The assumption is that a mobile home is like a car, and should be taxed accordingly. A conventional home, however, is not subjected to such a tax.

Florida carries the motor-vehicle classification of a mobile home even further. Each mobile home on a rental lot has to pay for yearly registration stickers, one for each mobile home section. Depending upon the length of the home, the tax may amount to $50 or more per section.

State laws vary in regard to sales tax. In Colorado, the sales tax is 3 percent, levied only once, at the initial purchase. Other states tax every time that the mobile home is sold. In addition, mobile homes located in rental parks have a tax levied yearly on such accessories as carport, sheds, awnings, screen rooms, and other appurtenances.

The percentage of sales tax levied varies with different states, but it may add a considerable amount to your mobile home purchase price. However, many states do not impose a sales tax on a mobile home resale if the mobile home is sold by the owner and not by a dealer. With few exceptions there are no other deductions allowed by the individual states in the imposition of the sales tax.

In some states, such as Florida, the sales tax is not supposed to be paid on the labor involved in the construction of such facilities as sheds, carports, and driveways, where the labor cost may be considerable. This saving to the buyer is lost when the mobile home is offered as a package deal, where the buyer is not given the breakdown of the various items but pays sales tax on the complete package, a practice which is definitely not in accordance with the spirit of the existing laws.

Table 12-1 gives the results of the author's survey of various states in regard to sales taxes on mobile homes.

TABLE 12–1

Sales Taxes by States

State	Sales Tax (%)	Resale Sales Tax (%)
Alabama	1½***	None*
Arizona	1.3	None*
Arkansas	3	None
California	6–6½	6–6½
Colorado	3 (plus any local)	None
Connecticut	7	7
Delaware	2 (documentary fee)	Yes
Florida	4 (rental parks)	None
	4 (lot owned)	None
Georgia	3–4	3–4
Idaho	3**	None
Illinois	4	None
Indiana	4	None*
Iowa	3 (use tax)	3 (use tax)
Kansas	3 (plus ½)	3 (plus ½)
Kentucky	5	None*
Louisiana	3½–6 (depending on location)	3¼–6
Maryland	5	5
Massachusetts	5	5*
Michigan	4	4
Minnesota	4	4
Mississippi	3	None*
Missouri	3	3***
Montana	None	None
Nebraska	3	None
Nevada	3 (plus ½)	None*
New Hampshire	None	None
New Jersey	5	5
New Mexico	3–¾	3–¾ (unless proved original tax paid)
New York	4 (plus up to 4% county tax and ¼% regional tax)	—
North Carolina	2 ($120 maximum)	None*
Ohio	4–5½	4–5½
Oklahoma	1 (plus registration fee)	—
Oregon	None	None
Pennsylvania	6	6
South Carolina	4	4
Tennessee	4½–7½	4½–7½
Texas	4	4
Utah	4¾–5	4¾–5
Vermont	3	None*
Virginia	3	3
Washington	4½ (plus local tax)	—
West Virginia	3	None*
Wisconsin	4	None
Wyoming	3	None

   * If resold by home owner.
  ** On less than listed price.
 *** Reduced by trade-in.

CHAPTER 13

MOBILE HOME IMPROVEMENTS

If you're handy with tools you can certainly improve your mobile home, just as you would have done had you elected to remain in a conventional home.

Some of the improvements described here can be accomplished with little effort but will nevertheless increase the value of your mobile home. Others will add to your safety in an emergency. Still others will help to eliminate the "sameness," such as paneling on all walls or carpeting over all the floor areas. For example, transforming your shed into a second livable area, while requiring considerable effort, will prove to be a worthwhile project for the person who spends considerable time on hobbies that require comfortable working space.

Roofs

Many mobile home roofs develop a rumble in high winds. This is caused by thin metal roof covering, which is either improperly secured to the roof trusses or too large for the area being covered. The better-built roofs are "stretched" at assembly.

The loose roof material "flaps in the breeze." Many people are mystified by the noise when they hear it for the first time. Small openings at the junction of the roof and walls allow air to enter beneath the roof surface, adding to the problem.

One repair method consists of fastening a C-shaped aluminum strip, about $\frac{1}{16}$-inch thick, long enough to span the loose roof material, to the roof trusses, with self-tapping screws. To accomplish this:

1. You must use caulking compound between the strip and the roof.

2. Cut the strip long enough to extend just beyond the roof trusses at each end of the repair area.

3. Drill clearance holes in the strip in line with the centerline of the roof trusses, for fastening screws.

4. As an additional precaution use caulking compound in each hole when attaching the strip to the roof surface.

Figure 13-1 shows such an installation. Notice the low spots on the higher roof side of the strip where it meets the roof. To prevent water leakage in this area, fill it with a mastic compound, high enough so that water will run off the ends of the obstruction.

Fig. 13-1. Two reinforcing strips stop roof rumble.

A Fire Escape Door

Occupants of a mobile home need some means to escape a fire which may block him or her from reaching the existing doors.

Escape windows. The so-called escape windows—special bedroom windows fitted with a removable window assembly for quick escape in case of fire (figure 13-2)—are now required by HUD in all new mobile homes. However, the high location required by HUD—3 feet above the floor, and 4 feet in older models—will prevent all but the most agile from being able to use them. The height necessitates a chair or another person to assist in reaching the window. An outside awning will further hamper an escape (figure 13-3). Also, there is the problem of dropping 5 or 6 feet to the ground without injury. For a handicapped person such an exit is a practical impossibility.

A workable substitute. Many a mobile home owner has installed a fire escape door himself. This is a far more practical escape means, suitable even for the handicapped. The door is generally installed in the main bedroom of the mobile home and requires only a 2-foot drop to the ground.

Choosing the location. It is important that such a

door be placed where it is easily reached. Some owners incorrectly install them in the outer wall of a closet, where access to the door is impeded by clothes and luggage.

To find a fire door in the dark, when one is suddenly wakened from a sound sleep by the smoke alarm, may be difficult for many persons. That's why the door should be placed in an open area, if possible, where not even a wastebasket can trip you in the darkness.

Fig. 13-2. Fire "escape" windows use two easily operable latches.

Fig. 13-3. An outside awning hampers escape from a window.

Selecting the door. The first step is to purchase the door, complete with the necessary exterior mounting screws. Fire doors are available at mobile home service stores or from other sources (figure 13–4). A rectangular door, approximately 24 by 50 inches, is better than the square escape hatch which one has to crawl through. Basically, it is an aluminum door on a piano hinge that swings outward within its own door frame. Check to see if it has a seal on the outside and if it is fitted with a built-in lock. It should have a key-operated lock on the outside and a flat handle latch inside. With these features the door can be locked from the outside when you're away; otherwise it is locked only by the inside latch.

Fig. 13-4. Fire escape doors are more practical than windows.

Installing the door. Follow the instructions carefully. If no detailed instructions come with the door, the installation steps are as follows:

1. Carefully measure the exterior of the door frame. This establishes the size of the opening to be cut through the wall, but add an extra ¼-inch in both vertical and horizontal dimensions. This allows some leeway in case of any error or if the frame is slightly out of shape.

2. Examine the exterior of the mobile home to be certain that there are no obstructions, such as the air conditioner, blocking the area selected for the door.

Check the space on the outside for the door by

measuring the expected door location on the inside to the nearest wall, and then measure on the outside, adding a 4-inch allowance for the wall thickness.

3. To save some work, locate one of the 2 by 4 wall studs, and use it as one member for mounting the door frame. Use a small drill to locate the edge, which will be the inner edge of the door frame. This becomes the starting point for the door frame.

The bottom edge of the door frame can be found by measuring a line approximately 1¾ inches above the floor. Again, use a small drill to locate the top surface of the floor's 2 by 4 plate.

These two locations, the vertical and horizontal, establish the exact door frame position on the inside. Lay out the external dimensions of the door frame on the inside paneling, adding the ¼-inch allowance mentioned previously. Use a 4-foot level to obtain square corners.

4. Cut out the paneling on the marked lines with a fine keyhole saw or a hacksaw blade. Use a series of small holes along one of the layout lines to start cutting.

Save the paneling. You may want to use it later to cover the door (figure 13–5).

You will have to cut off the 2 by 4 stud you will find when you remove the paneling. Cut it off carefully at the top, even with the top edge of the door opening, and save it to use as the other vertical wall member when mounting the door frame.

5. After the inside wall opening has been completed, use it as a guide to locate the opening in the outside aluminum skin.

Drill four small holes in the skin, as square as possible, from the four corners of the inside opening.

Draw lines on the outside skin between these four holes and check to see if the opening space agrees with door frame dimensions. Cut out the skin opening (figure 13–6). This can be done with a fine hacksaw blade, using a few small holes to start. The door assembly frame should fit readily into this cutout.

Fig. 13-6. Skin opening for the fire door.

6. The next step is to frame the opening with 2 by 4s. You can use the reserved 2 by 4 to serve as the other vertical member, and purchase a short 2 by 4 to serve as two horizontal members, one on each side of the vertical 2 by 4 which remained in the wall after you cut off the 2 by 4 left in the opening. Thus, you will have a complete wooden frame into which the

Fig. 13-5. The inside of the fire escape door reuses the paneling cut away for the installation.

door frame will fit (figure 13–7). Angle-nail the 2 by 4s, and also use nails through the paneling to hold the paneling edges to this framework.

Fig. 13-7. Framing for a fire escape door.

7. Once the framework has been completed, you are ready to mount the door in place. Place caulking sealing compound around the outer edge of the door opening in the skin. This will compress the skin when the door frame is fastened in place with the self-tapping screws and prevent water from getting between the back of the door frame and the skin. It will also keep water from following the mounting screws inside, and thus achieve a complete seal.

8. You have now reached the halfway point on the job. You can leave the door exposed inside if it is inconspicuous. A simple way to improve appearance is to hang some light-colored fabric over it. In a fire emergency it can be torn off.

9. If the door is in an exposed area, where appearance counts, you may want to finish the installation by remounting the original piece of paneling on the inside of the door, flush with the interior paneling.

This requires building a frame for the door, slightly smaller than the opening on the inside. The height of the frame should be about $3/16$ inch less than that of the closed door, to allow for the thickness of the paneling (figure 13–8).

The frame width has to be about $3/4$ inch less than

Fig. 13-8. Edge view of the fire escape door.

the door width to allow clearance when the door swings outward. Mount the frame temporarily to the door and check for clearance as the door swings outward before you fasten it permanently to the door with small angle brackets. The mounting screws should not project through the outer skin of the door.

10. Mount the paneling with the door closed within the wall opening. Allow for some clearance as the door swings outward. Again, mount temporarily before nailing the paneling permanently to the door frame.

11. Once the door assembly is complete, you will need a lock on the inside to work the outside lock. A T-handled lock with an extension (figure 13–9) can

Fig. 13-9. A T-handle fire escape door lock.

be mounted on the door paneling and connected to the outer lock. A small, saddle-type bracket can be used to support the end. Make a slot in this extension to fit over the latch handle so it can be turned remotely by the lock's T-handle from the inside and locked by a key on the inside.

12. After the door assembly has been completed, nail a one-inch wide flat molding strip on the wall opening to cover the small open clearance space between the door edge and the wall opening next to it (see figure 13–5).

A small aluminum strip, about 1½ inches wide, commonly known as an "eyebrow," should be mounted just above the top edge of the door to prevent water leakage into the door opening outside.

A Finished Shed

The size of such a shed in feet may be 8 by 8, 8 by 12, 10 by 12, or more. It is generally finished in baked enamel in a color to match the exterior of the home. Most sheds are constructed of aluminum sections that are readily assembled by companies specializing in this sort of work.

Shed caulking. It is advisable to caulk the outer perimeter of the shed at the floor level to prevent the entrance of water that may collect during heavy rains. The same process should be repeated on the inside as double insurance against leaks. Otherwise the interior will become musty and accumulate mold and mildew. Occasional airing also helps.

It is advisable to caulk joints between wall channels of sections abutting each other as well as any other areas where there is a possibility of rain getting inside the walls.

Shelving. This may consist of ⅝-inch plywood board, supported by aluminum angles, and a vertical 1-inch-square aluminum section in the center (figure 13–10). Well-planned shelving will increase the utilization of the interior space.

Finishing the interior. The basic temperature deficiencies of sheds—cold in the winter and hot in the summer—may be improved to make a comfortable interior if the owner is handy with tools. It can also serve as a temporary retreat, if the home's air conditioning unit fails, on a hot weekend, for instance.

Before starting the construction you will have to remove any shelving and also the washer and dryer if they are installed in the shed. All walls must be clear of any obstructions to expedite the work.

If you plan to finish the shed after moving into the

Fig. 13-10. Shed shelving.

mobile home, make arrangements with the park to have electrical service brought in. This can be done by having a ¾-inch pipe installed under the mobile home and carport and into the shed itself. The pipe is used as a conduit to bring in the wiring for electrical service in the shed, and is connected to a circuit breaker in the panel box in the mobile home.

A junction box should be installed in the shed to extend future wiring for lights and power tools. Additional outlets can be installed later if you decide to put in a washer and dryer.

The start. The first step is to build a framework, for each wall, of 1½ by 2 inch furring strips, to provide a sturdy wall structure. They are separated on 16-inch centers for the vertical members.

First, get the inside dimensions, both top and bottom, of each wall. Many sheds are not perfect cubes, hence the double measurements. If the shed walls are assembled from channel members, specially shaped flat strips (figure 13–11) are slipped over their edges. The dimensions are taken from the top surfaces of these strips.

Make a rough pencil layout of each wall framing (figure 13–12) for reference later. With the vertical members on 16-inch centers, it will be possible to use the standard 4-foot wide paneling for the walls.

Electrical receptacle boxes. These can be anchored to the vertical studs and should be at least 2 feet above the floor. They should be installed with all the necessary wiring, by an electrician, and project ¼ inch above the framework.

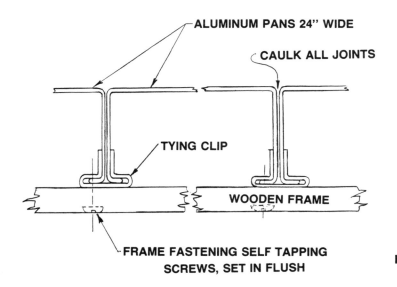

Fig. 13-11. Details of shed's walls.

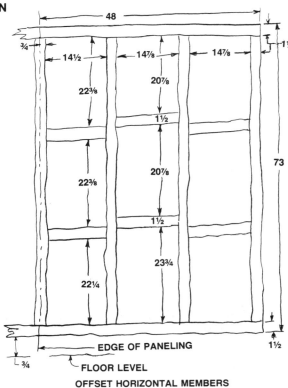

Fig. 13-12. A rough layout of the wall framing.

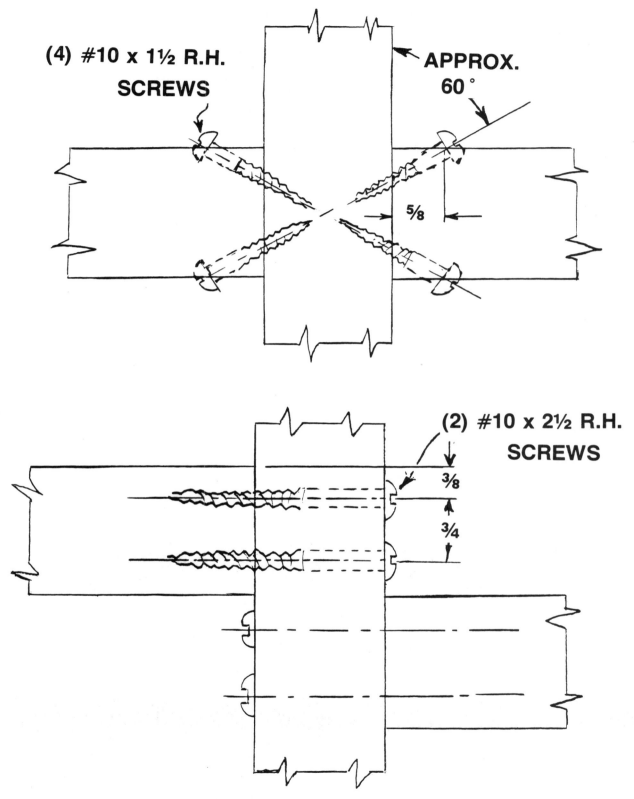

(4) #10 x 1½ R.H. SCREWS

APPROX. 60°

⁵⁄₈

(2) #10 x 2½ R.H. SCREWS

³⁄₈

³⁄₄

Figs. 13-13, 14. Horizontal frame members may be fastened with long wood screws at a 60-degree angle (left) or horizontally.

Outlet placement. Outlets should be placed in the areas where they will be used. One outlet box should be located above the expected height of the finished ceiling to connect an overhead built-in light. Others should be located near the workbench if you plan to have one to take care of the bench light and power tools and near the washer and dryer, if located in the shed. Do not forget to install an outlet box by the door for a switch to turn the lights on and off.

Framework. Once you have the dimensions of the complete frame for each wall, they can be built in the carport, in sections not exceeding 7 feet wide, so that they can be carried through the door of the shed.

The height will be determined by the ceiling height that can be accommodated at the lowest point of the shed roof. Some extra space will be desirable for installing a false ceiling and an overhead light. A ceiling height of 7½ to 8 feet is ample. The framework should extend from about ½ or ¾ inch above the floor to 3 inches above the finished ceiling. The floor within the shed is likely to slope for drainage and hence the tolerance for the framework to keep it square and level.

There should be two cross- or horizontal members across the framework to provide adequate anchoring of the wall panels and to give it rigidity.

Framework members are butted flush with the vertical members. To save a lot of extra work, they are fastened with long wood screws at a 60-degree angle (figure 13–13). They can also be offset with screws driven horizontally into them (figure 13–14). The main objective is to have the framework rigid once it is assembled. The framework also leaves space to install 4-inch-thick insulating batts.

Make the framework for the two opposite walls and secure them to the flat strips on the shed's walls with flat-head, self-tapping screws.

Then measure the space left from one framework to the other to establish the dimensions of the third framework. Again, measure at both top and bottom in case the walls are not square. Lay out and make a similar frame for the third and fourth walls, allowing for windows and a door in the frames requiring them.

Insulation. The electrical wiring should be completed and receptacle boxes installed prior to placing the insulation..

This construction allows space for standard 16-inch wall insulation, 4-inches thick. It is put in place between the vertical members, after being cut to length to fit between the various cross members. It is placed with the paper side toward the interior of the shed.

Paneling. *Do not* use the 5/32-inch luan paneling, but use the standard ¼-inch type. The thinner panel-

ing is definitely a fire hazard and will not stand up under use. The ¼-inch paneling will also strengthen the walls. These concerns are as important in your shed as they are in the construction of your mobile home.

Once the insulation has been installed the next step is to cut the paneling to length. The standard paneling length is 8 feet, so your framework should be no larger than that. If the framework for each wall has been planned right, the joints of the panels will occur at the center of the vertical strips. The paneling should be about ½-inch short of the floor. This space is covered with floor molding later.

Use the edge of your framework as a reference line to locate the receptacle boxes in the paneling. These should project ¼ of an inch above the framwork surface to be flush with the top surface of the paneling.

Holes in the paneling should be made slightly larger to allow for errors in measurement.

There should be an opening in the paneling to allow access to the junction box. It can be covered with a plate made from the paneling. The paneling is nailed to the framework with colored nails available for this purpose.

The door. A similar framework should be attached to the door so as to mount paneling on it. It should be thick enough so the paneling is flush within the wall on which the door is mounted (figure 13–15). Provision should be made for a new lock to extend through the thicker door. Again, insulation should be placed within the framework.

Fig. 13-15. The shed paneling and door blend together.

To complete the paneling installation, floor trim can be nailed along the bottom of the shed's walls, leaving ⅛-inch clearance between the trim and the floor.

Drop ceiling. Because the carport roof over the shed is not generally insulated, it's advisable to install a drop ceiling. Such a ceiling uses metal angles, available in home improvement centers, to support the 2-by-4-foot ceiling tiles. The same 4-inch-thick batts, 16 inches wide, are used to insulate the space above the ceiling tiles.

Prior to placing the ceiling tiles, a large fluorescent light fixture can be installed within one of the tile spaces to provide adequate lighting in the shed (figure 13–16). An additional fluorescent light fixture can be installed over the workbench (figures 13–17, 18).

Figs. 13-16, 17, 18. In addition to a ceiling light fixture (left), a light over a workbench is very useful.

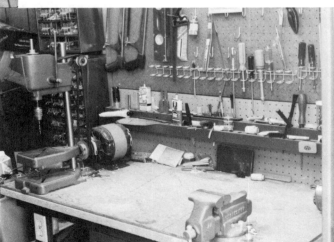

An air conditioner. As a real comfort item, an air conditioner, of 5,000- to 7,000-BTU capacity, can be mounted in the wall opposite the door, fairly high to obtain maximum cooling benefit. It is mounted flush on the inside so that its rear projects from the outside of the shed (figures 13–19, 20).

If you expect to install an air conditioner, make provision for it in the wall framing. The framework should tip slightly downward to allow for water drainage.

Figs. 13-19, 20. An air conditioner in the shed—inside and outside views.

A receptacle box should be installed below it for the power supply. Make a small metal frame to fit around the air conditioner on the outside, and seal space between the air conditioner and the shed's opening with caulking compound.

Floor. The concrete carport floor within the shed will be improved by covering it with asphalt tiles. The mastic should be of the water-resistant type. Such a floor (figure 13–21) can be laid down readily with a tile kit available for this purpose.

nate the possibility of grooves showing through. Allow a day after filling the grooves before hanging wallpaper.

There are many types of wallpaper on the market; the ones with vinyl coating are preferred as they are more easily cleaned. Wallpaper supply stores carry complete sets of instructions for hanging wallpaper, as well as the necessary tools.

The reflective surfaces of many wallpapers tend to accentuate any wall imperfections. It is therefore

Fig. 13-21. A shed vinyl tile floor.

Wall Papering

Paneling on all the walls of a mobile home often becomes tiresome to some people. They would welcome relief from the uniformity. One of the easiest and most practical means is covering the paneling with wallpaper in such areas as kitchens and bathrooms.

Two types of paneling are used in mobile homes: grooved and grooveless. In either case the paneling should be free of grease. The grooveless type can be used as is. The grooved type requires some preparation to prevent the grooves from showing through the wallpaper.

Spackling method. Spackling compound, available in most hardware or paint stores, will fill the grooves level with the paneling surface. The only tool needed is a small putty knife. Grooves should be filled above the paneling surface so that they can be sanded flush with it once the compound has set. The use of a heavier wallpaper is recommended to elimi-

advisable to select your wallpaper carefully. Always try to use full or textured patterns and avoid glossy finishes.

A Mirrored Room

You can create the appearance of a larger room by mounting mirror tiles on one wall. They come 12 inches square and are available in various designs.

The thicker tiles, about 3/32 to 1/8 inch thick, available in glass shops, are recommended in preference to the thinner tiles sold in cut-rate stores. They are less likely to crack and easier to cut to size.

The tiles are mounted with two-sided, sticky tape sold with the tiles. This method is better than using self-adhesive-back tiles because the paneling may not be perfectly flat, and thus part of the adhesion surface is lost.

Receptacles. One problem that may present itself, especially in a dining room, is a wall or switch receptacle located within the wall area to be covered.

The easiest solution is to lay out the area to be

covered to scale, with the receptacle or switch opening located in one tile corner (figure 13–22). Be sure to shut off the power to the receptacle or switch while you are doing the work.

Making the layout. Measure the dimensions to which the tiles will have to be cut on your layout, which can be made on graph paper. Since it is impractical to make an opening cutout in the middle of a tile, it has to be made in one corner by cutting the tile straight, vertically and horizontally.

From the layout you can determine the sizes to which the perimeter tiles will have to be cut and also how the tile with the receptacle cutout will have to be cut (figure 13–23).

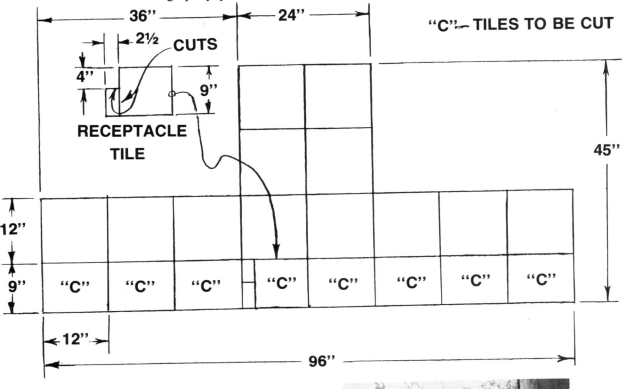

Figs. 13-22, 23. Make a mirror-tile layout and locate the receptacle switch plate in one tile corner.

You will have to determine which corner is best for placing the cutout. This placement determines the dimensions to which the perimeter tiles will have to be cut. If possible, avoid the tiles in narrow widths; they will be difficult to cut and might crack after the installation. A tile strip an inch or less in width is too difficult to cut.

Cutting tiles. The glass shop where you purchase the tiles can cut them to size if you make your layout prior to purchase. You will be able to give them the exact dimensions to which the receptacle cutout and perimeter tiles are to be cut.

While the receptacle cutout shown appears to be larger than necessary, it is needed to raise the receptacle or switch forward so it will be almost flush with the top surface of the tile. Small metal washers under the mounting lugs that will raise it 3/32 to 1/8 inch are the easiest to use for this purpose.

Mounting the tiles. Use a plumb bob and a chalked string or a 4-foot carpenter's level to establish a vertical line as a starting point for the tile containing the cutout. Start mounting the tiles, beginning with the cutout tile, along the vertical line. Press the mounting tape on the back of each tile's corner and press the tile in place. It will take only a short time to get all of the tiles mounted.

Replace the receptacle or switch cover plate. Again press on each tile to make sure it is adhering to the wall. If it is, your job is finished.

Replacing Hallway Paneling

The hallway in the center of a mobile home is narrow and, if covered with 5/32-inch luan paneling, could be hazardous in a fire. Replacing the existing paneling with gypsum wallboard ⅜ inch thick will make it safer. Gypsum wallboard comes in 4 by 8 foot sheets that have to be cut to fit by using the existing luan paneling as the pattern.

Shut off the electric power to any switches or lights in the hall area. Release the electrical switch boxes from the paneling. They are generally mounted by two screws, one on each side of the box. You can determine the right rotation by turning them in one or the opposite direction until the box starts to loosen.

The start. The first step is to remove all trim at the ceiling, floor, and doors. Mark each piece and make a list, identifying the position of each trim piece. Remove all electrical cover plates and light fixtures.

Remove one wall panel at a time. They are generally stapled to the wall studs. Mark each to indicate its relative position along the hallway. The panels will

be your patterns to make the gypsum panels later. Cover all open receptacle boxes with duct tape.

Place a piece of plywood on top of two sawhorses to support the wallboard. Place the first wallboard, face up, on top and then set the #1 panel over it. Outline the various openings and the overall length and width in the wallboard in pencil.

Cutting the wallboard. Cut the openings with a keyhole saw and the outside edge with an ordinary saw or hacksaw blade. It is also possible to crack the wallboard to size after it has been scored on the front, instead of having to saw the outer edge. This saves time and energy.

Mark the vertical stud positions on the wallboard so you don't have to nail it in place blindly. Use the special nails available for this purpose. Anchor the electrical receptacle boxes as you attach the wallboard.

After all the panels have been nailed in place, the vertical joints will have to be covered. This is done with special gauze and paste. The paste will have to be applied two or three times. Sand the joint each time and raise it higher until it is flush with the remainder of the wallboard.

You can then decorate the wallboard by painting or wallpapering.

Because the wallboard is thicker than the original paneling, you'll need to make some additional trim pieces to complete the installation.

A Cedar Closet

Closets can be improved by nailing tongue-and-groove red cedar boards over the walls. Red cedar is moth repellent and thus provides year-round protection for furs, blankets, and other valuable garments. Cedar-lining a small closet may take only a weekend and requires only a hammer, saw, and nails. Because cedar is highly moisture resistant, it prevents a mildew problem.

Cedar paneling. Red cedar boards are ⅜-inch thick, 4 inches wide, and come in random lengths. They are generally sold as a package of 16 square feet and they have tongue-and-groove on all four sides. That means that the horizontal joints don't have to be over the wall studs.

Applying the paneling. Cedar lining is applied horizontally over the existing wall paneling after removing the bottom trim. Start with the first piece, placed with the grooved side down. Then continue straight up, row by row, until you have covered the entire wall. Boards should be tapped together, horizontally and at the end joints, to achieve a tight fit.

Reinstall the trim around the walls after they have been lined with cedar.

To obtain the maximum benefit from cedar lining it should not be painted, varnished, or shellacked. Otherwise its moth-repellent quality will be ruined.

After a few years, when the aroma begins to disappear, it can be brought back by sanding the cedar with coarse sandpaper.

A Parquet Floor

If you have a floor area you'd like to dress up, parquet may be the answer. There are few floor treatments that excel parquet tile in appearance (figure 13–24). It's possible to put down the tiles with a special mastic, provided your present floor is plywood. Putting parquet tiles over a particle-board floor is not recommended by manufacturers of parquet flooring. Particle board will chip and have no holding power if parquet tiles are laid over it. The parquet tiles are prefinished so your job is completed as soon as the tiles have been laid.

Fig. 13-24. A parquet floor.

Parquet tools. Tiles come in a variety of sizes, finishes, and thicknesses. The 6-inch-square tiles, only 5/16-inch thick, are adequate and will not project much above any adacent carpeting they may abut.

You'll need the following installation tools: (1) a big-tooth trowel or an asphalt tile trowel; (2) special mastic; (3) cork; (4) a softwood stick, about 8 inches long.

Layout. Remove the trim or shoe molding prior to measuring the area to be covered. The procedure is similar to laying asphalt or vinyl tiles. Measure equal distance from each end of one wall to establish the end points of a center line, line No. 1. Then tighten a chalked string between the two points and snap it onto the floor surface.

You'll need to locate another line at right angles to line 1. There are any number of ways to go about constructing a perpendicular; perhaps you recall them from plane geometry class in high school. In any event, you will be certain that your line 2 is exactly perpendicular to line 1 when you can measure sides of a triangle, 4 feet along line 1, 3 feet along line 2, and 5 feet across the diagonal (figure 13–25). These

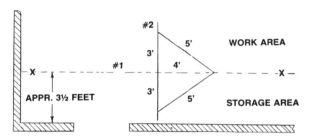

Fig. 13-25. A tile area layout.

two lines are necessary to lay the parquet tiles straight. "Storage area" on the diagram simply shows where you will keep your materials for this job. "Work area" is the side of line 1 where you will lay tiles first.

When measuring the tile space, determine if the last row of tile will be only 1 to 2 inches wide. If this is the case, shift the center line two inches to one side so that the end row tiles will be more than half a tile wide.

By measuring the area, you can determine the number of tiles required, since there are four tiles for each square foot. Count each partial tile needed as a full one.

One recommended practice is to buy and take home your tiles at least one week prior to installing them. They will be then able to adjust to humidity conditions in the room and are less likely to be affected later.

Spread the mastic with the special trowel (see "Details," below) and let it stand one or two hours before starting to place the tiles. Leave a narrow space along both chalk lines clear of mastic so that they can be seen to start the tile rows.

Laying tiles. Predrill small holes in the "tongue" at one edge of the tiles used in the first row so they can be temporarily nailed in place. Start with the first tile at the center, nail it temporarily, and then drive the second tile against it. Tap it with the softwood stick to get a tight joint. Do not slide the tiles; tip them into place, so they will not scoop up the mastic.

Tiles should be laid in a pyramid fashion (figure 13–26) to keep the pattern square, working up one

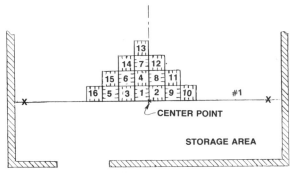

Fig. 13-26. Sequence of laying tiles.

side and down the other. Lay all tiles on one side of the chalk line before starting on the other side. Follow the numbered scheme to maintain the pyramid.

Details. The mastic trowel can be made from an asphalt tile trowel by using its plain edge to make the notches required for parquet tile. These notches are ½ inch apart, ¼ inch deep, and ³/₁₆ inch wide. They can be made easily with a file after they have been marked on the trowel.

Cork expansion strips permit the tiles to alter in size with changes in humidity or temperature. These can be made from cork ¼ inch thick, ¾ inch wide, and 2 inches long, and should be placed at every other tile joint.

Fig. 13-27. A "brick" wall.

Accent with Bricks

The look of brick can accent a wall in your mobile home: not real brick but imitation decorative brick that resembles the real thing without the weight or the effort required to put it up (figure 13-27).

These "bricks" can be put up by a handy man with very little work. The materials and tools required are adhesive mortar, a trowel, a cutting knife, and clear acrylic sealer.

Wall preparation. The type of the wall surface determines the preparation needed to install the bricks.

If the wall material is ¼-inch-thick plywood, it will only be necessary to roughen it with coarse sandpaper prior to applying the adhesive mortar.

If the wall material is luan paneling, ⁵/₃₂ inch thick, then it is necessary to apply ⅜-inch thick-gypsum board first. Unless the paneling is protected by gypsum board there is danger that the luan paneling will bow out or otherwise distort.

The bricks are 2¼ inches by 8 inches by ½ inch thick. They come in cartons each containing 30 bricks. Each carton will cover 5 to 6 square feet. They are available in aged, rustic, or modern brick styles. Carton weight varies from modern brick at 4 pounds to 9 pounds for aged-looking brick. Corner bricks are available in the aged style.

Installation. The adhesive mortar is applied to the surface to be covered, and to the back surface of each brick by "buttering" it. You have 30 minutes to press the brick onto the wall before the mortar starts to set. The sealer can be applied after a day's wait. It will protect the surface and help to keep the bricks clean.

Fixing Your Lawn Mower

Many electric-start gas mowers, which use a battery pack for starting, develop trouble due to short battery life.

Most of these mowers start readily if the mower is in top condition, if the weather is warm, and if the mower needs only a few turns from the starter to get under way. The battery pack on virtually all of the electric-start mowers I've encountered is only good for a few fast turns of the starter motor. If the engine fails to catch immediately, the battery power drops, and you're likely to have to face the prospect of a battery-pack replacement at a cost of about $30.

Making the adapter. Your lawn mower can be started with your car's 12-volt battery, which has a much greater capacity than the battery pack. The conversion can be made readily by anyone.

The following will be needed:

1. A 6-foot, #12 three-wire air conditioner exten-

sion cord. It has a three-terminal plug at one end and a receptacle at the other.

2. Two large alligator clips.

3. Some rubber tape.

Proceed as follows:

1. Remove the battery pack and cut off the wires leading from the electric starter motor to the pack, leaving them about 18 inches long and strip their ends about ½ inch.

2. Cut the three-wire extension cord in two, about a foot from the plug end. Strip the two large wire ends on the short cord and attach to the two wires coming from the starter motor (figure 13–28). Solder the two joints, if possible, and

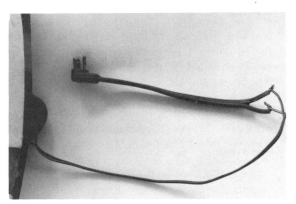

Fig. 13-28. The short cable is attached to the starter motor wires.

tape securely. Cut off the small wire back several inches from the joint.

3. Strip the wires on the cord with the receptacle about ½ inch and attach the two alligator clips to them (figure 13–29). Again, solder the joints and tape them.

Fig. 13-29. The long cable has alligator clips.

4. Tape the shorter cord assembly to a convenient place on the mower.

Using the cord. Plug the shorter cord with the plug into the longer cord with the alligator clips. The reason for splitting the cord is to eliminate having the full length stay with the mower once it has been started.

Put your mower control into the *start* position. You will then have to attach the two alligator clips to the battery to start the mower by trial. If the mower starter motor merely spins, instead of cranking the engine, reverse the two clips on the battery. Mark the clip connected to the ground terminal of the battery for future reference (figure 13–30).

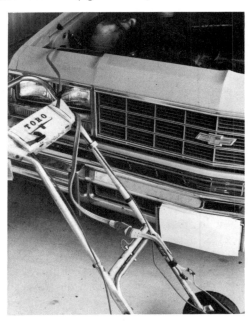

Fig. 13-30. A complete starting hook-up.

Remove the longer part of the cord once the mower starts.

Cold weather start. In cold weather, when starting time is longer than usual, start up the car engine before trying to start the mower. The higher battery voltage with the engine running will help to start the mower quickly. This method is useful in any weather if the mower is hard to start.

A Lawn Sprayer

A handy, mist-producing, rectangular-area lawn sprayer can be assembled from a few, readily available parts (figure 13–31). It consists of one or more sections of ¾-inch plastic pipe, plugged at one end, and a garden hose adapter at the other (figures 13–32, 33).

3. Snap a chalk line down the length of the pipe assembly for reference. Drill holes along this line, about one foot apart, of the diameter required to mount the nozzles.

4. Drive in the nozzles (figure 13–34). They are available at lawn-sprinkler-system stores.

Figs. 13–31, 32, 33, 34. A lawn mist sprayer (top left) has one plugged end (top right) and the other end coupled to a garden hose (bottom left). Sprayer nozzles are driven into the pipe (bottom right).

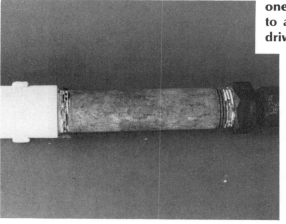

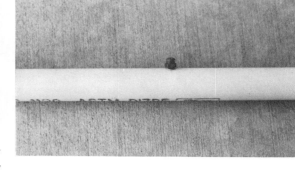

Construction. Spaced about a foot apart are tiny plastic nozzles, which create the misty spray. The big advantage of this sprayer is that the width of the area being sprayed can be controlled simply by turning the pipe, or you can spray on either side of the pipe. Also, it is more durable than a conventional plastic hose with its tiny holes that plug up, or the hose itself splitting open.

The construction follows:

1. Select two or three approximately 6 foot lengths of ¾-inch plastic pipe. Connect them by means of a ¾-inch coupling, and place another coupling at one end of the pipe assembly into which a removable pipe plug has been fitted. This is used to clean out the pipe when necessary.

2. Into the other end, insert a 6-inch-long metal nipple, to which is attached a regular garden hose coupling (figure 13–33).

This completes the assembly, and it is ready for use by connecting it to the garden hose. Rotating the pipe assembly will give you the desired spray width.

Noisy Ducts

Most mobile homes use aluminum air ducts. They stay quiet on the cooling cycle, but they are apt to make "snapping" sounds on the heating cycle because of duct expansion.

A usually successful remedy is to put stress on the ducts at their register openings. It can be done by using 2 by 4 inch pieces of wood, about ¼-inch thick, at the top and bottom duct surfaces. Another piece of wood of similar thickness is used as a wedge between these pieces (figure 13–35). The wedge should be facing in the same direction as the air flow and should be long enough to distort the duct slightly and keep the horizontal pieces in place. The distortion is what keeps the ducts from moving in the floor assembly.

Fig. 13-35. Wood blocks stop air duct noise.

CHAPTER 14

TENANT PROTECTION

The mobile home owner residing in a rental park certainly has one distinct disadvantage compared to apartment house dwellers. The latter only have to move their furniture if they are displeased with their landlord for raising their rent, for not keeping up the property, or for renting to undesirable neighbors.

The mobile home owner, in addition to having to move his furniture, has a mobile home, shed, air conditioner, carport roof, skirting, and other items to move. The mobile home, weighing 6 to 8 tons or more, is not exactly an easily movable object, despite its name. In fact, most "mobile" homes are practically immovable.

Lack of Tenant Protection

This immobility has resulted in the passage of some laws, in Florida and California as well as other states, to protect mobile home owners. The laws are aimed at the rent gouging that has become so commonplace, especially by profiteering corporations. As the longest rental lease is for only one year in most states, there has been little to prevent an annual increase of rents.

The courts in Florida have been very lax in protecting tenants in rental mobile home parks. In one county, for example, a park owner increased the monthly rent from $101 to $161 and the local judge allowed the increase. Another small-town judge has decreed that a mobile home owner can be expelled from the park, mobile home included, in one year *without cause,* and the higher state courts have upheld his decision.

Such incidents highlight the need for protection of the thousands upon thousands of tenants in rental parks, many of whom have invested their life savings in their homes and then find themselves unprotected by the law. Many tenants, living on fixed incomes, find themselves unable to keep up with the large yearly rent increases.

Associations

These abuses have led to creation of mobile home owners' associations. The largest is the Golden State Mobilehome Owners League, Inc. (GSMOL) in California, consisting of nearly 200,000 members, followed by the Federation of Mobile Home Owners of Florida with approximately 104,000 members. Although the park owners have fought such associations in court and in the state legislatures, much has been accomplished by the tenant associations. The biggest goal of the associations have been rent control laws. Some towns and cities in California have now instituted such laws and the association's aim is to secure passage of a statewide law on rents in California. The abuses have been widespread and only a law with teeth in it will protect the tenants. The large corporations set the pace for rent increases. The locally owned parks tend to follow their practices.

Your rights

In a small way, some laws have been enacted to protect the mobile home owner on a rental lot. They have been passed as the result of many management abuses of tenants and the subsequent storm of righteous resentment.

The California State legislature has enacted the Mobilehome Residency Law; Chapter 2.5 of which covers rental agreements, rules and regulations, fees and charges, tenant meetings, termination of tenancy, transfer of mobile homes, and actions, proceedings, and penalties. A summary of its provisions follows.

Rental agreements. A rental agreement shall be in writing and include:
1. The term of tenancy and rental charge
2. Rules and park regulations
3. Management to provide and maintain in good working order all common facilities
4. Management to meet and consult with the tenants on amendments to park rules and regulations. Meeting to be held not less than ten days after notice has been given to the tenants.

5. A rental agreement, not in excess of one year, shall be given to the tenant whose rights may not be waived.

Rules and regulations. A tenant shall be given a written notice of amendment of park regulations, with or without his consent, such notice being given a minimum of six months in advance. The management has no right of entry into a mobile home without the written consent of its occupant, except in cases of emergency or when the mobile home has been abandoned.

Fees and charges. These six points pertain:

1. The tenant must be notified by a written notice, at least 60 days prior to date of rent increase.

2. No additional fee may be charged outside of rent.

3. No extra charge for pets unless special facilities are provided.

4. A tenant may not be charged any extra guest fee if the guest remains only a maximum of 14 days in a calendar month, nor is such a guest required to register with the management.

5. A tenant shall not be charged a fee based on the number of members in his immediate family.

6. No entry fee shall be charged.

Tenant meetings. Tenants shall be permitted to hold meetings related to mobile home living.

Termination of tenancy. A tenancy may be terminated for one or more of these reasons:

1. Failure to comply with local or state laws.
2. Creating substantial annoyance to other tenants.
3. Failure to comply with park rules or regulations within seven days of receipt of written notice.
4. Nonpayment of rent.
5. Condemnation of the park.
6. Change in park use, provided park management gives 12 months' notice of the proposed change.
7. No tenancy can be terminated to make the site available to a person who has purchased a mobile home from the park.

Transfer of mobile home. Here the basic points are as follows:

1. A tenant may advertise his mobile home for sale displaying a sign in the window, which can be at least 12 by 12 inches.

2. The management shall not charge the tenant a transfer or selling fee.

3. The management may require approval of the new purchaser of the mobile home offered for sale.

4. Management may restrict the new owner to complying with park rules that limit residence only to adults.

Actions, proceedings, and penalties. In any legal action the loser has to pay all reasonable attorney's fees and court costs.

Florida regulations. In Florida the law specifies that a mobile home tenant may be evicted for:

1. Nonpayment of rent
2. Violation of Federal, state, or local ordinances which are considered detrimental to the safety and welfare of other tenants
3. Violation of park rules
4. Change in use of park land

No one will quarrel with the fact that park owners have to increase their rents to cope with creeping inflation, higher taxes, and other expenses. However, there is little justification for doubling rents, or worse, in a period as short as five years. Tenants also notice that park rents tend to rise in unison, especially when parks are filled.

While some people decry rent controls, they forget that mobile home tenants have a limited ability to move to a new location without large expense. The lobbying efforts by the park owners' and state dealers' associations have preserved the status quo of existing laws that favor their interests. The tenants have unwillingly helped to support these efforts because part of their rent payments have been used to underwrite that lobbying.

The growing membership in California and Florida tenants' protective associations confirms that tenants are finally discovering the need to work for their interests.

CHAPTER 15

SELLING OR MOVING YOUR MOBILE HOME

Circumstances may arise which force you to move. In that case you will have to decide whether to sell your mobile home and buy another at a new location or move the one you have.

Since moving is likely to be expensive, you should carefully consider both options. The type of park in which your present home is located will heavily influence the price you'll be able to get for it. If it is a modern park, with mostly double-wides, your chances for fast sale and a good price will be better than if it is located in a park full of single-wides.

Before setting a price for your mobile home check the prices others in the park have received for homes similar to yours.

If possible it is best to sell your home *before* you move out so prospective buyers can see it with furniture in place. Many people find it hard to visualize; and mobile homes look worse empty than do conventional homes.

Selling Your Present Home

Your present mobile home can be sold in several ways:

1. If you have ample time you can do it yourself by advertising in the local papers, putting a FOR SALE BY OWNER sign in your window when permitted; telling friend's and neighbors, both in and out of the park about your "resale"—as it is popularly known, and letting the park manager approve the new buyer before he signs the bill of sale.

2. The park manager or the person delegated to handle resales may offer to sell your home for a fixed fee. He'll list it in the office or clubhouse, and arrange to take prospects to see your home.

3. A regular real estate office, with salesmen qualified in mobile home sales will have lists of prescreened prospects, just as is done in selling a conventional house. The charge is generally about six percent of the sale price.

Remember to ask to be notified before the salesman brings the prospective buyers. Even the appearance of the home's occupants has been known to lose a sale.

Helpful Hints

As in selling a car, you should spend some time and possibly some money to bring your home to tiptop appearance. Cleaning the carpeting, washing down the outside walls, and windows, cleaning the yard area and planters, and other beautification will make your home more desirable to a prospect.

Repair any visible damage, such as stains on a rug in an enclosed porch. Even if its been caused by nothing more than an accidental spill, your prospect may believe that such damage is the result of a leaky porch roof. If necessary, replace the rug. The buyer has probably inspected other mobile homes on the market and he will make his decision on the basis of appearance as well as price. A bad appearance warns the buyer to look more closely at other items before deciding to make an offer.

If you expect to buy new furniture, consider selling the present furniture to the prospect at a reasonable price. It may close the sale. You may also sell all items you won't need to neighbors.

Commercial Guides

There are publications that serve to establish used mobile home prices: *Mobile Home Blue Book* and *N.A.D.A. Appraisal Guide.* Their publishers sell them to such business establishments as banks, appraisers, mobile home dealers, county assessors, and others involved with used mobile homes. But the publishers refuse to sell them to the general public, the people who do the actual buying. The seller then has the advantage of having the information necessary to price his product, set up loan values, and offer it to the prospective used mobile home buyer. The latter will have to do some research to determine if the offering price is reasonable or not.

Copies of the *N.A.D.A. Appraisal Guide* may be found in reference sections of some public libraries or in assessors' offices. If available, use it to establish the price of the mobile home you are selling, in line with the current market.

A Comparison

When considering selling your home you should make a quick comparison of the costs involved by adding the separate items in the two columns in Tables 15–1 and 15–2. Neither should you neglect the extra fees and costs listed in the paragraphs following these tables.

Insurance. You are already carrying insurance on your mobile home. Now you must either transfer the policy to the buyer, if this is agreeable with the insurance company, or cancel the policy and secure a refund. (More on insurance is found in Chapter 6.)

If the buyer is financing the purchase, he will be required to have it insured at least from fire and theft as soon as the papers transferring ownership are

TABLE 15–1	
Sell Present Mobile Home	**Move Home to a New Location**
Selling price _____	Carport and apron _____
Less { Commission (if sold by others) _____	Shed erection (unless included in moving costs) _____
Exit fee* _____	Re-anchoring _____
Total	Planter & plants _____
	Labor costs _____
	Moving costs _____
	Entrance fee* _____
	Total

*These fees are illegal in many states.

By buying a new or used mobile home at your new location your cost is:

TABLE 15–2	
New Home in New Park	**Used Home in New Park**
Basic cost _____	Basic cost _____
Carport & apron _____	Expected repairs _____
Shed _____	Improvements _____
Air conditioner/ heat pump _____	Total
Anchoring _____	
Skirting _____	
Planter & plants _____	
Total	

Selling Problems

In addition to locating a buyer for your present mobile home, you'll have several other concerns to take care of. These are insurance, legal fees, and service contracts. They also apply if you buy a used mobile home in the new park.

signed. The amount of insurance has to be sufficient to cover the value of the loan. (Financing is discussed in more detail in Chapter 6.)

Transfer papers. If your mobile home is in a rental park where no lot sale is involved, the transfer process is quite simple. In many states, the mobile home is titled like a car, with the same type of title. Notarization of the title transfer probably will be required.

Existing service contracts. You may already have service contracts on the air-conditioning/heating unit, or heat pump, and on appliances such as the refrigerator, electric range and oven, washer and dryer, and others. The simplest method is to have the service companies transfer them to the buyer, if both agree. Otherwise, ask for a refund on your existing policies, closing out the coverage on the day of the transfer. When you made the service contracts in the first place, you will have been wise to make certain that these agreements carried written provision for refund.

Moving

When mobile homes were all single-wides, 8 or 10 feet across, moving them was relatively easy. They could be picked up by attaching the hitch and tow bar as well as axles and wheels once the home had been jacked up on its site and the supports removed (figure 15–1).

The double- and triple-wides present a much greater problem if they are to be moved. They have to be disassembled into their respective sections and electrical wiring and plumbing separated; and such large items as air-conditioning/heating unit and shed have to be moved as well.

If it is to be moved to a colder climate your present home may not have sufficient insulation or furnace capacity to keep you comfortable. Some states have standards that do not allow in mobile homes built in other states. Check the regulations of the state to which you are moving and also the regulations of the states the mobile home will travel through before you decide to move. Your mover should have this information available.

Locating a new park. Before you decide to move your mobile home you will need to locate a site or park that is willing to accept the home you plan to move. The park will determine if the make, size, age, and appearance of your home will be consistent with the other mobile homes in the park.

Some parks will not permit an owner to take up residence unless an "entrance fee" is paid, or they may not accept used homes at all. So you will have to shop around for a site well in advance of your move. Your present park may request an "exit fee" on or before your departure. Be certain about the law and the practice in your area so that you don't have a rude shock come moving day.

Fig. 15-1. Moving a mobile home.

A new park in the area you are moving to may be listed in Woodall's or other reference periodicals, together with rates, park details, management, facilities, and so forth. If possible, visit the park personally when contemplating the move. Consumer protection agencies (see Appendix) will be helpful in determining a desirable park. Local Business Bureaus will also advise if complaints have been received about a given park.

The mover. As noted earlier, moving a mobile home is a complicated affair. The moving company should be licensed, bonded, and insured. Moving mobile home sections over long distances is not recommended because their structural integrity may be impaired.

Find out if the moving company you're considering handles interstate or only intrastate moves. Interstate moving companies are more likely to be reliable, and their rates are regulated by the Interstate Commerce Commission. A company that is not reliable can damage the home or its contents through careless driving and handling.

Transit insurance should be purchased on the home for fire, collision, and personal property damage.

Since multi-wides are a job for professional movers, it will be necessary to select the company with considerable care. These specialized movers are listed in the Yellow Pages of the telephone directory. Get estimates from several major companies. Reservations may have to be made considerably ahead of the moving date because certain months of the year are the movers' busiest. Depend not only on the mover's reputation but also upon reports from other customers.

Preparation. Once your new site has been selected, you should arrange with the park manager or an outside contractor to set up the mobile home, install the carport and its apron to the street, provide anchoring and skirting, have electrical and plumbing connections made, and build a planter if one is required by the park.

All of these arrangements have to be made before the truck delivers your mobile home, or its sections if it is a multi-wide.

Although leaving the hitch, tow bar, and the wheels with the mobile home is a thing of the past, they still must be attached by the mover so the sections can be maneuvered into position for travel and setup. They can be used by the mover again and again, and therefore, you should have to pay only a nominal price for their use during the move.

Be sure that the mover has all the necessary papers, such as registration, in his possession. Your home will have to be reregistered if it is going to another state.

Appliances. Your washer and dryer should be serviced before the move. The serviceman will block the washer's rotor properly to avoid damage to the driving mechanism. You will have to block the washer and dryer to prevent them from being upset or breaking connecting hoses on the washer.

Hot water heaters should also be blocked to avoid breaking the pipes during the move.

Dishes and other loose objects. You will need cartons to pack dishes and other breakable items, books, records, and other loose items. "Duct" tape, available in 1½-, 2-, and 3-inch widths, will be helpful in taping windows, doors, and mirrors.

Removable items. Items such as the air conditioners, connecting plastic air ducts, and television antennas will have to be removed and trucked separately.

Awnings, carport roofs, and skirting must be removed, but perhaps can be moved by you in a rented vehicle.

Piping. All piping under the home should be drained and blocked to prevent damage and leaky joints.

Other precautions. All loose items, such as the drawers in the kitchen, should be taped shut. The refrigerator should be emptied and defrosted, and the drawers and outer door taped. It should be blocked in place in the same manner as it was when the home was originally delivered. The contents of the kitchen cabinets should be packed in cartons.

Your mover will advise you how you should place the boxed items and the best method of protecting your television set, stereo system, radios, and other electrical equipment.

If you plan to pack your dishes and other fragile items yourself be sure to ask whether the mover will guarantee their safe arrival.

The following will have to be removed: contents of medicine cabinets, toilet tank covers, items on walls or shelves, such as pictures, plaques, antique plates, and other items of a similar nature. They can be wrapped in blankets or other heavy material and placed in the bathtub.

The mover will give you a list of items to take care of prior to moving. When he arrives to move your mobile home, he will give you a check list prior to travel.

As with conventional house furniture moving, you will have to have an estimate for the move. Upon arrival at the new site the mover will expect you to pay in cash, money order, or a certified check. He will not accept a personal check, and therefore, you should arrange to have the payment ready. In many instances, the final charge may exceed the original estimate. Thus it is a good idea to have extra funds available to speed up the settlement. Any claims by the mover for additional payment should be covered by invoices.

Damage claims, if any, should be made once the setup has been completed and the furniture placed in its premove locations. Examine all fragile pieces carefully for signs of damage. If you do not receive timely satisfaction you may want to seek recourse through a state consumer protection agency or through the Interstate Commerce Commission.

CHAPTER 16

MOBILE HOME PUBLICATIONS

Introduction

As the number of mobile home residents has grown, several mobile home publications have appeared, regional in nature, and supported by advertisements of mobile home manufacturers, dealers, parts makers, mobile home parks, and service industries.

These papers publish local news of events in the various parks, supplied by correspondents in the parks. However, because of extensive advertising, the news in many papers is slanted toward the advertisers, with park notes buried in the back pages.

Since papers are delivered to the parks in bulk for free distribution, some park managements have attempted to censor unfavorable articles by refusing to allow distribution on their property.

In one recent case, an advertiser (a mobile home dealer) was upset when a newspaper, not a mobile home paper, published a picture of mobile homes upset by a windstorm. He threatened to stop advertising in the paper unless it stopped printing such pictures.

In still another instance, a park manager applied pressure on the park contributor to only send in news that was to his liking.

Listing of Trade Papers

Some of the trade papers (and their annual sub-scription prices and frequency of appearance) are as follows:

The Manufactured Housing Reporter
$12—monthly
P.O. Box 34475
Dallas, TX 75234

This is a Texas newspaper, with advertisements by mobile home manufacturers, dealers, and suppliers, and up-to-date industry news.

Mobile Home Merchandiser $24—monthly
203 N. Wabash
Chicago, IL 60601

The foregoing publication is strictly a mobile home industry magazine. It presents the industry's views, through the manufacturers' associations and dealers, on the subject of mobile home selling, lobbying in Congress, details of forthcoming trade shows, financing, and other viewpoints.

Some of the newspaper-type publications that are regional in character with occasional news of interest to park residents are:

Arizona Mobile Citizen $10.55—weekly
4110 E. Van Buren
Phoenix, AZ 85008

This is a newspaper devoted to mobile home advertisements by manufacturers, parks, dealers, classified want ads; also gives park news.

Mobile Home News $15—weekly
P.O. Box 1219
Altamonte Springs, FL 32701

This is a newspaper with mobile home advertising by manufacturers, dealers, and parks, industry news, and items sent in by correspondents from various mobile home parks in the vicinity. Also has an RV section.

Nevada Times $5—biweekly
P.O. Box 4142
Las Vegas, NV 89030
This newspaper carries mobile home advertising by manufacturers, parks, industry show information, some mobile home park news.

Western Mobile News $7.50—weekly
4043 Irving Place
Culver City, CA 90230
This newspaper has advertisements by mobile home manufacturers, parks, and industry news as well as a want ad section.

A list of other publications follows:

Recreation and Mobile Home News
                                 $4—bimonthly
225 Guler Street
Seattle, WA 98119

Mobile Living in Canada/
Manufactured Homes Canada $7—monthly
925 23rd Ave. N.W.
Calgary, Alta.
Canada T2m 1T5

CHAPTER 17

THE FUTURE OF MOBILE HOMES

Fig. 17-1. Poor mobile home housekeeping is objectionable to others.

Mobile home manufacturers, parks, and dealers will have better prospects of enlarging their percentage of the housing market IF they change many of their present attitudes about selling their product and correct some of the worst problems.

Here's a list of some of the problems that prospective buyers will still have to face in the future, unless remedial legislation is enacted. The mobile home industry, tightly knit in various associations, is not likely to produce a better product unless forced to do so.

Community resistance. Park owners and development corporations continue to press for land rezoning for mobile home parks. They fail to understand the reluctance and resistance of the zoning boards and are even trying to enlist the assistance of HUD to get zoning restrictions removed. The zoning boards, whose primary members are conventional housing developers and local residents, have taken a dim view of a different type of housing abutting existing conventional housing. Since most mobile homes are indeed unattractive compared to most conventional homes, one must expect antipathy from those who may have to live next door. In addition, many parks are poorly managed and poorly kept up. Figure 17–1 illustrates the nightmare of many a conventional home owner who fears just such an eyesore will destroy his view and his own property value.

Rents. In some rental parks rents have doubled in five years. The outlook for the future, in jurisdictions with no controls, is for more of the same. This abets the growing tendency toward lot ownership, where there is also less regimentation and no threat of eviction.

Although rent control in rental mobile home parks has been fought by the park owners' associations, it is the way of the future in many states.

Tenants are organizing nation-wide to control soaring rents. They have been "captive" too long.

Exteriors. For many years, the mobile home industry has relied upon vertical siding, or "skin." At last, the use of insulated horizontal siding, like that on conventional houses, is increasing, with even more widespread use expected in the future.

Roof designs are finally changing from low angle, metal construction to one with a steeper pitch and shingle covering, and this will increase in the future. A twenty-year shingled roof, free of maintenance problems, is now on the market.

The vented concrete block system of skirting, which creates the appearance of temporary housing will give way in the future to complete enclosures that constitute a far better method of anchoring mobile homes.

Garages will start replacing carports and improve the appearance of many mobile home parks.

Interiors. It will take time; but, hopefully, government regulations will eventually be imposed to prohibit the use of luan paneling and particle-board floors. Both are the source of formaldehyde vapors, and both constitute a high fire hazard and contribute to high insurance costs.

Lots. In the future, mobile home lots are likely to increase in size to accommodate the larger and better-built homes. Lot prices can also be expected to rise, and there will be an increase in rents in rental parks as a result.

"Package" price. Government regulations are likely to be passed making it mandatory to provide the buyer with a complete breakdown of the total or "package" price. Outrage at deceptive practices in the car industry forced the government to require that

buyers be able to see the prices of the various items that make up the total. It will eliminate instances where a mobile home, by the same manufacturer, with the same options, is sold at different prices by various parks.

Also, it is likely that rental park management will one day no longer be allowed to force a prospective purchaser to accept only one make of mobile home if he wants to live there. This will enhance price competition.

Also on the bright side are some new developments that will become widespread in the near future. They will solve some of today's most vexing problems.

Mobile homes for the handicapped. One of the problems faced by would-be mobile home buyers who are confined to wheelchairs is that mobile homes have, until now, offered limited physical accessibility.

A new approach by one of the large mobile home manufacturers has been to replace conventional steps to the home with approach ramps. Floor coverings have been selected for easy wheelchair mobility. The kitchen, bathrooms, shower, closets, counters, and appliances have all been designed to provide comfortable and efficient use by persons in wheelchairs.

Now, many thousands of these handicapped persons will be able to purchase a mobile home specially designed for their needs (figure 17-2). Appearance

Fig. 17-2. Ramps make for easy access by handicapped people.

Fig. 17-3. Many facilities are specially designed for the handicapped, such as low electric range tops.

has not been sacrificed in this newly developed home, nor has luxury or comfort. Available in several versions, it enables several persons to live independently of each other within the same modified structure. The counters and appliances are low, doors are wide, closets and showers are roll-in (figures 17–3, 4, 5).

Fig. 17-4. A low wall oven is accessible from a wheelchair.

Fig. 17-5. Special showers can include built-in seats and railings.

Another concept. A new concept in mobile home housing has been developed by the Immobile Home® Company in California. It has issued licenses to several selected mobile home manufacturers to produce homes in accordance with this concept.

A complete absence of windows on one side of each home, and the inclusion of a one- or two-car garage on the opposite side in front, replacing the usual carport, is one part of this approach (figure 17–6). Thus, it is possible to create a private courtyard or a patio (figure 17–7) on the side of each home, between it and the blank sidewall of the adjacent home.

Figs. 17-6, 7. The Immobile Home® may include a garage (above) or a private courtyard.

In high-density parks, the home is placed near the side lot line, as in conventional mobile home arrangement. In low-density parks, the homes may be set parallel to the street, with the garage located at either end of the home, so as to give a conventional home appearance. In either type the garage has direct access to the street.

A floor plan of one home model is shown in figure 17-8.

In the May 20, 1981, issue of *The New York Times,* Tom Collier, a former deputy assistant secretary of the Department of Housing and Urban Development, called mobile homes "the best-kept secret bargain in America." "Those who take our housing shortage seriously should embrace this resource," he said.

Maybe. Maybe not.

But the harder the mobile home industry tries to match its product with conventional housing, the brighter will be its future in the housing market.

The mobile home construction standard issued by HUD in 1976 is widely quoted by the mobile home industry in its press releases. Yet that government document needs substantial revision. It should incorporate new regulations in such areas as fire safety, construction materials, and overall structural design, as well as installation of single- and multi-wides and their site inspection. It should also mandate elimination of such undesirable features as metal roofs and materials containing excessive amounts of formaldehyde, and the replacement of pier supporting structures by solid foundations.

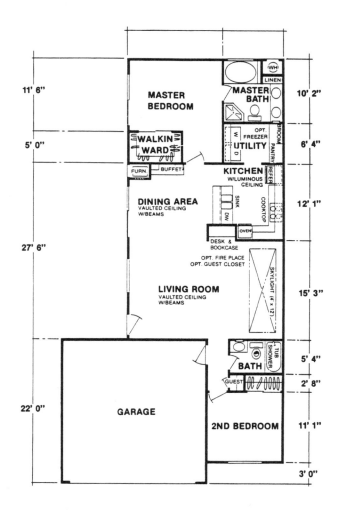

All dimensions approximate. Specifications subject to change. © 1979 The Immobile Home Company. PATENT PENDING.

Fig. 17-8. A floor plan.

APPENDIX

STATE CONSUMER PROTECTION AGENCIES

ALABAMA
Office of Consumer Protection
544 Martha Street
Montgomery, AL 36104

ARIZONA
Office of Economic Planning & Development
505 State Capitol
1700 W. Washington Street
Phoenix, AZ 85007

ARKANSAS
Consumer Protection Division
Office of the Attorney General
Justice Building
Little Rock, AR 72201

CALIFORNIA
Department of Consumer Affairs
1020 N Street
Sacramento, CA 95814

COLORADO
Consumer Section
Office of the Attorney General
Department of Law
State Services Building
1525 Sherman Street
Denver, CO 80203

CONNECTICUT
Department of Consumer Protection
State Office Building
165 Capitol Avenue
Hartford, CT 06115

DELAWARE
Division of Consumer Affairs
Delaware State Building
820 N. French Street
Wilmington, DE 19801

FLORIDA
Division of Consumer Services
Department of Agriculture & Consumer Services
110 Mayo Building
Tallahassee, FL 32301

GEORGIA
Office of Consumer Affairs
225 Peachtree Street, N.E.
Atlanta, GA 30303

IDAHO
Business Regulation/Consumer Protection
  Section
Office of the Attorney General
Statehouse
700 W. Jefferson Street
Boise, ID 83702

ILLINOIS
Consumer Fraud & Protection Division
Office of the Attorney General
134 N. LaSalle Street
Chicago, IL 60602

INDIANA
Consumer Protection Division
Offices of the Attorney General
219 State House
Indianapolis, IN 46204

IOWA
Consumer Protection Division
Iowa Department of Justice
1209 E. Court
Des Moines, IA 50309

KANSAS
Consumer Protection Division
Office of the Attorney General
State Capitol Building
Topeka, KS 66612

KENTUCKY
Consumer Protection Division
Office of the Attorney General
204 St. Clair Street
Frankfort, KY 40601

LOUISIANA
Consumer Protection Section
1885 Wooddale Boulevard
Baton Rouge, LA 70806

MAINE
Bureau of Consumer Protection
Department of Business Regulation
State House
Augusta, ME 04330

MARYLAND
Division of Consumer Protection
Office of the Attorney General
1 S. Calvert Street
Baltimore, MD 21202

MASSACHUSETTS
Executive Office of Consumer Affairs
1 Ashburton Place
Boston, MA 02108

MICHIGAN
Consumers Council
Hollister Building
108 W. Allegan Street
Lansing, MI 48933

MINNESOTA
Office of Consumer Services
Metro Square Building
7th & Roberts Streets
St. Paul, MN 55103

MISSISSIPPI
Consumer Protection Division
Office of the Attorney General
550 High Street
Jackson, MS 39203

MISSOURI
Office of Consumer Services
Department of Consumer Affairs
505 Missouri Boulevard
Jefferson City, MO 65101

MONTANA
Consumer Affairs Division
Department of Business Regulation
805 North Main
Helena, MT 59601

NEBRASKA
Consumer Protection Division
Department of Justice
State Capitol
Lincoln, NE 68509

NEVADA
Consumer Affairs Division
Department of Commerce
2501 East Sahara
Las Vegas, NV 89104

NEW HAMPSHIRE
Consumer Protection Division
The Attorney General
State House Annex
25 Capitol Street
Concord, NH 03301

NEW JERSEY
Department of Consumer Affairs
Office of Consumer Protection
1100 Raymond Boulevard
Newark, NJ 07102

NEW MEXICO
Consumer Protection Division
Office of the Attorney General
Bataan Memorial Building
Santa Fe, NM 87501

NEW YORK
Consumer Protection Board
99 Washington Avenue
Albany, NY 12210

NORTH CAROLINA
Consumer Protection Section
Department of Justice
Justice Building
Raleigh, NC 27611

NORTH DAKOTA
Department of State Laboratories & Consumer
    Affairs
26th & Main Streets
Bismarck, ND 58501

OHIO
Division of Consumer Protection
Department of Commerce
180 E. Broad Street
Columbus, OH 43215

OKLAHOMA
Department of Consumer Affairs
460 Jim Thorpe Office Building
2101 N. Lincoln Boulevard
Oklahoma City, OK 73105

OREGON
Consumer Services Division
Department of Commerce
Labor & Industries Building
Salem, OR 97310

PENNSYLVANIA
Bureau of Consumer Protection
Office of the Attorney General
301 Market Street
Harrisburg, Pa 17101

RHODE ISLAND
Consumer's Council
365 Broadway
Providence, RI 02909

SOUTH CAROLINA
Department of Consumer Affairs
2221 Devine Street
Columbia, SC 29250

SOUTH DAKOTA
Division of Consumer Protection

Department of Commerce & Consumer Affairs
State Capitol
Pierre, SD 57501

TENNESSEE
Division of Consumer Affairs
Ellington Agricultural Center
Box 40627, Melrose Station
Nashville, TN 37211

TEXAS
Consumer Protection Division
Office of the Attorney General
121 W. 14th Street
Austin, TX 78701

UTAH
Consumer Protection Division
Office of the Attorney General
236 State Capitol
Salt Lake City, UT 84114

VERMONT
Consumer Protection Division
Office of the Attorney General
109 State Street
Montpelier, VT 05602

VIRGINIA
Office of Consumer Affairs
Department of Agriculture & Commerce
P.O. Box 1163
Richmond, VA 23209

WASHINGTON
Consumer Protection & Antitrust Division
Office of the Attorney General
Dexter Horton Building
Seattle, WA 98104

WEST VIRGINIA
Consumer Protection Division
Office of the Attorney General
1800 Kanawha Boulevard, E.
Charleston, WV 25305

WISCONSIN
Governor's Council for Consumer Affairs
16 N. Carrol
Madison, WI 53703

WYOMING
Consumer Affairs Division
Wyoming Attorney General's Office
123 Capitol Building
Cheyenne, WY 82002

SELECTED BIBLIOGRAPHY

Books

Center for Auto Safety, The. *Mobile Homes—The Low-Cost Housing Hoax.* New York: Grossman Publishers, 1975.

Condon, Kaye. *Complete Guide to Mobile Homes.* Garden City, NY: Doubleday & Co., 1976.

Nulsen, Robert, and Nulsen, David. *Mobile Home Encyclopedia—Recreational Vehicle.* Beverly Hills: Trailer-R-Club of America (Box 1376, CA 90213), 1978.

Oaks, Marian C. *Mobile Home Living.* New York: Tower Publications, 1975.

Purdy, Anita. *How to Buy a Mobile Home.* Northwest Trailer & Mobile Home News, 1979.

Guides

California Mobile Home Park Guide. Western Mobile News, 4043 Irving Place, Culver City, CA 90230. Annually.

Florida and Southern States Retirement and Resort Communities. Woodall Publishing Co., 500 Hyacinth Place, Highland Park, IL 60035. Annually.

Florida's Mobile Home Guide. Mobile Home News, P.O. Box 1219, Altamonte Springs, FL 32701. Annually.

Pacific Northwest Mobile Home Park Guide. Western Mobile Home News, 4043 Irving Place, Culver City, CA 90230. Annually.

INDEX